IMAGES
of America

CADES COVE

ON THE COVER: In a typical picture of a Cades Cove child on a normal day, Otis Tipton is shown here in his everyday overalls, wearing no shoes at all, and walking in this field with his calf. Cove children were required to do many chores such as feeding livestock, milking, gathering eggs, hoeing the garden, and many, many more tasks on a daily basis. Because children had to do so much work on the farm, school was only in session during the winter months. This picture was taken in the 1920s. (Courtesy of Margaret Oliver, John W. Oliver collection.)

IMAGES
of America

CADES COVE

Missy Tipton Green and Paulette Ledbetter

ARCADIA
PUBLISHING

ISBN 978-0-7385-8822-3

Published by Arcadia Publishing
Charleston, South Carolina

Printed in the United States of America

Library of Congress Control Number: 2011930142

For all general information, please contact Arcadia Publishing:
Telephone 843-853-2070
Fax 843-853-0044
E-mail sales@arcadiapublishing.com
For customer service and orders:
Toll-Free 1-888-313-2665

Visit us on the Internet at www.arcadiapublishing.com

Contents

Dedication and Acknowledgments

This book is dedicated to the authors' good friend and cousin, Dave Post, who passed away in December 2009, and to Missy Tipton Green's brother, Tim Tipton, who passed away on December 20, 2010.

Dave spent countless hours researching his Cades Cove lineage and put it into various collections for others to enjoy. Hiking was something that Dave loved to do, and he would hike to many of the old homesites in the cove just to be on the land that was once occupied by cove families. In 2001, when the Cades Cove Preservation Association Inc. was established, Dave was a charter member of the organization. Never did he complain about all of the hard work he put in to making the organization a success, and he was responsible for the good name that was acquired by the association. Dave was the son of William M. and Margaret Clark Post. The authors are proud to have known Dave Post and all of the precious memories that they have of him.

Tim was also a proud descendant of many cove families. He loved to fish and spent lots of his time doing just that. Tim went to schools in Blount County, attending Walland High School until its closure in 1977 and then Porter High School, where he graduated in 1979. He played football at both schools and was a member of the Walland High School football team that won the Tennessee State Championship in 1975. Tim's parents are Faye Everett Tipton and Wayne and Belle Tipton.

On June 8, 2011, Wayne Arnold Tipton, Missy Tipton Green's father, passed away. This book is also dedicated to him not only for being Missy's father, but also for his love of Cades Cove. He was born August 31, 1934, to Roy and Myrtle Nuchols Tipton. Roy was born and lived most of his childhood years in the cove. He was the son of Preacher Johnnie and Louisa Myers Tipton. Wayne grew up in Maryville, Tennessee, and went to school there, graduating from Everett High School. He worked for the Maryville Police Department for 36 years: his first years as a patrol officer and the last 16 as a detective. He served his country proudly in the US Army and the US Army National Guard. He was also a member of the New Providence Masonic Lodge and a charter member of the Maryville Fraternal Order of Police. His love for music was shown in many ways. He could play any instrument he picked up, and he was in the Kinsmen gospel quartet, singing one of the best tenor parts you could hear. He was very proud of his Cades Cove heritage and would share many stories with his family. He loved God and his family very much.

Without the help of many individuals contributing to the book, there is no way it would be as informative. Many thanks go to Margaret Oliver for the John W. Oliver collection, Leon and Johnnie Bryant Sparks, Lois Kay Sparks Russell, Verna Lee Burchfield Myers, Dale Sparks, George Shields, Sylvia Garland Galde, Nancy Webber, Ruth Caughron Davis, Roy Coada collection, and the National Park Service Archives (NPS). All of these contributed many wonderful pictures that tell the story of life in Cades Cove.

Introduction

Blount County was established in 1795 when it was voted into existence by the legislature of the Territory South of the Ohio River. The next year, Tennessee became a state. At this time, Cades Cove was not open for settlement; it was included in a sizable amount of land that still belonged to the Cherokees. There had been white settlers venturing into this fertile land known as Cades Cove, but none could legally lay claim until the Cherokees gave up their rights in 1819 under the Calhoun Treaty. The first known white family to settle in the cove traveled a crude Indian road from Carter County around 1818. John Oliver brought his wife, Luraney Frazier Oliver, with one small child and another one on the way. Many more families would later migrate to Cades Cove and started their homes and farms. They had many churches, schools, mills, and stores and lived life to its fullest. They were very self-sufficient and did not have to travel out of the cove very often.

In 1821, William Tipton was granted 1,280 acres, the first recorded legal land title in Cades Cove following the Calhoun Treaty. Tipton, along with his brothers Abraham and Thomas, began acquiring land on the valley floor. This area was established as the 16th Civil District of Blount County and was described in the minutes of the Blount County Court as "including all the inhabitants in Cades Cove, and in the Chestnut Flats, also all those living on or near the road from the Rich Gap to Cades Cove, which bounds shall constitute the 16th District, and we designate the house of Captain Jacob Tipton as the place for holding elections in the said district."

Others began to acquire parcels of the fertile valley known as Cades Cove. By 1850, the population of the cove was 685 individuals in 132 households, but by 1860, there were only 45 households with 275 individuals. The change was due simply to farm families moving on to other locations. The population began to increase again by the 1900, with 125 families and 708 individuals. Around 1928, though, land sales began for a national park, and many families decided to sell and move out immediately. Some families chose to sell but stayed on as lessees of the national park. In 1936, the 16th District ceased to exist when the property was obtained by eminent domain and made part of Great Smoky Mountains National Park. Having a lifetime lease, Kermit Caughron and his wife, Lois Shuler Caughron, were the last family to live in the cove. Kermit passed away in 1999, and Lois moved out, leaving no remaining people living in the cove.

Visitors travel to Cades Cove each year in great abundance to view this community of yesteryear. There are some signs still remaining, as well as cabins, churches, and a mill. This book will highlight houses not seen when you visit the cove. It will show the families that lived in these homes. There was more in Cades Cove than what meets the eye today.

One

Churches and Schools

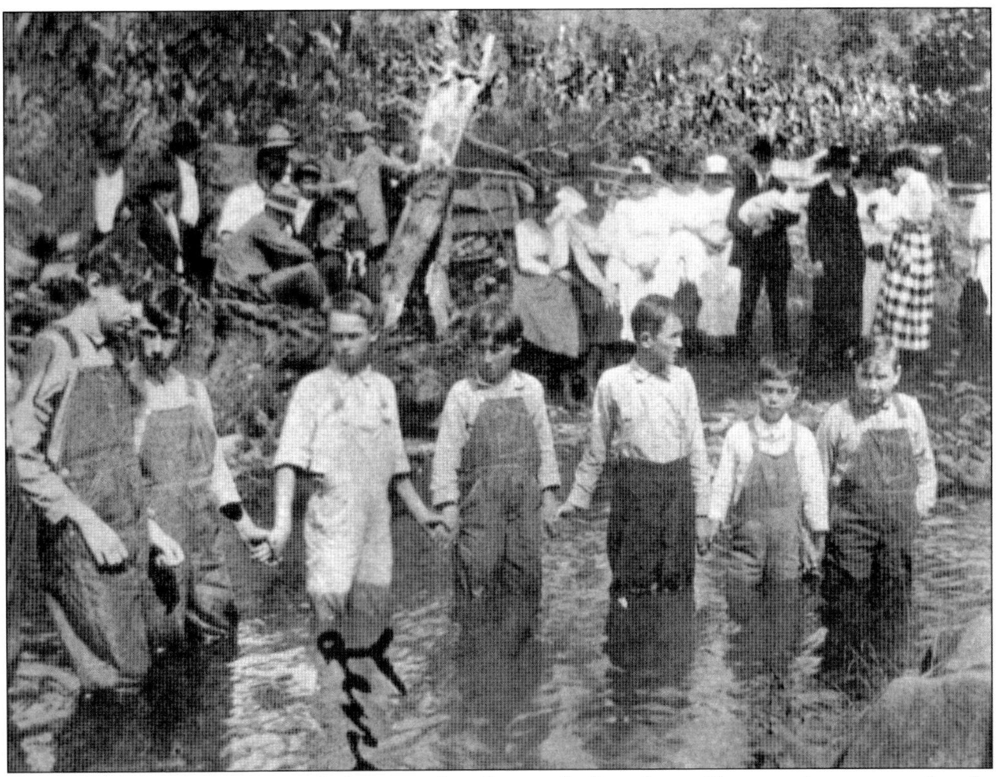

A Cades Cove baptism, a symbolic way of professing faith in Jesus Christ and joining a church, is seen here. Not all baptisms were held in a large river; sometimes, a smaller creek was used. There were many water spots in the cove known as "baptizing holes," and the baptisms were well attended by cove residents. Many of these residents followed in the believer's baptism, which is the Christian practice of his or her profession of faith and an admission into a local community of faith. (Courtesy of Margaret Oliver, John W. Oliver collection.)

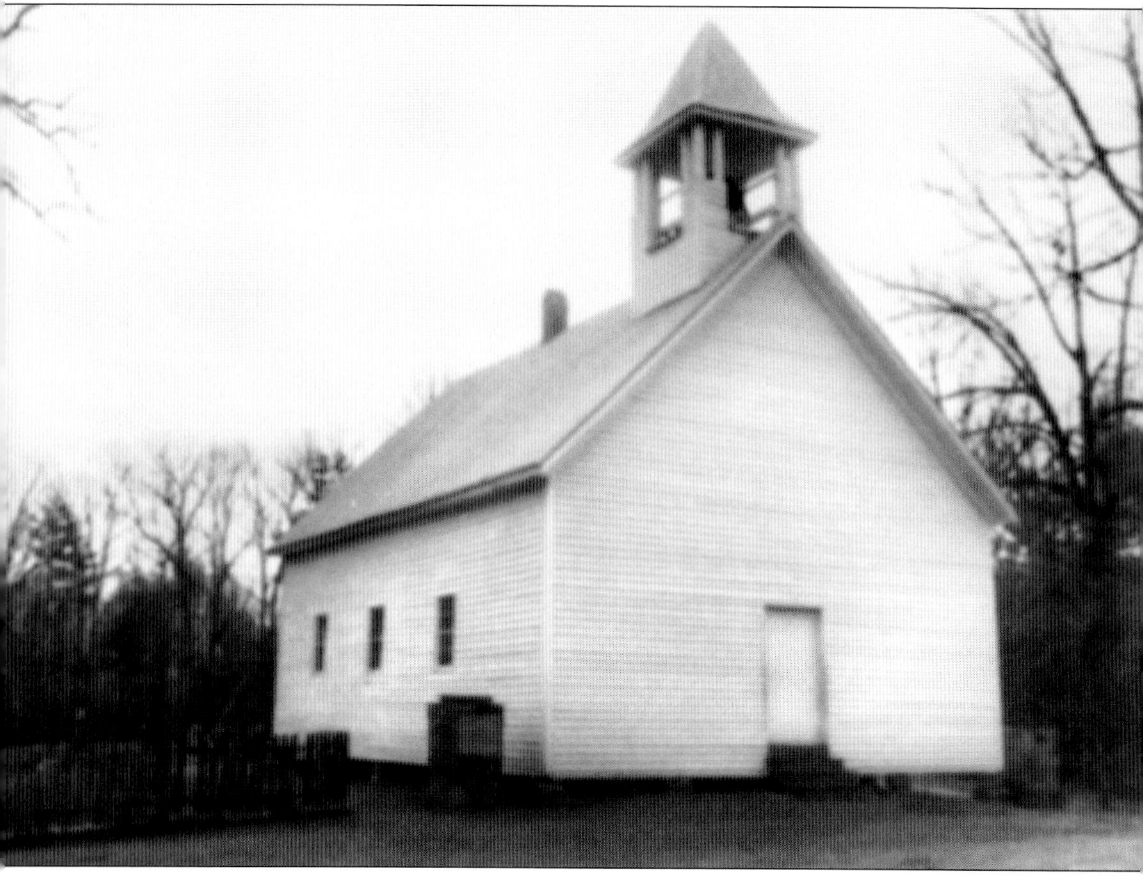

In June 1825, the Cades Cove Primitive Baptist Church was known as the Church of Christ of Miller's Cove. On June 16, 1827, the first meeting of a group of Cades Cove residents started the formation of the church; they were Calvinistic and believed in complete separation of church and state. On June 19, 1829, the church became independent and was called Cades Cove Baptist Church. As recorded on page 178 in Blount County Deed Book M, William Tipton deeded a half acre to the church. The first meeting place was constructed of crude logs in 1832, with the current building erected in 1887 to replace the log structure. By 1841, the church was known as the Cades Cove Primitive Baptist Church. The church and the land were conveyed to the National Park Service by condemnation action by the State of Tennessee on December 8, 1939, as recorded in Blount County, Tennessee, Miscellaneous Book 5, page 574. (Courtesy of NPS.)

Cades Cove Methodist Church was listed as one of five churches on Holston's Little River Circuit in 1830; however, the church did not have a structure until 1840, when three acres of land were deeded to the Methodist trustees. The first building was described as a structure of very crude nature, made with logs. The building had no floor, but later puncheon floors were added. Like other cove churches, the Methodist church was inactive during the Civil War era. Around 1902, the log structure was replaced by the frame building that stands today, which was constructed by Rev. John McCampbell of Tuckaleechee. He was paid $115 for the 115 days it took to complete the structure. The cemetery at this church is the second-oldest cemetery in Cades Cove. The trustees sold the church on December 29, 1936, according to the Blount County, Tennessee, Deed Book 118, page 43. (Courtesy of Margaret Oliver, John W. Oliver collection.)

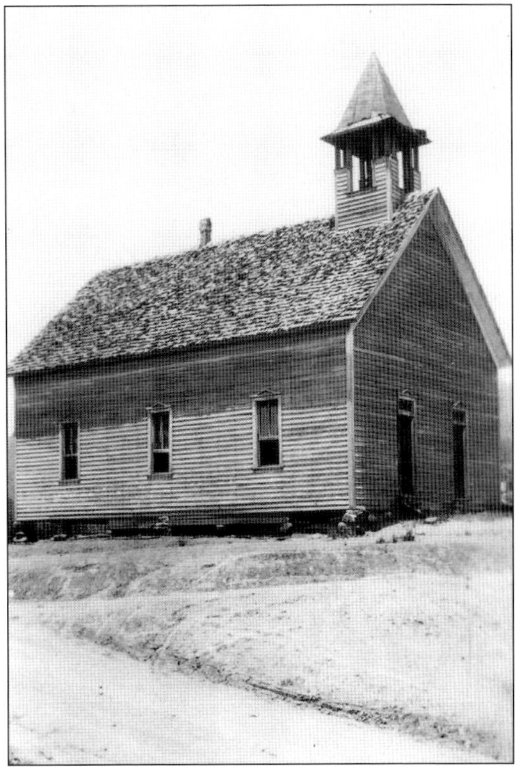

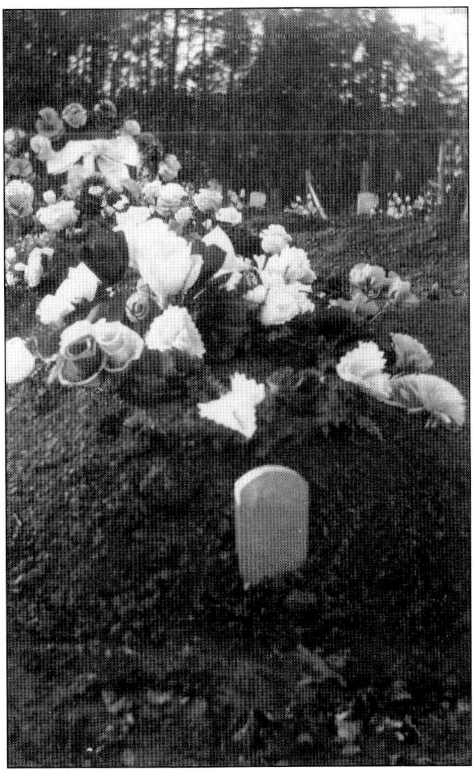

This photograph shows the many paper flowers that were made by cove families and placed upon a new grave. Hours of preparation were put into the making of these flowers. Paper flowers were often dipped in paraffin to prevent the rain from destroying them after placement on a grave. (Courtesy of NPS.)

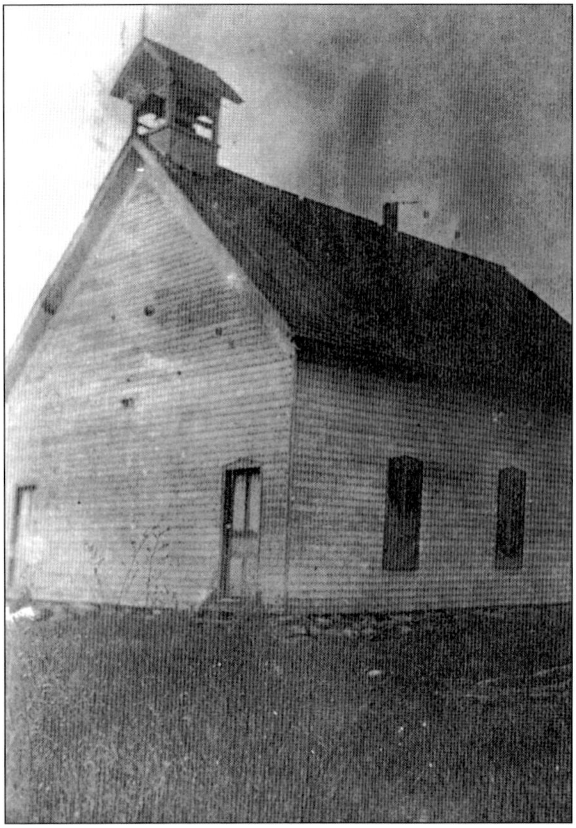

Hyatt Hill Missionary Baptist Church was built in 1895 on what is known today as Hyatt Lane. This was a result of the split from the Cades Cove Primitive Baptist Church by members who were dismissed over the mission-support issue. Some members did not want to support missions, and some did. The older Primitive Baptists did not believe in giving help for any mission projects. The split resulted in the organization of a Missionary Baptist Church in 1838. Meetings were held at members' homes or were shared at the current Primitive Baptist Church or Methodist church buildings until the completion of the Hyatt Hill structure. In 1898, a Sunday school was started, ongoing until 1944 when the doors to the Cades Cove Missionary Baptist Church closed. (Both, courtesy of NPS.)

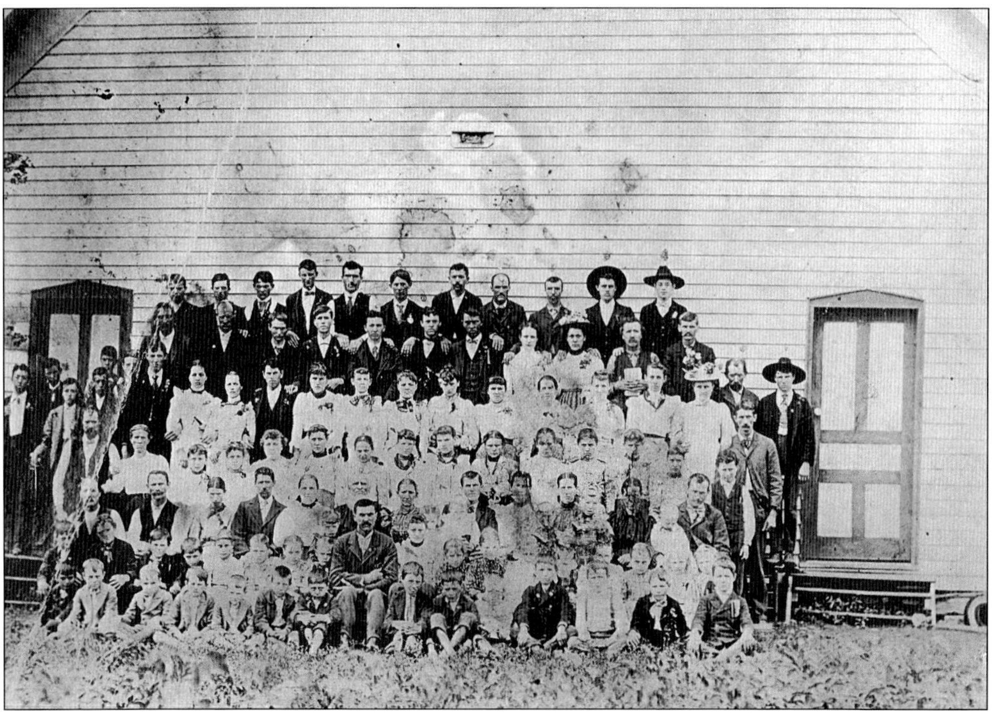

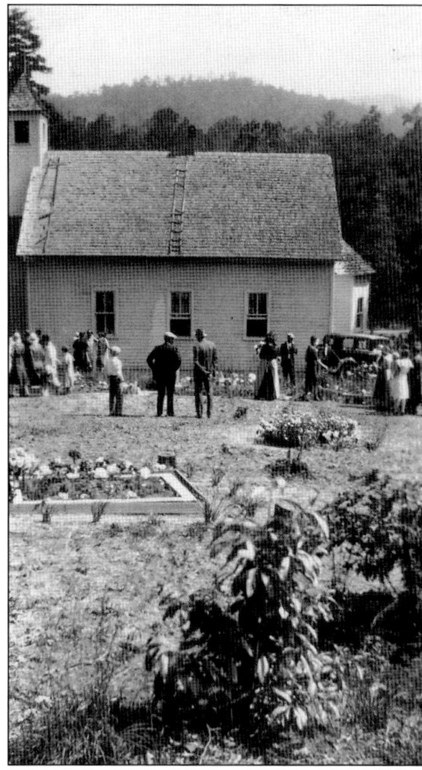

Decoration Day, which possibly originated when Southern women began scattering spring flowers on the graves of soldiers during the Civil War, was one of the largest social events in Cades Cove. There was much to do to get ready for this day: cleaning the graveyards and cemeteries; meetings at church; worshipping with each other in prayer, songs, and preaching services; and placing paper flowers, made by the women and children of the cove during the winter months and stored until Decoration Day, or fresh flowers, which the women had grown at their homes, on the graves. For some people, it meant coming home to the cove. It also meant fellowship with family and friends. The photograph on the right was taken at Missionary Baptist Church. Below is Cades Cove Methodist Church. (Both, courtesy of Margaret Oliver, John W. Oliver collection.)

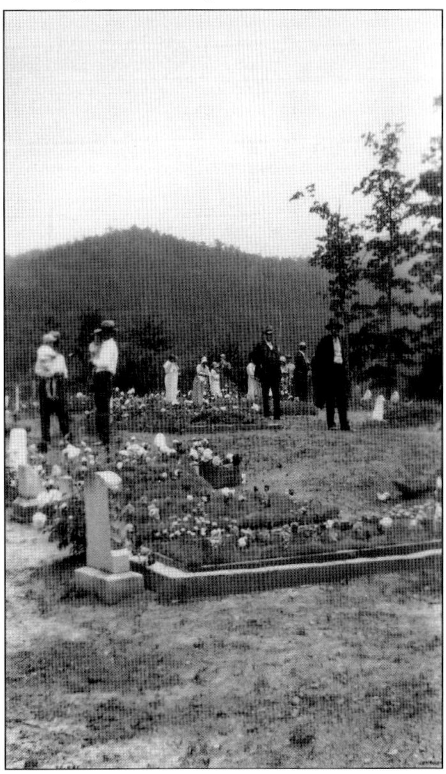

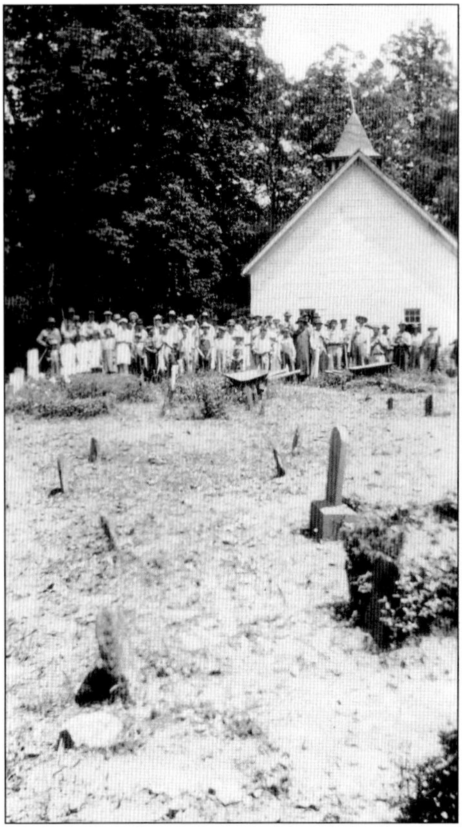

The photograph at left shows the community getting ready to clean up the Cades Cove Primitive Baptist Church cemetery, which would take about a day. Below, cove families place flowers at the Cades Cove Methodist Church. In the early morning on Decoration Day, many cove families arrived at Cades Cove Missionary Baptist Church, either in a buggy or on foot, carrying flowers and baskets of food for the dinner to be held later in the day. The first service would begin with much singing, poems recited by the children, and a sermon. The same kind of program would next be held at Cades Cove Methodist Church. Families would then proceed to Cades Cove Primitive Baptist Church, where the much anticipated dinner on the ground was held at the Consolidated School area and the last service of the day at the church. (Both, courtesy of Margaret Oliver, John W. Oliver collection.)

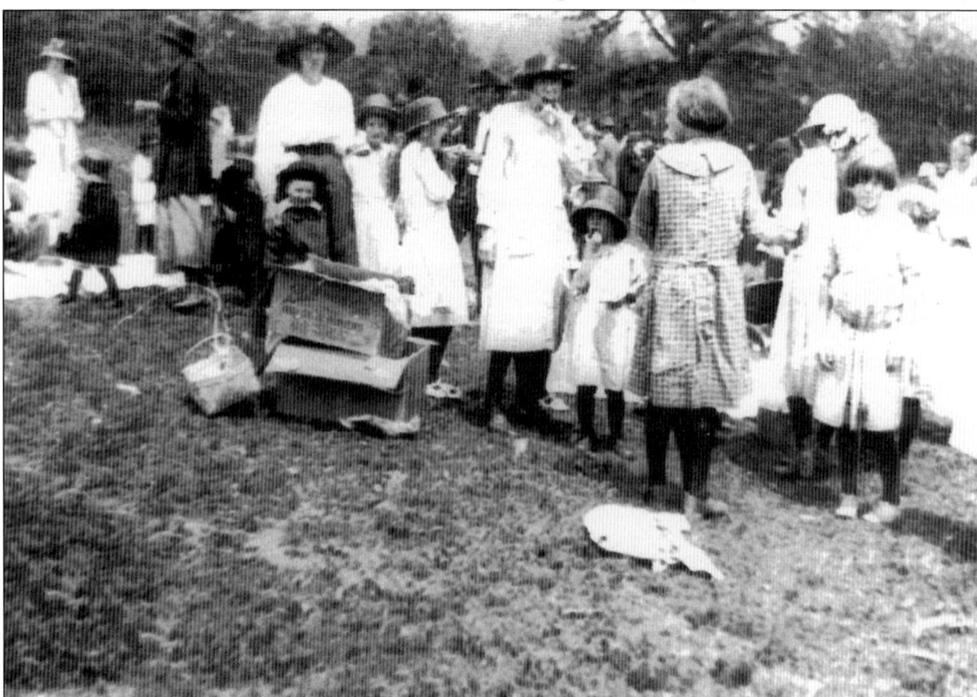

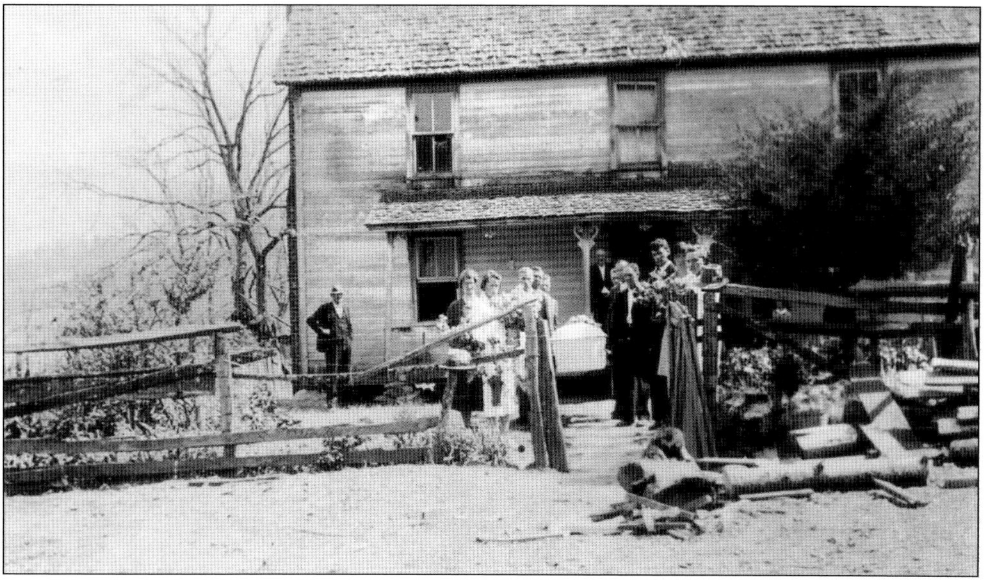

The tolling of the church bells let the cove residents know when a death had occurred in the community. The bell would toll first to get the attention of the community, and then it would toll the age of the deceased. All work would stop, men would help to dig the grave, and women would prepare food to be taken to the home of the deceased. Preparations had to be made for the laying out of the body and sitting up with it. The community would take charge and make sure everything was taken care of for the family that had lost their loved one. After the burial was completed, daily activity resumed. The above photograph shows Sarah Burchfield's coffin being carried out of her home by family and friends. Below is the funeral march for Sarah Burchfield at the Cades Cove Missionary Baptist Church. (Both, courtesy of Margaret Oliver, John W. Oliver collection.)

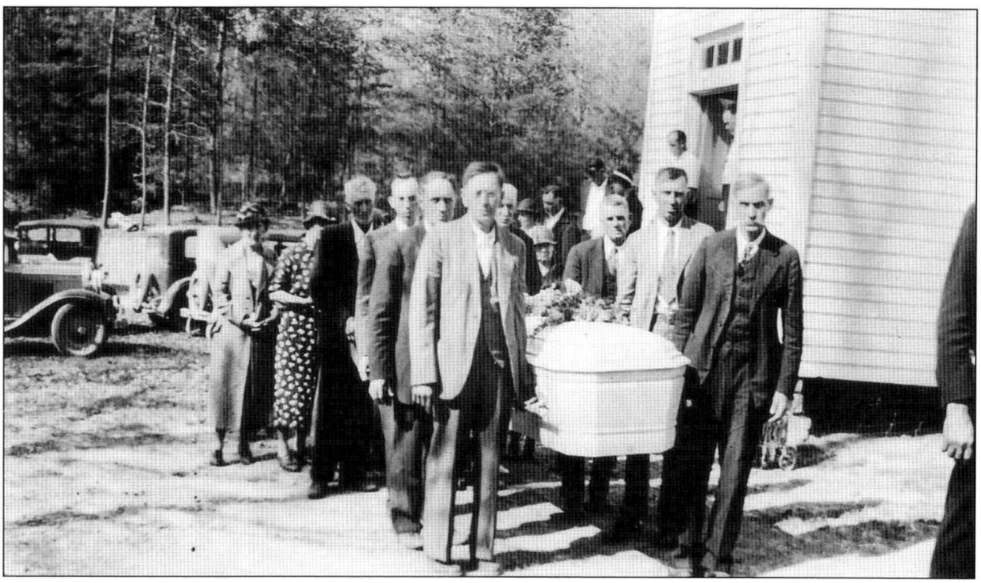

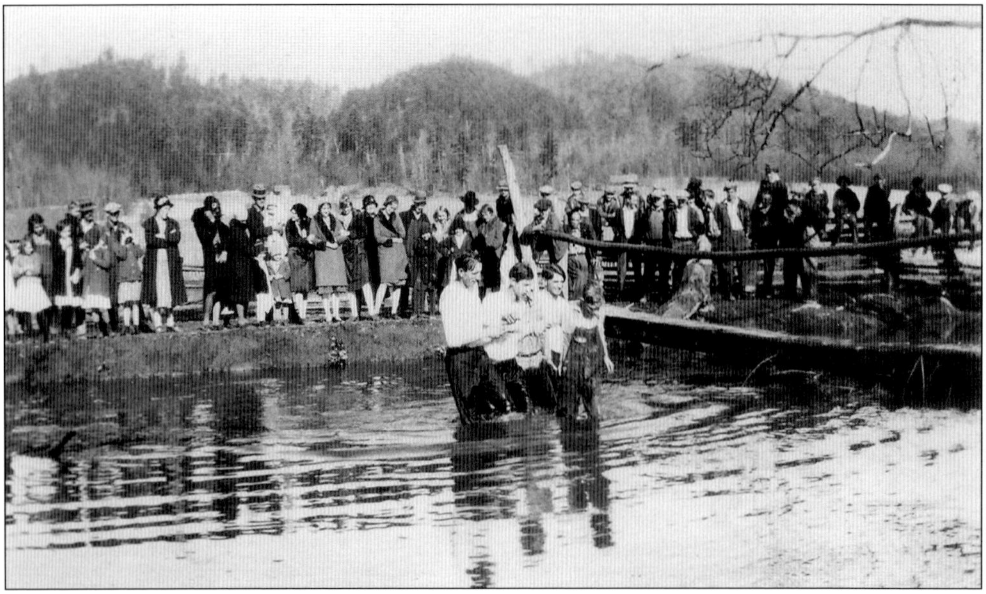

Being baptized at the Noah Burchfield farm in the cove are, from left to right, Townsend Garland, Arthur Wright, Joe Tipton, and Arley Tipton. Rev. Joe Boring is in the background. Baptism is a symbolic representation of the inner conversion a person being baptized makes and is also a public expression of faith. (Courtesy of Margaret Oliver, John W. Oliver collection.)

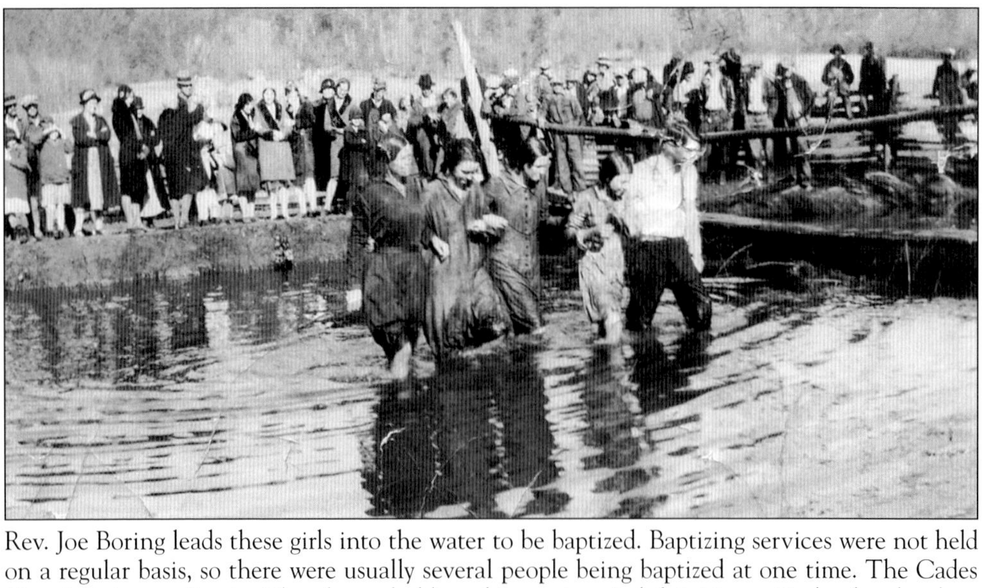

Rev. Joe Boring leads these girls into the water to be baptized. Baptizing services were not held on a regular basis, so there were usually several people being baptized at one time. The Cades Cove Missionary Baptist Church was holding this service. At left is Nancy Garland, a daughter of Jake and Sarah Garland. (Courtesy of Sylvia Garland Galde.)

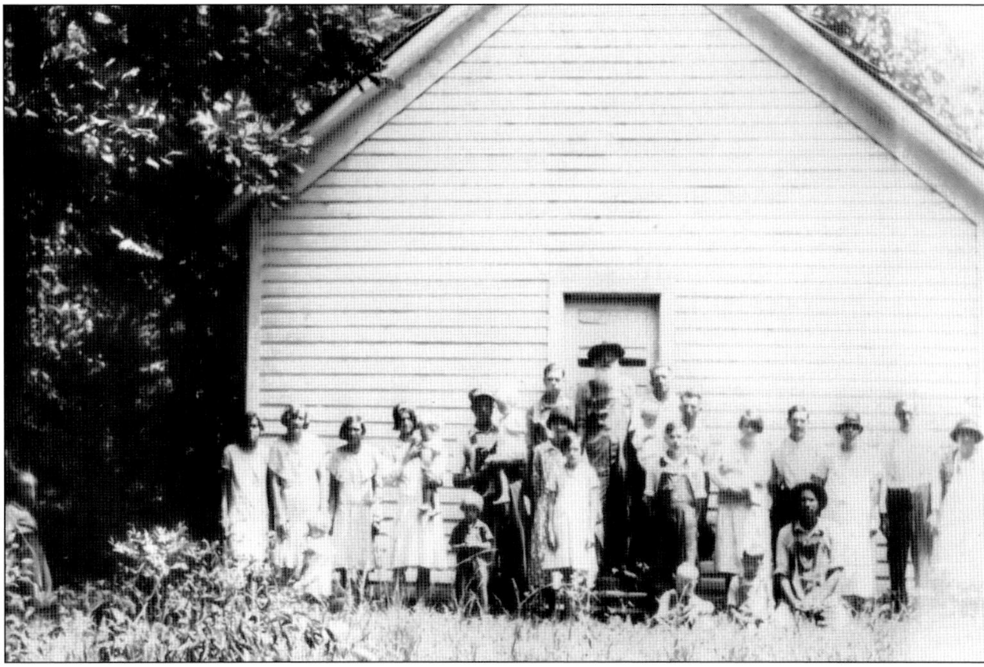

Spruce Flats School was established in 1900 about a fourth of a mile east of the current Cades Cove picnic area. This school was built because of the student population along the Anthony Creek area and was also known as the Crib Gap School. The school was dismantled in 1917 and relocated to the east end of the current picnic area, probably because of a change in the population of students. (Courtesy of Margaret Oliver, John W. Oliver collection.)

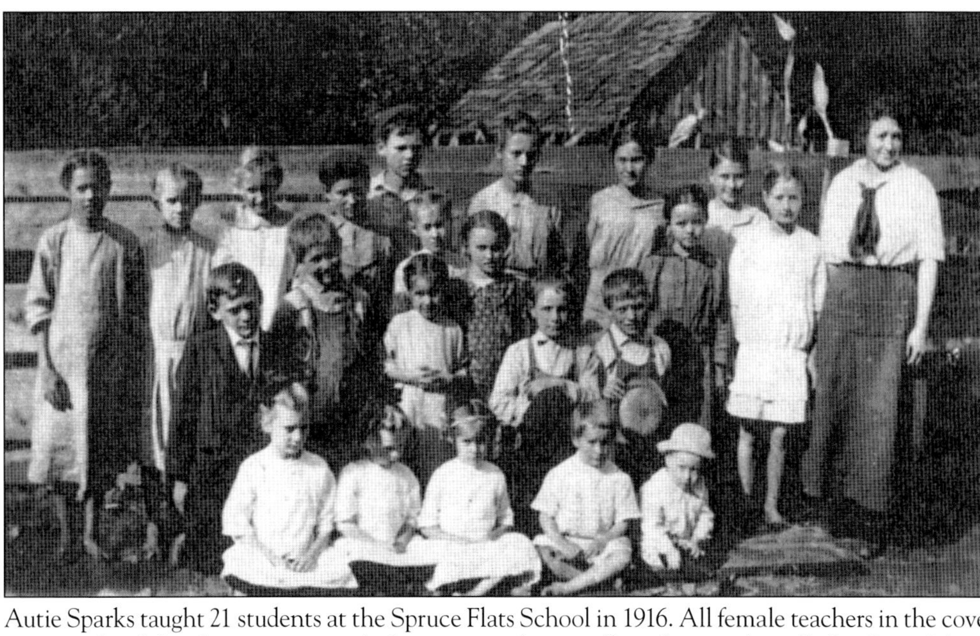

Autie Sparks taught 21 students at the Spruce Flats School in 1916. All female teachers in the cove were single; if they became married, they were no longer allowed to teach in Cades Cove. Many of the teachers would board with a student's family. (Courtesy of Geraldine Cooper Waters.)

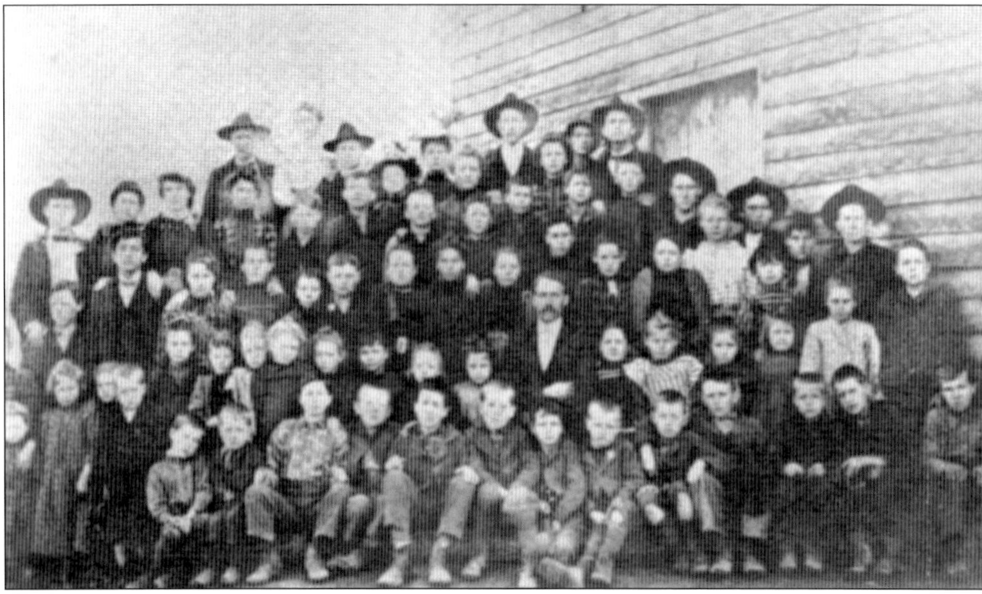

The Upper School of Cades Cove was located in the Sparks Lane area. James R. "Jim" Oliver (middle of second row) is the teacher in this 1901 photograph. Whether it was spelling bees, baseball, or basketball, there was always a great rivalry between the Upper and Lower Schools. This school closed with the completion of the Cades Cove Consolidated School. (Courtesy of NPS.)

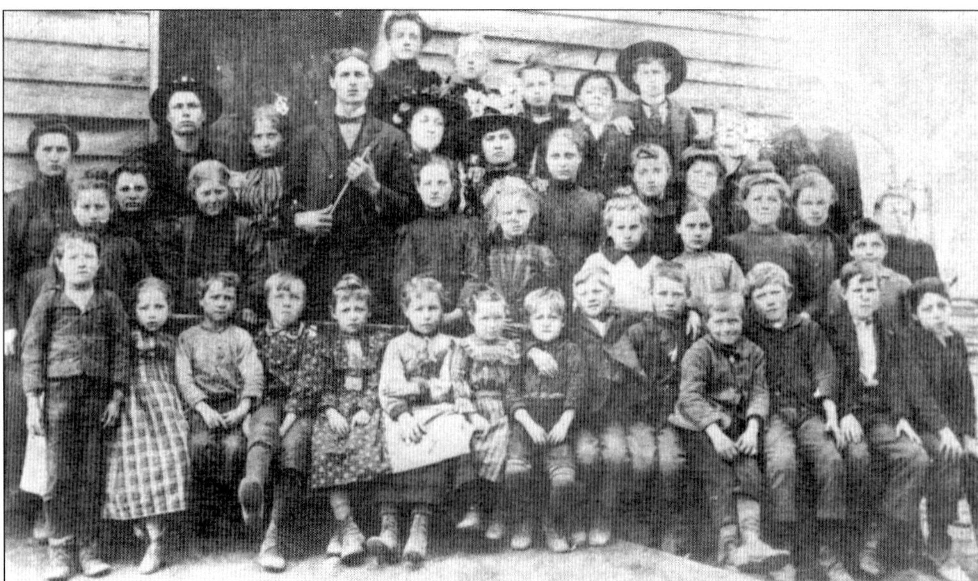

The Lower School of Cades Cove was located in the vicinity of the Cable Mill; it was a one-room building that housed grades one through eight. This school was in session in 1896 but ceased operation when the Cades Cove Consolidated School was built in 1915 to combine both of the cove schools. In 1901, the teacher for this school group is John W. Oliver. (Courtesy of NPS.)

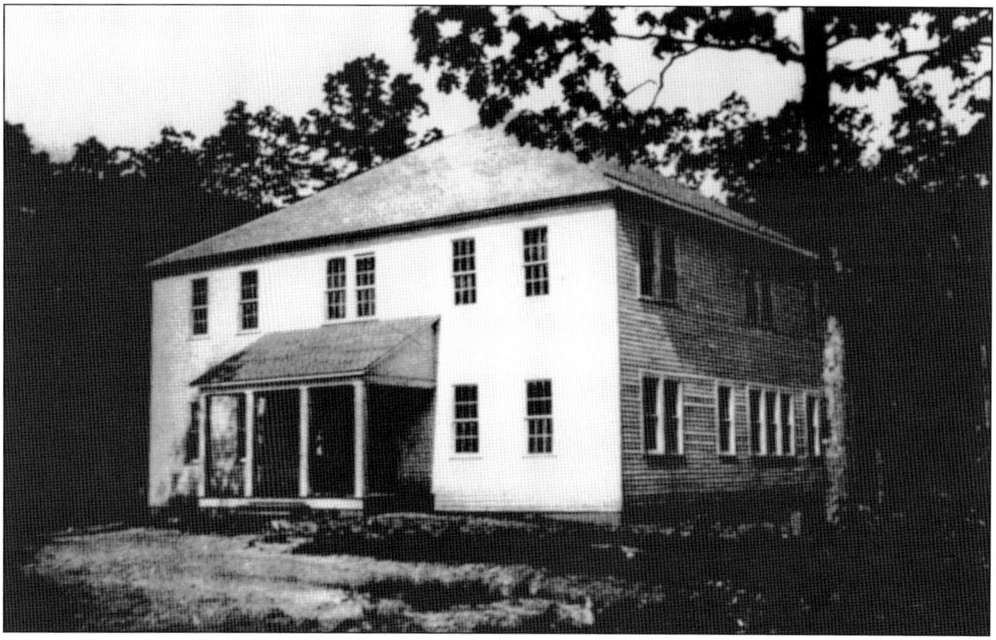

Built on land donated by Witt Shields in 1915, the Cades Cove Consolidated School was constructed to promote progress and efficiency. It was located east of the Cades Cove Primitive Baptist Church. The *Maryville Times* reported that the school was constructed with modern methods and both lighted and heated, with water from a mountain spring and educational advantages for the boys and girls of the cove. It was a two-story frame structure (above) with the upper level serving as a chapel, assembly area, and basketball court. The school term was only five months, usually completed before Christmas. Damages from severe weather in 1925 resulted in the loss of the upper floor, and it became a three-room, one-level building (below). Grades one through eight continued to attend the school. Teachers at cove schools often boarded with families. Cades Cove Consolidated School ceased to operate after 20 years, with students transferring to the Cable School. (Both, courtesy of Margaret Oliver, John W. Oliver collection.)

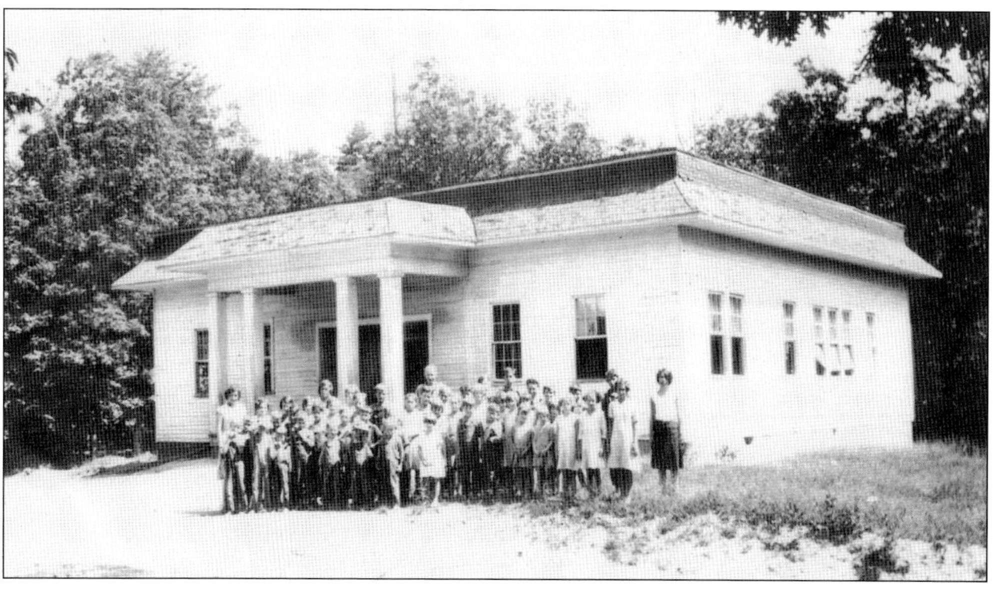

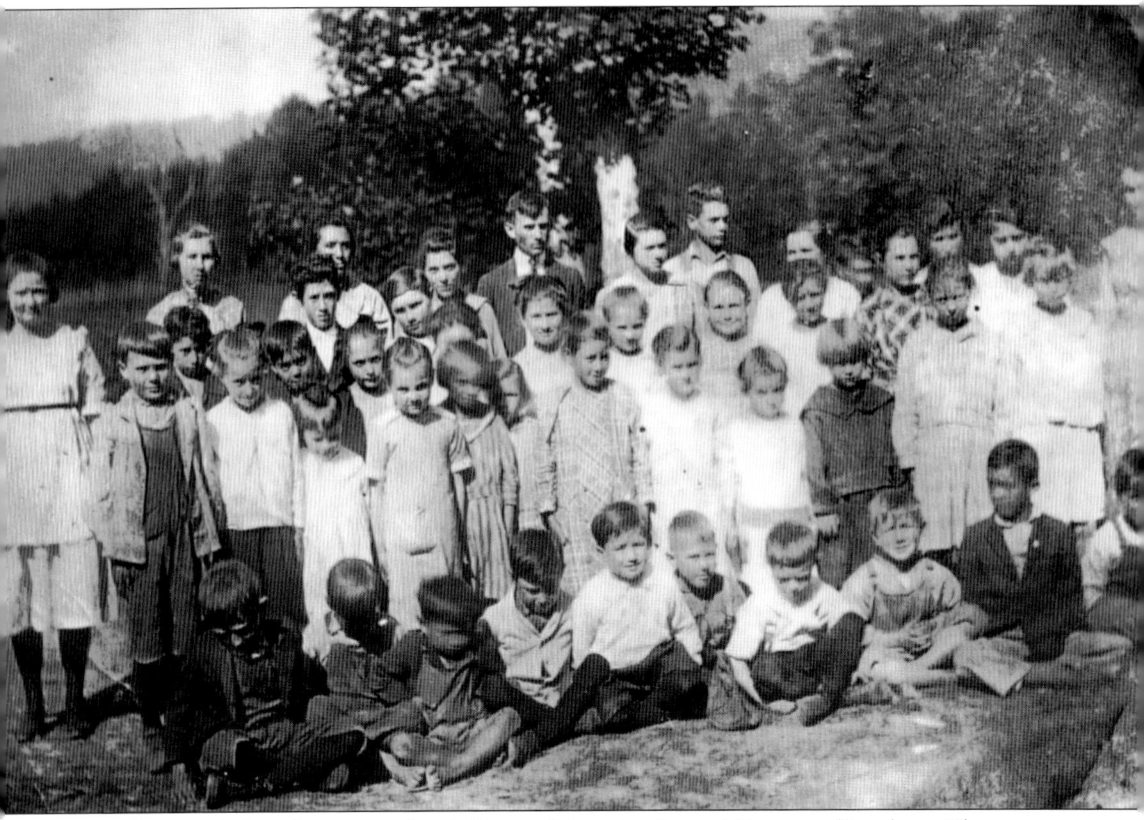

Often on Friday afternoons, the children of the schools would have spelling bees. The seats were arranged in two parallel rows on opposite sides of the room, and two students would be chosen to pick sides, which would include all students. The teacher pronounced a word, starting at one end of one side and moving to the other end, crossing over to the other side, and then repeating the process. Every word was repeated until it was spelled correctly. When a student spelled one of the missed words correctly, he would be moved ahead in the line to where the student that misspelled the word sat. This was often known as turning down or moving ahead of the person or persons who missed the word. When the student got to the front of the line and spelled his next word correctly, he would move over to the other side. A tally was then awarded to that team, and at the end of the session, the side with the largest tally score won the spelling bee. (Courtesy of Margaret Oliver, John W. Oliver collection.)

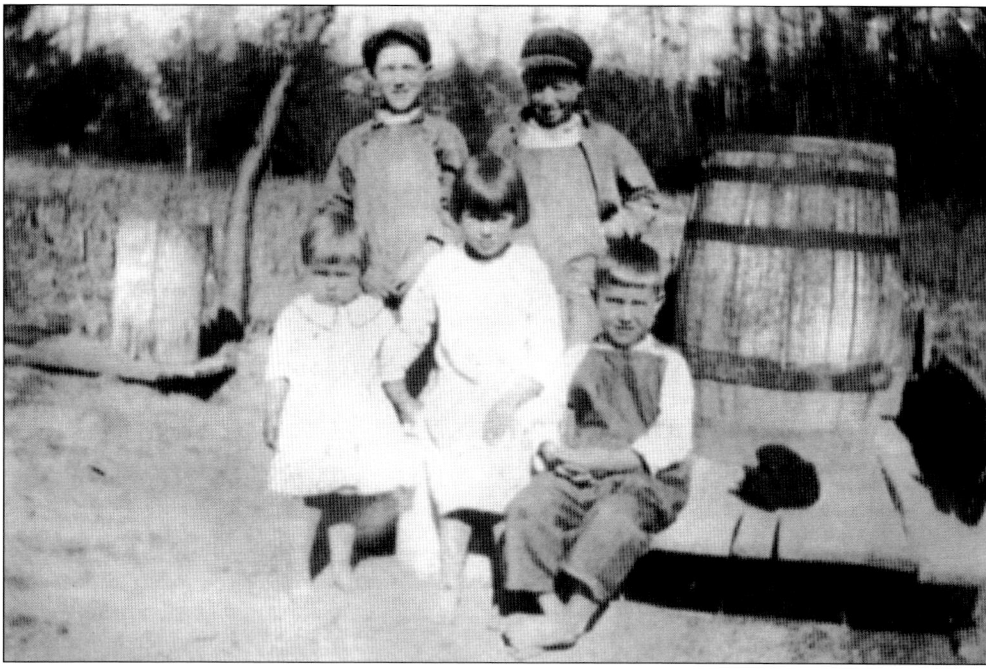

From left to right, Lois, Roy, Ruth, Vernie, and Lee Tipton were the children of Preacher Johnnie and Louisa Myers Tipton. At one time, they lived at the headwaters of Tater Branch in a section known as Cooper Hollow. Lee Tipton remembers a school day from 8:00 a.m. until 4:00 p.m., with one hour for lunch and a 15-minute recess. Families ate together because mothers only packed one basket; the Tipton children would eat under a white oak tree. Their basket or lard can could hold baked sweet potatoes, corn bread, molasses in a pint jar, butter, or fried Irish potatoes. Because of the distance to the school from their home, cove children often had to walk for an hour to and from the school every day. (Courtesy of Tipton family collection.)

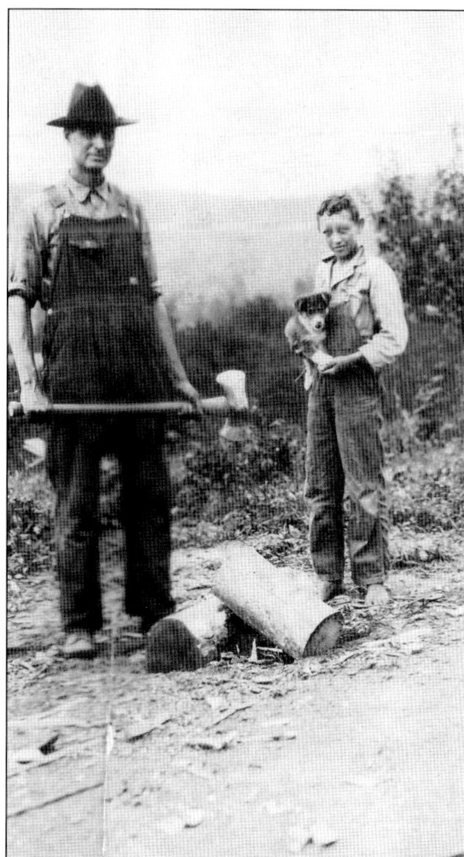

Pictured are John W. Oliver and his son Henry Clay Oliver with Henry's puppy, Grey Dawn. There was much work to do on the Oliver farm. The children were always involved in the daily chores, and some days in the months when the crops were ready to be harvested, children were kept home from school to help get this job completed. Some schools would close down during the busy harvest season and start back up when it was completed. (Courtesy of Margaret Oliver, John W. Oliver collection.)

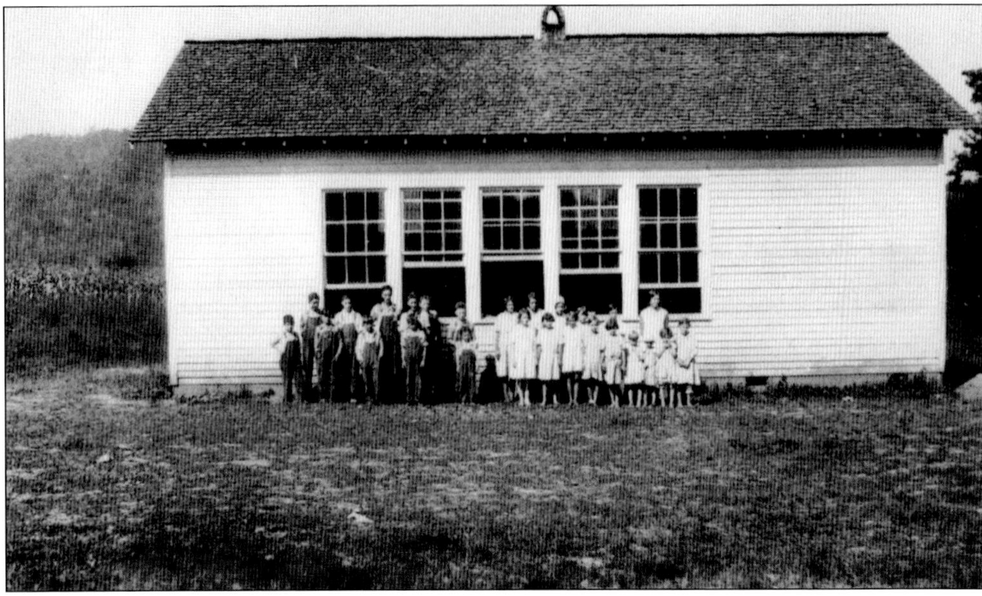

About 1927, there was a need for a school in the southwestern region of the cove. Rebecca "Aunt Becky" Cable donated the land for the construction of the building. Laurel Springs School, which was located in the Chestnut Flats area, was dismantled and materials were recycled for the Cable School. With the use of Aunt Becky's wagon and a team of mules, the materials were transported to the new site. The steps for the school were constructed of concrete, which was made by using sand removed from Forge Creek. Eight grades attended the one-room school until it closed in 1944. Pictured above are students at the school. Below is the back of the school. (Both, courtesy of Margaret Oliver, John W. Oliver collection.)

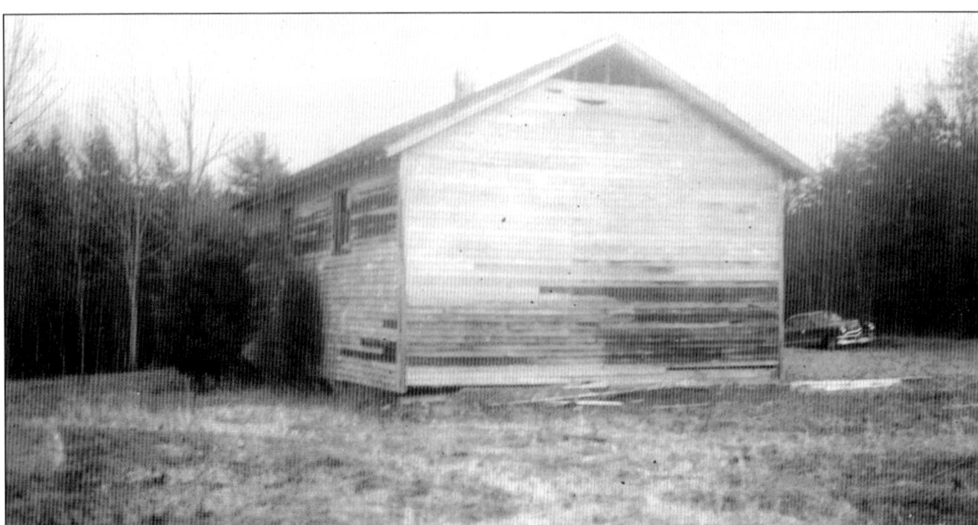

Two

STORES AND MILLS

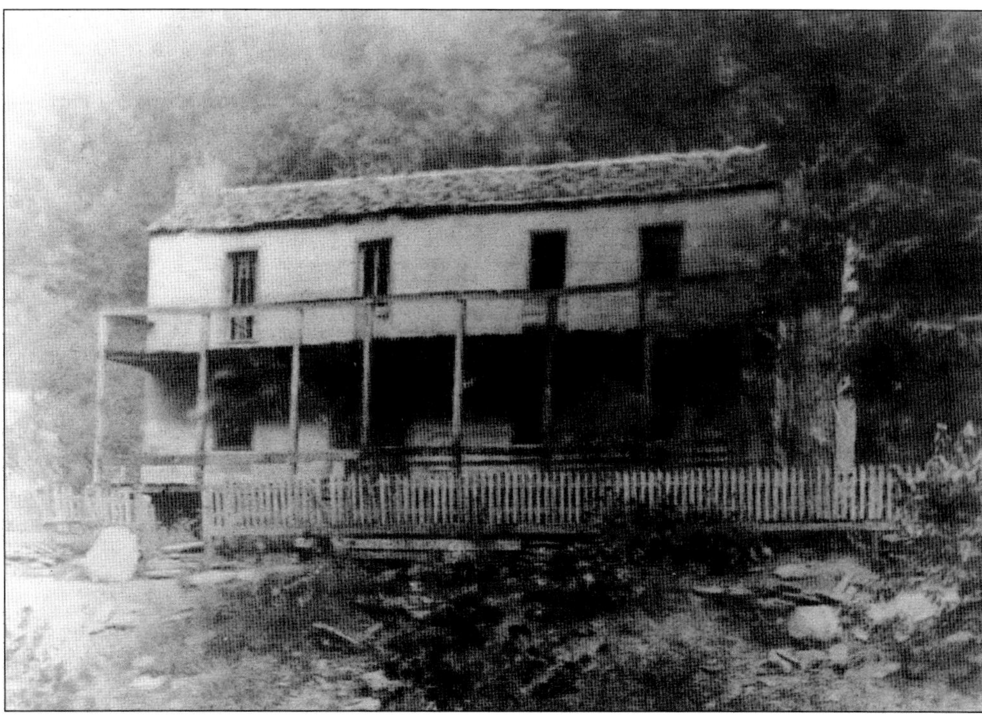

In 1873, Leason Gregg established the first documented store in Cades Cove. The location of the business was on Forge Creek Road at Mill Creek in the western area of the cove. A room on the lower floor of the building was used as the store. Around 1887, Rebecca Cable purchased the storehouse and continued operation until about 1900. (Courtesy of NPS.)

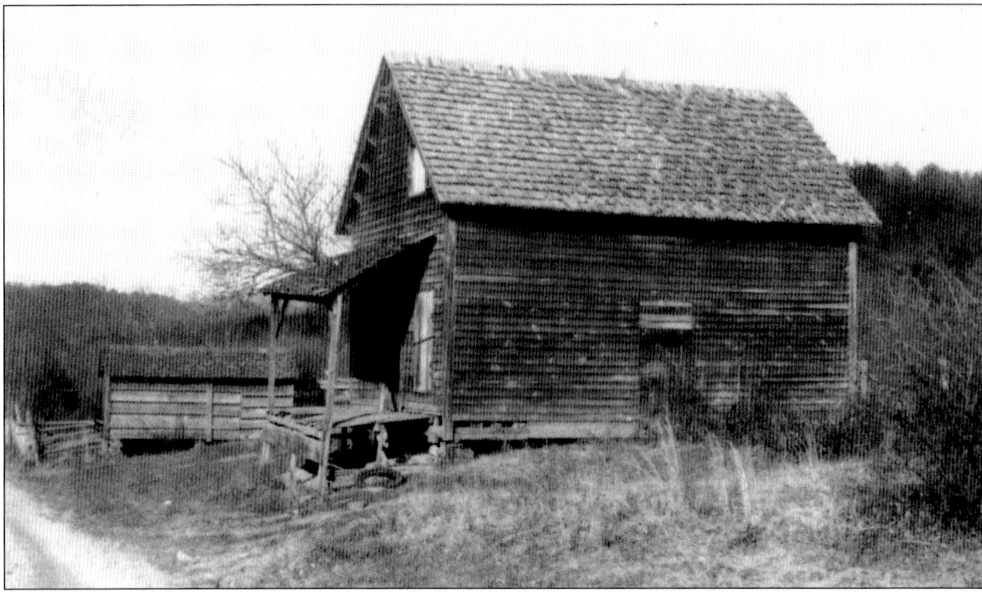

Russell and Jane Burchfield operated this store, located on Forge Creek Road not far from the Gregg-Cable store. Items for sell here from 1911 to 1913 included tobacco, shoestrings, cough syrup, coffee, cloth, soda, coal oil, handkerchiefs, lard, sugar, and many other things. Individuals paid in different ways—by credit, by cash, or by bartering. Credit was given for eggs, chickens, and corn. Often, running credit was given and paid for as soon as possible by the purchaser. (Courtesy of NPS.)

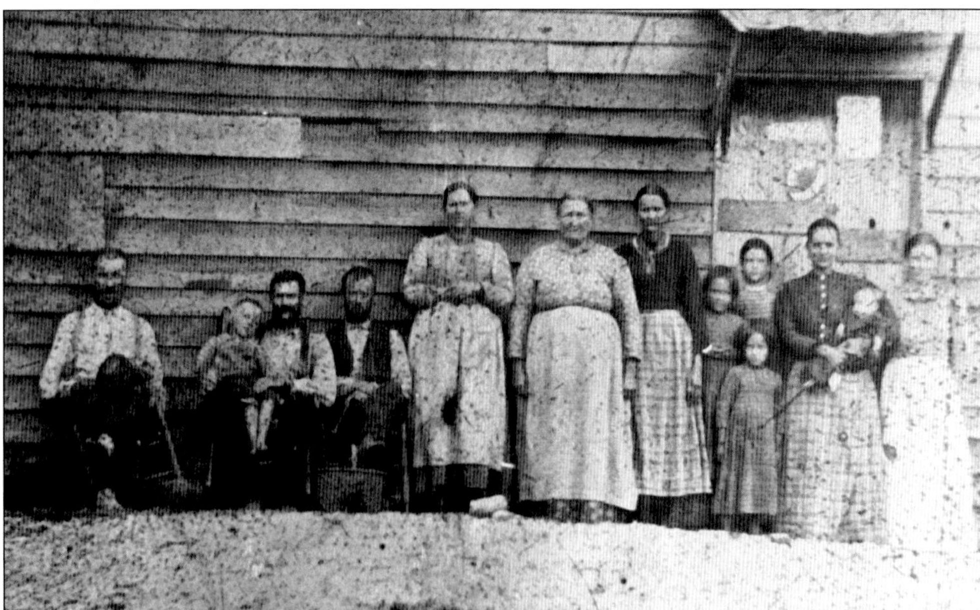

Lazarus Anthony was a prominent storekeeper with a store located near Abrams Creek and Sparks Lane in the eastern end of the cove. It was often used as a gathering place for cove residents to catch up on community news. Men would sit, talk, and whittle while the women were shopping. This store was later known as the "Bud" Gregory store. The Anthony family and friends are pictured here. (Courtesy of Margaret Oliver, John W. Oliver collection.)

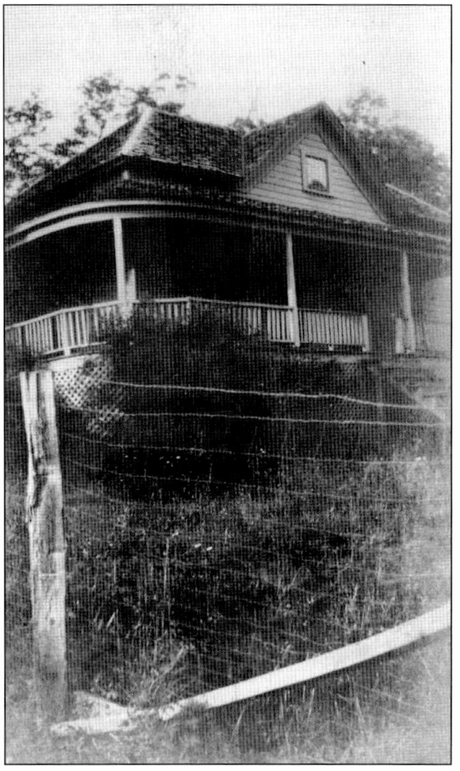

On the main roadway in the cove, opposite the road to the Cades Cove Primitive Baptist Church, sat the Albert Hill home and store. Like many of the cove stores, it was located in the residence. Rolling stores also operated in the cove, bringing items that could not be purchased at the local store. Cove residents would also sell items such as eggs, chickens, and honey to the rolling store. This was known as bartering, and people would purchase what they needed with what they earned for their items sold. This store was located in the north central area of the cove and was the last to operate in Cades Cove. Pictured below are, from left to right, Martha, Elmo, Albert, Ruth, and Mabel Hill. (Both, courtesy of Margaret Oliver, John W. Oliver collection.)

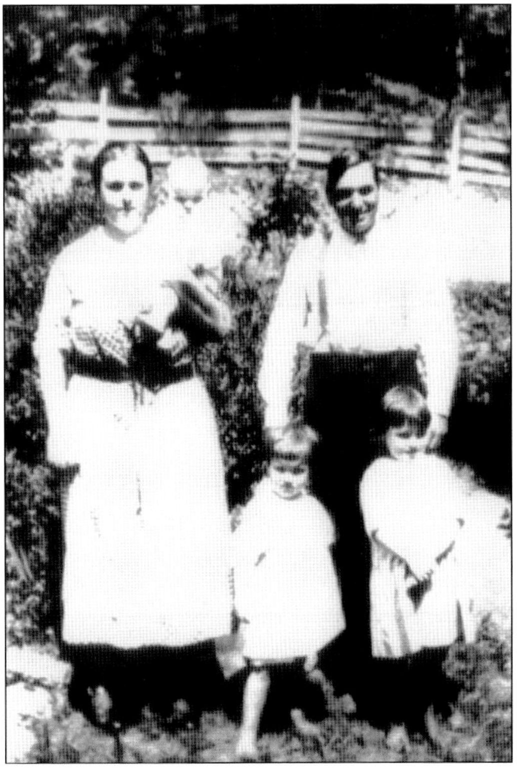

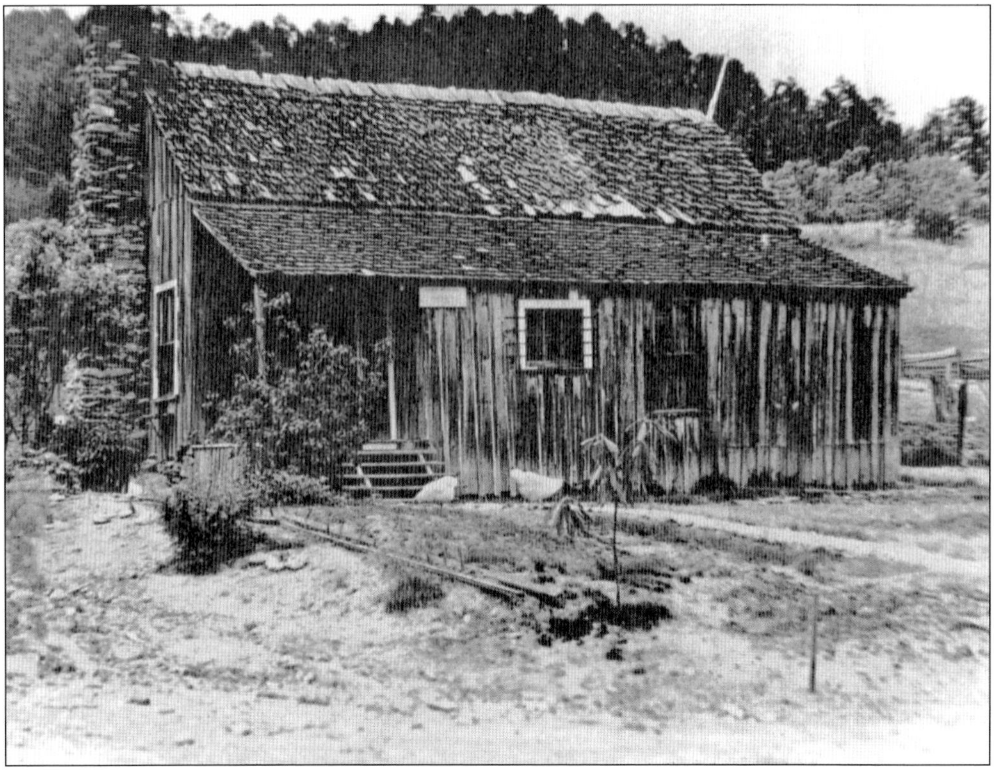

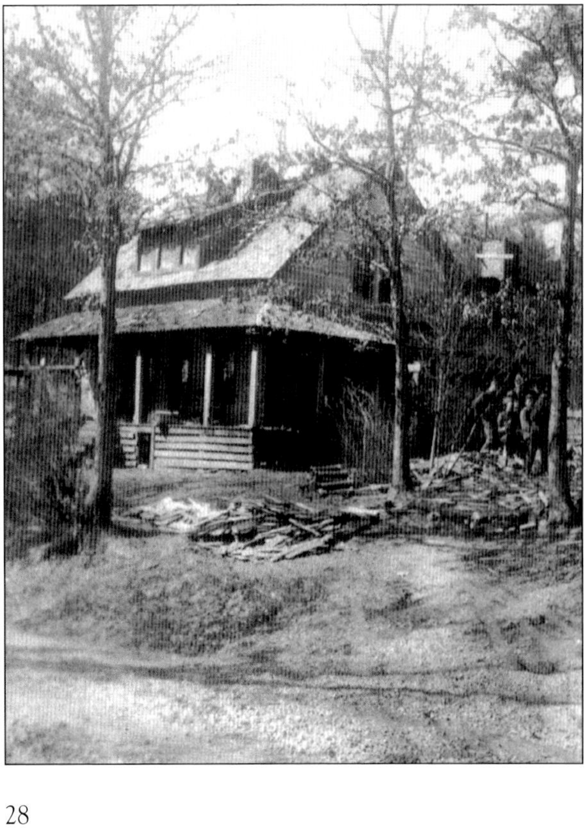

Pictured is the first home and store of Jonathan Myers, located in the north central area of the cove. Myers was also a postmaster, and the cove's post office was located in this house. Myers purchased items for inventory from J.N. Badgett Company, Rockford Overalls Company, E. L. Wilkinson, Maryville Bottling Company, and Kaiser Brothers. Myers was also a well-known local photographer. (Courtesy of NPS.)

Jonathan Myers moved his store, home, and post office to a different site, located opposite the Cades Cove Missionary Baptist Church. To be able to make purchases, cove residents often had to use the barter system. Goods received by the store clerk could be honey, eggs, seng (ginseng), chickens, a calf, wheat, wool, or other items. (Courtesy of Verna Lee Burchfield Myers.)

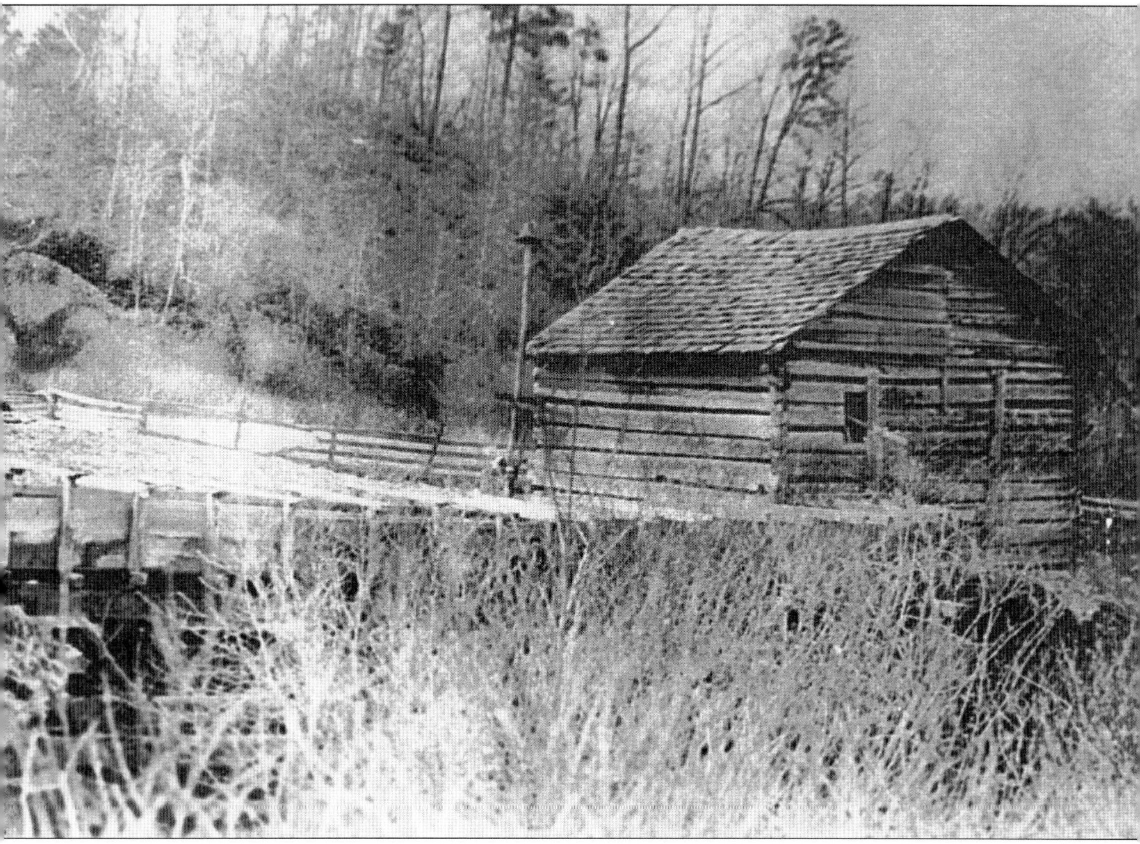

Robert Shields purchased land in 1831 in the western end of Cades Cove and, along with David Emmett, built a large waterpowered mill for sawing lumber and milling wheat and corn. There were separate rocks used for grinding corn and wheat. Pioneer settlers of Cades Cove imported life-sustaining skills, knowledge, and values to establish and maintain the community. These included agricultural methods and processes for conversion of agricultural products to foodstuffs. One of the most critical processes was that of transforming grains grown in the cove, primarily corn and wheat, into meal and flour for the preparation of bread, typically consumed morning, noon, and evening. The location of this mill was on Mill Creek just off Forge Creek Road, and it operated with an overshot wheel, which functions wholly by gravity with water filling buckets from the top. (Courtesy of NPS.)

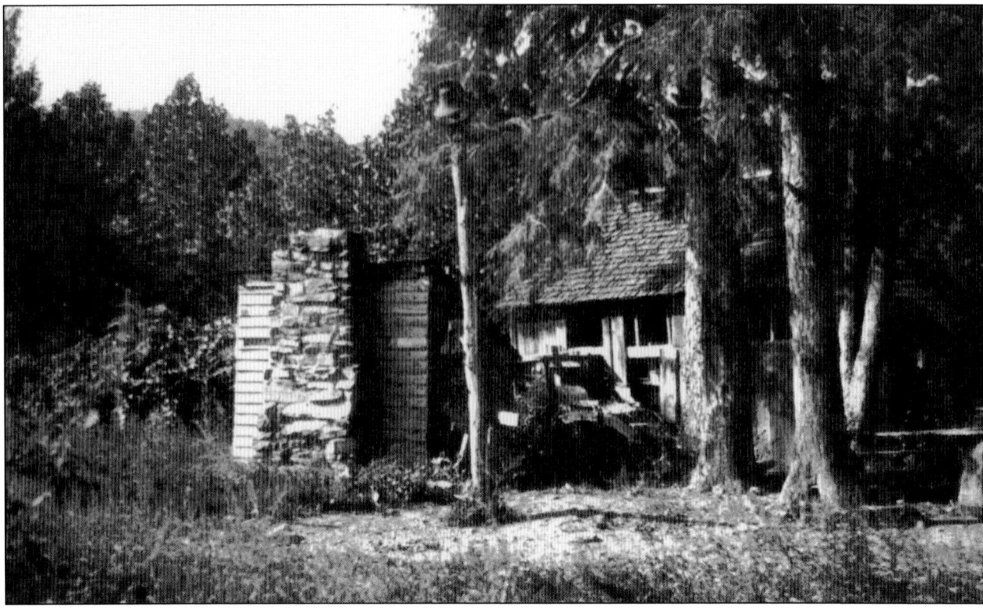

John P. Cable moved to Cades Cove from Carter County, Tennessee, and built his gristmill from about 1870 to 1875. With its small dam, long race and flume, and vertical overshot wheel, it turned out to be typical of the small custom mills in the area. Cove residents would take their corn to be ground; the charge would be 1/8 of the completed meal. Cable Mill is located in the lower part of Cades Cove. The water in Mill Creek reached a really low level at one time, and there was not enough water flowing to keep the mill going. A diversion was made behind the mill for water from Forge Creek to flow to the mill to keep it operating. (Both, courtesy of NPS.)

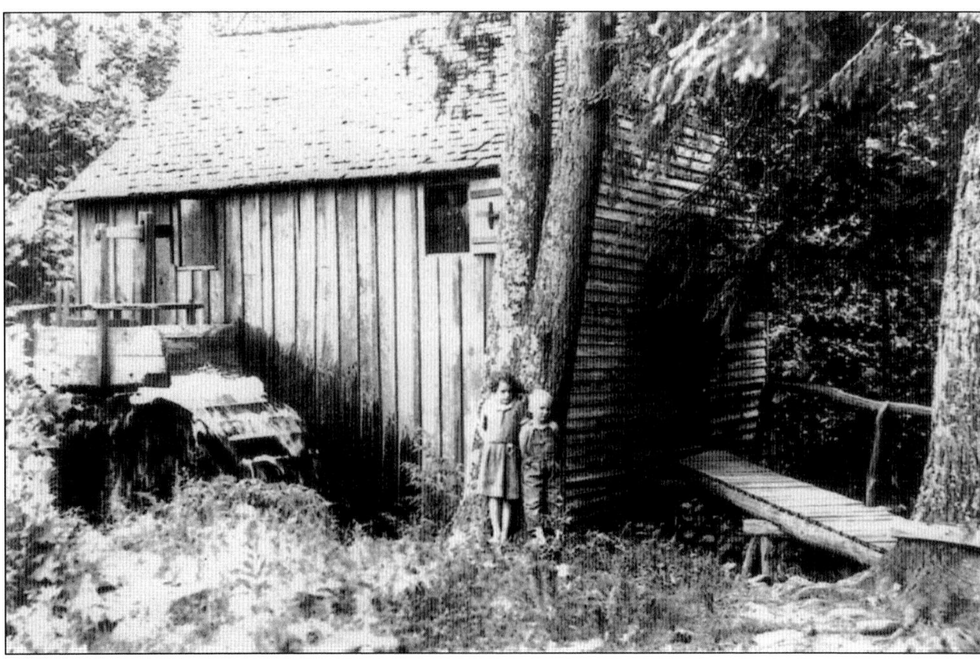

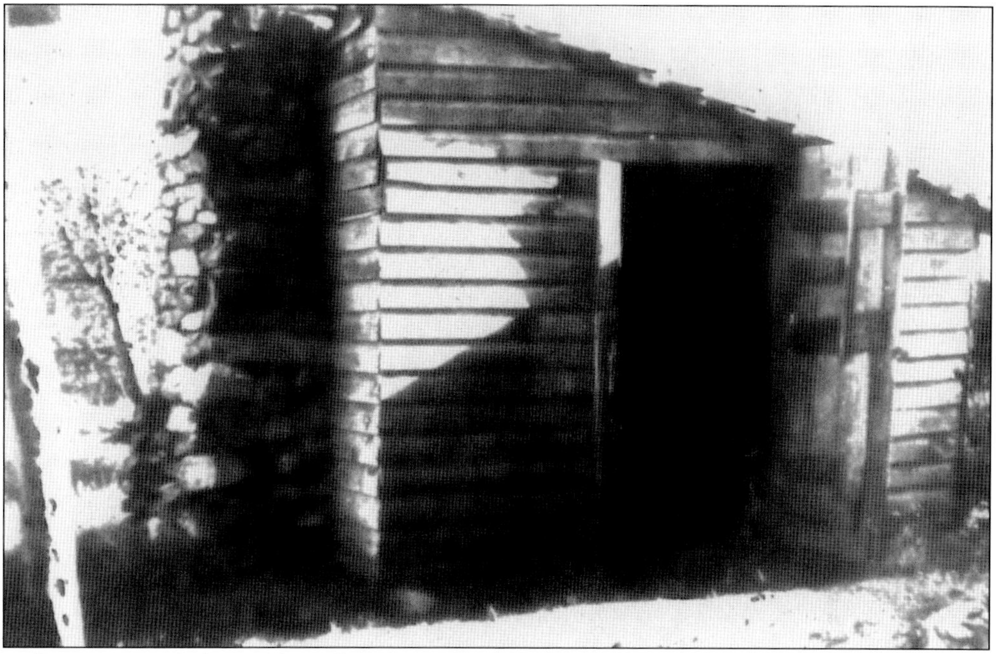

Mill patrons used the Cable Mill warming shed, where an open fire was burning, to stay warm while their corn was being ground into meal. There was also a bell located beside the shed to summon the miller, who lived close to the mill. Fred LeQuire, a grandson of Peter Cable, built the warming shed. (Courtesy of NPS.)

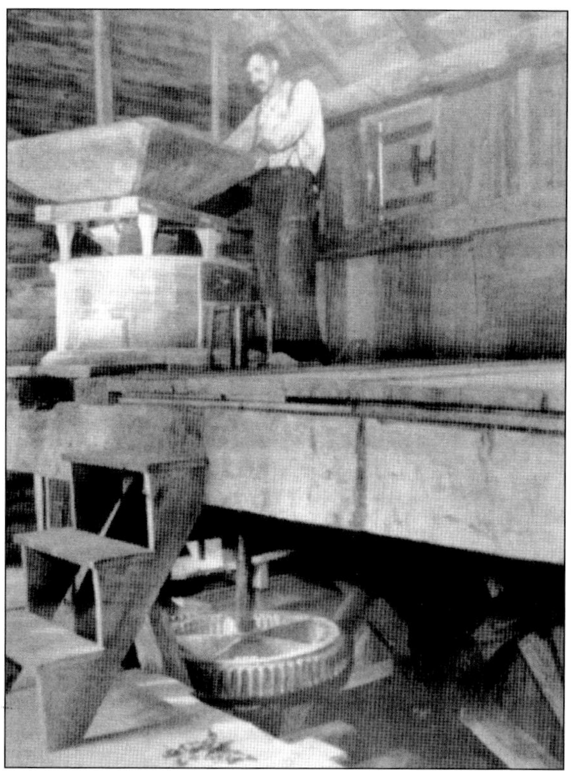

Pictured here is the inside of the Cable Mill, with details of the hopper, shoe, and millstone hoop used to grind meal from corn. John Gull Tipton is feeding the corn into the hopper. Many cove children had the chore of taking corn to the mill. In the summer months; many enjoyed fishing while waiting on the meal. When the job of grinding the corn was finished, the miller summoned the customer and he put the meal sacks full of the finished product on the customer's horse, one bag on each side, and the journey back home was started. (Courtesy of NPS.)

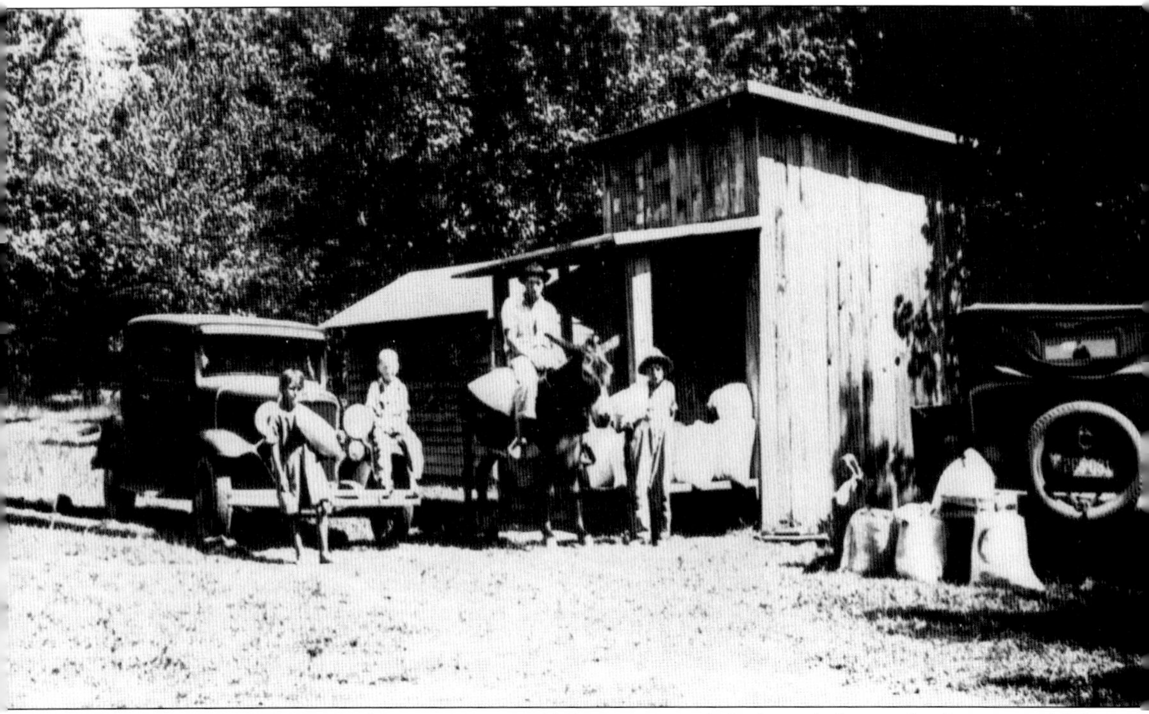

The pioneer settlers of Cades Cove imported life-sustaining skills, knowledge, and values to establish and maintain the community. These included agricultural methods and processes for conversion of agricultural products to food. One of the most critical conversions was that of transforming grains, corn and wheat, into meal and flour. In the latter days of the active community of Cades Cove, waterpowered mills were supplemented with mills powered by internal combustion engines. The skilled craftsmen who built and operated the mills utilized knowledge and talents passed down through generations to provide family and community with critical food products. John W. Oliver bought this grain mill and moved it to his Cades Cove farm in the mid-1920s. (Courtesy of Margaret Oliver, John W. Oliver collection.)

Three

Buildings and Families

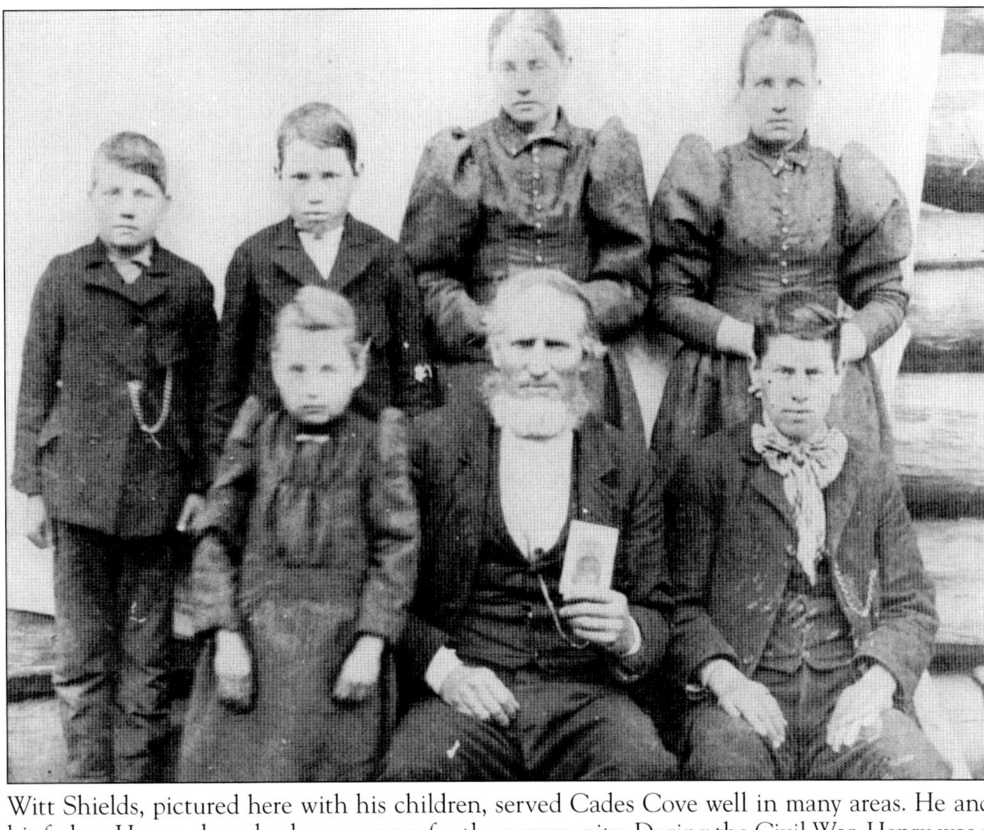

Witt Shields, pictured here with his children, served Cades Cove well in many areas. He and his father, Henry, shared a deep concern for the community. During the Civil War, Henry was a staunch supporter of the Union and a leader for the "home guard," organized to protect the cove from Confederate raids. He was wounded while serving in this capacity. Witt's highly successful farm adjoined the Primitive Baptist church. He was a very innovative and progressive farmer, improving his soil condition through application of pulverized limestone mined on the farm. (Courtesy of Margaret Oliver, John W. Oliver collection.)

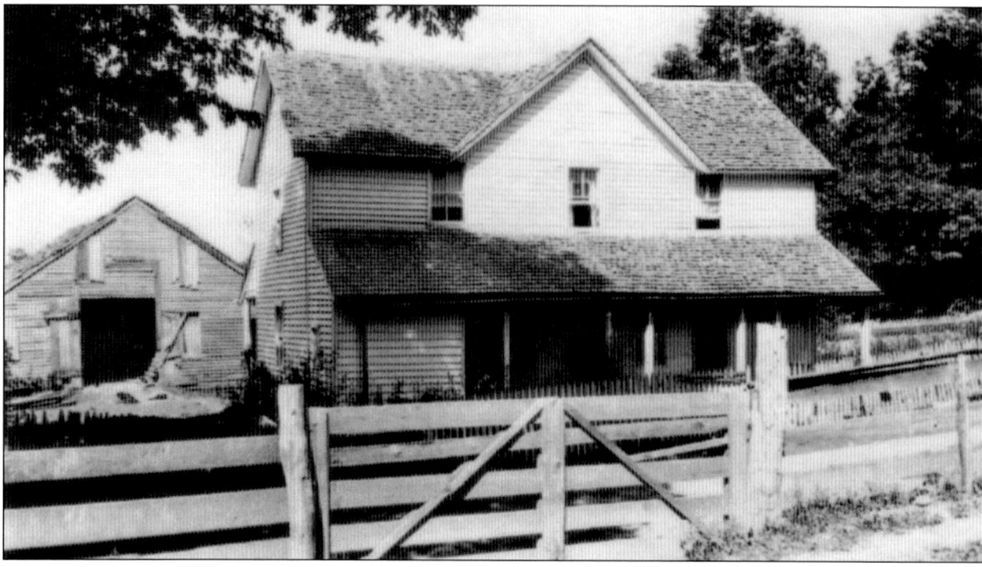

Witt Shields's barn was a standard of the community, to the extent that it was thoroughly documented before its destruction. Witt's original house was of log construction. According to Dave Post's research, after Shields built "the best frame house in the Cove" in 1900, this small cabin became known as the "coffin house." Here, Witt crafted coffins for grieving relatives and neighbors. His new house was "the envy of the Cove," complete with running water. Springwater was piped from the Carter Shields cabin vicinity to a "concrete refrigerator" on Witt's back porch. Witt also established a mill and general store at his home. His industrial skills served the community well. Pictured above is Witt's house; below is the coffin house. (Above, courtesy of Margaret Oliver, John W. Oliver collection; below, courtesy of NPS.)

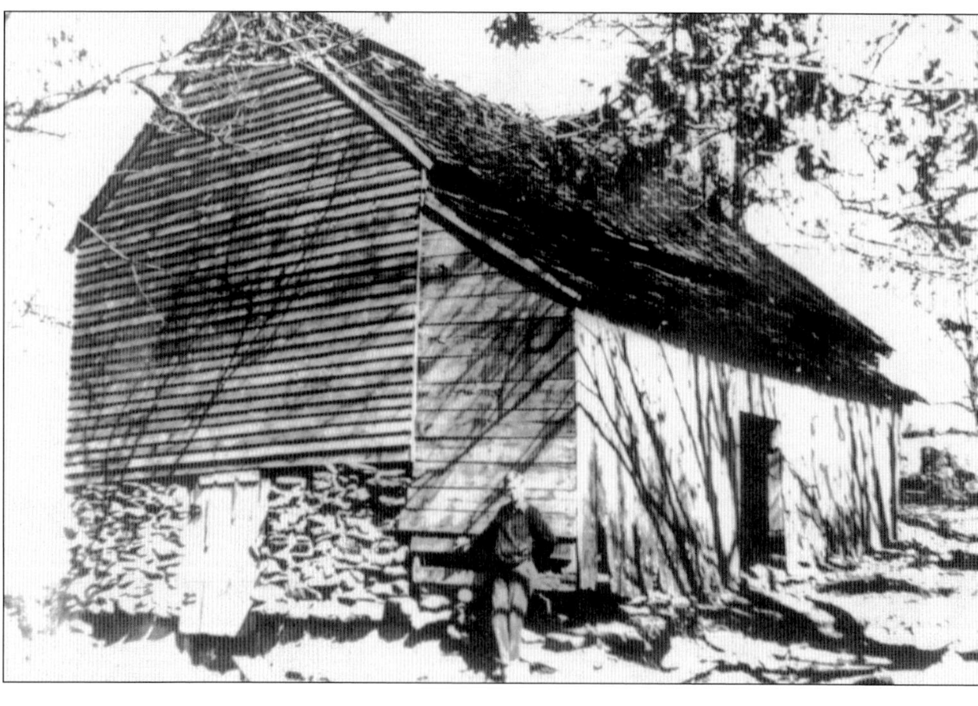

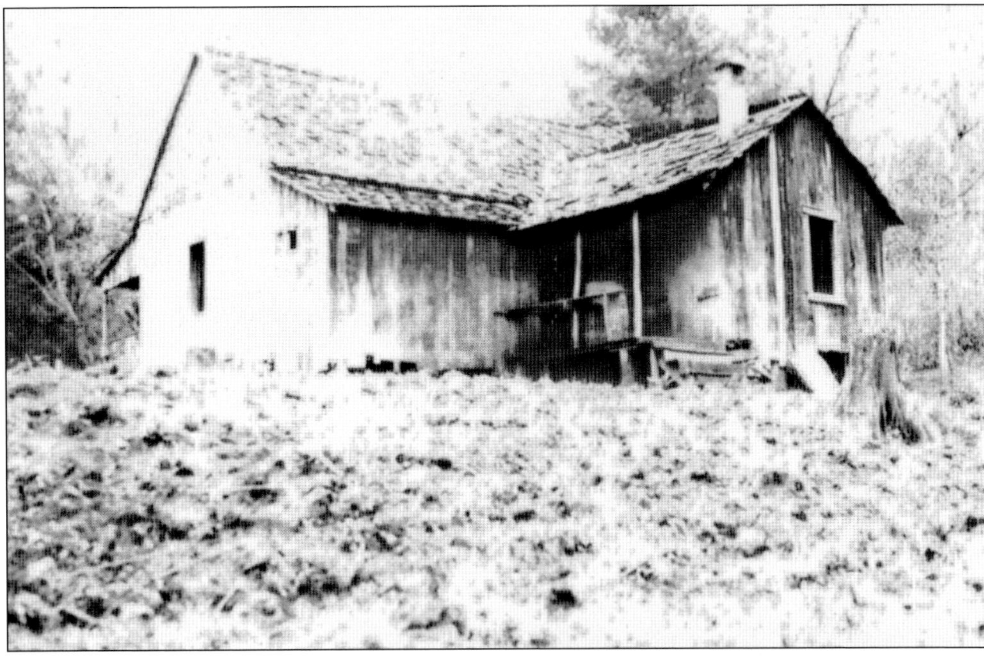

William T. "Will" Shuler was the son of Henry T. and Mary Laura Fisher Shuler. In 1920, Will married Laura Angeline Anthony, the daughter of John T. and Sarah LeQuire Anthony. The house that the Shuler family lived in, seen above, was behind what is now known as the Tipton-Oliver place in the cove. From left to right, Laura Anthony Shuler, William T. "Will," Edward, and Dorothy Shuler are pictured at right. (Above, courtesy of Margaret Oliver, John W. Oliver collection; right, courtesy of NPS.)

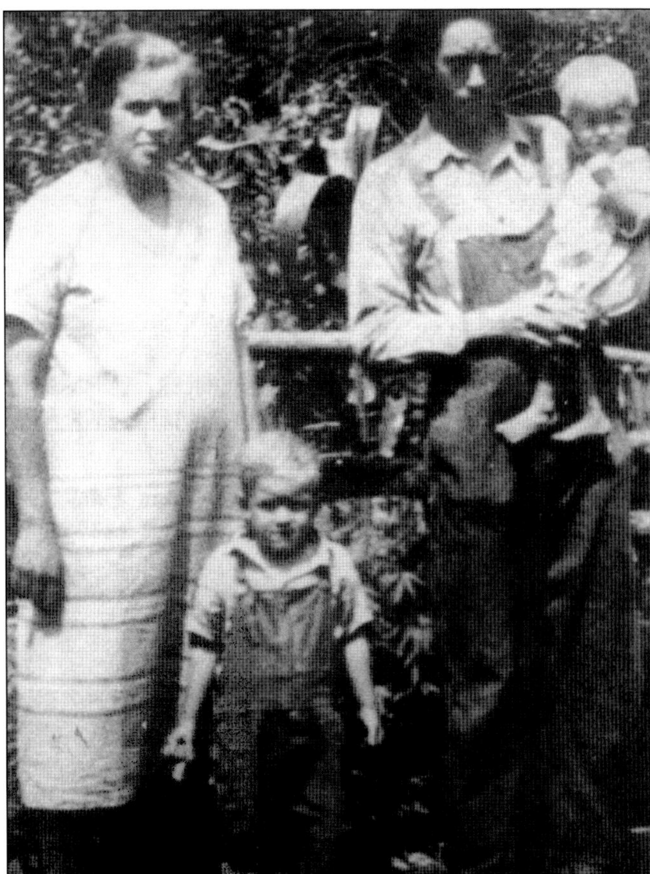

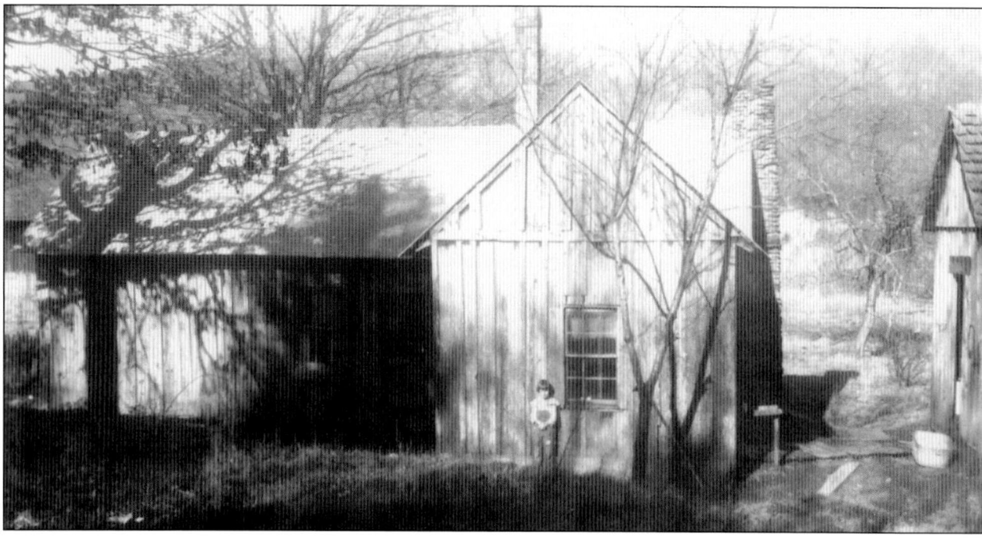

The Cades Cove census records show that John R. Cooper and his wife, Margaret Rowan Cooper, were living in Cades Cove with a daughter Mary, who was one year old. Cooper married Margaret in 1848, so the move into the cove came shortly after their marriage. They had four more children, which was shown in the 1860 census. By the time of the 1870 census, Margaret had passed away, and John R. had married Hannah J. Greer. Together, they had two sons, John Thomas and James Franklin. James Franklin married Martha Miranda LeQuire, a daughter of Isaac and Harriet Bowers LeQuire. Their son Wiley married Julia A. Lane. Above is a picture of the Wiley Cooper house in Cades Cove. Pictured below are, from left to right, Wiley Cooper, Julia Lane Cooper, Martha Miranda LeQuire Cooper, James Franklin Cooper, and J.T. Cooper. (Both, courtesy of NPS.)

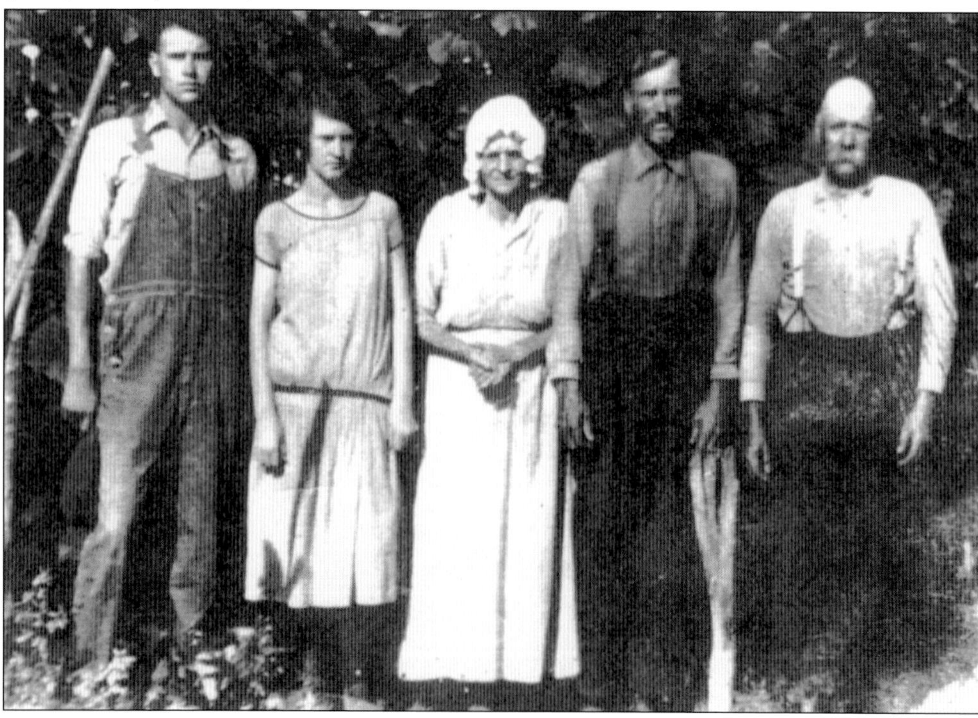

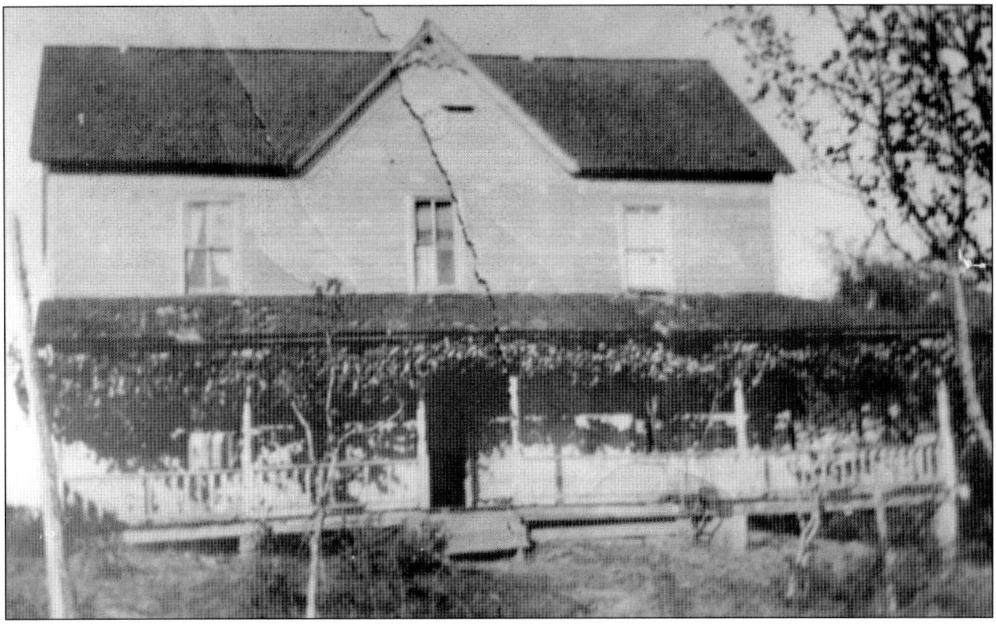

John Thomas "Tom" Sparks was the son of Cades Cove pioneer Nathan Sparks and Jane Potter Sparks. Tom married Hannah Whitehead, and they had eight children born and raised in Cades Cove. Their house was located on Sparks Lane, where Tom farmed his land. He was also one of the legendary herders who worked in the Spence Field area. Sparks would be responsible for as many as 600 cattle, 100 horses and mules, and as many as 1,000 sheep for the summer months. His charge was $1.50 for cattle per head, $2 for horses and mules, and 25¢ for sheep. Sparks lost his life in 1926 when a visitor to his Spence Field cabin shot him over a disagreement. Pictured above is the family home located on Sparks Land. Below is the Tom and Hannah Whitehead Sparks family. (Both, courtesy of Leon Sparks, Sparks family collection.)

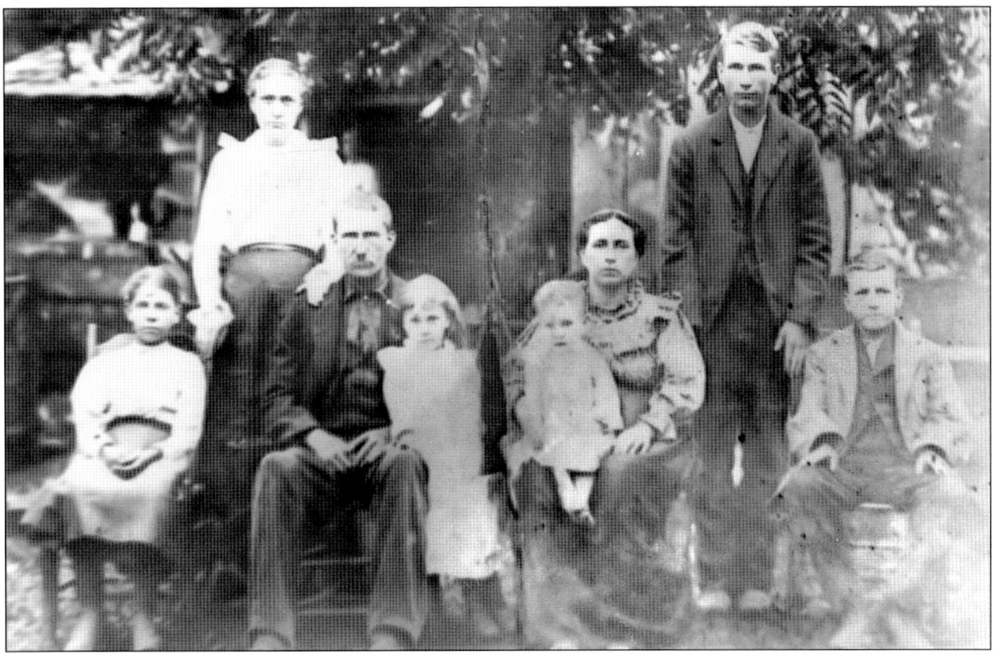

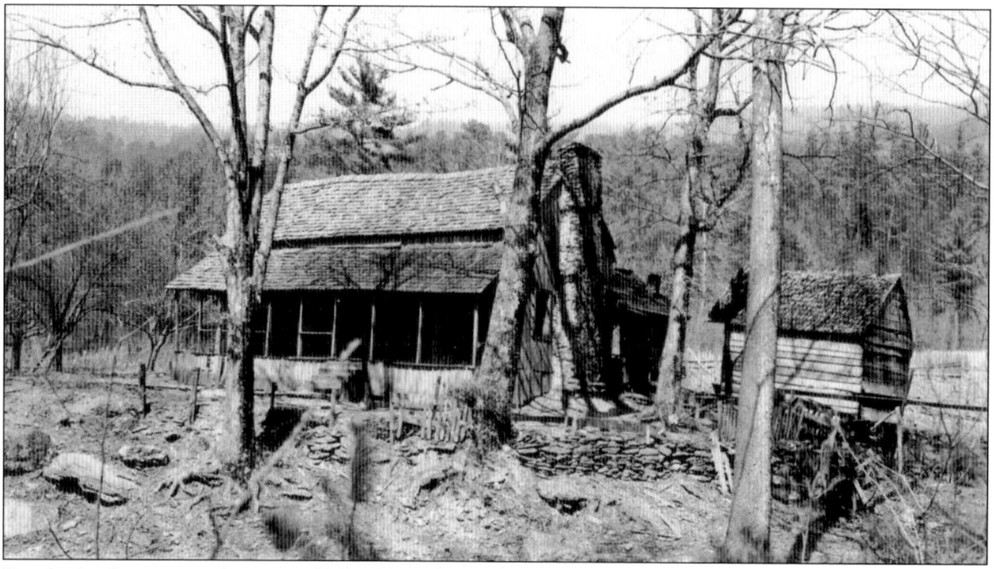

Pearly Anthony was the son of John T. and Sarah LeQuire Anthony and lived on land that was handed down from his parents, who probably built the original house. In National Park Service records, it states that this was known as the Pearly Anthony home, probably because he was the last to live there. The Anthony family was among the pioneers of Cades Cove, and their land is located to the right just as one enters the Cades Cove Loop Road. Pictured above is the Anthony house. Below are, from left to right, John T., Sarah, Ethel, Jack, and Pearly Anthony, and Kenneth Jones. (Both, courtesy of NPS.)

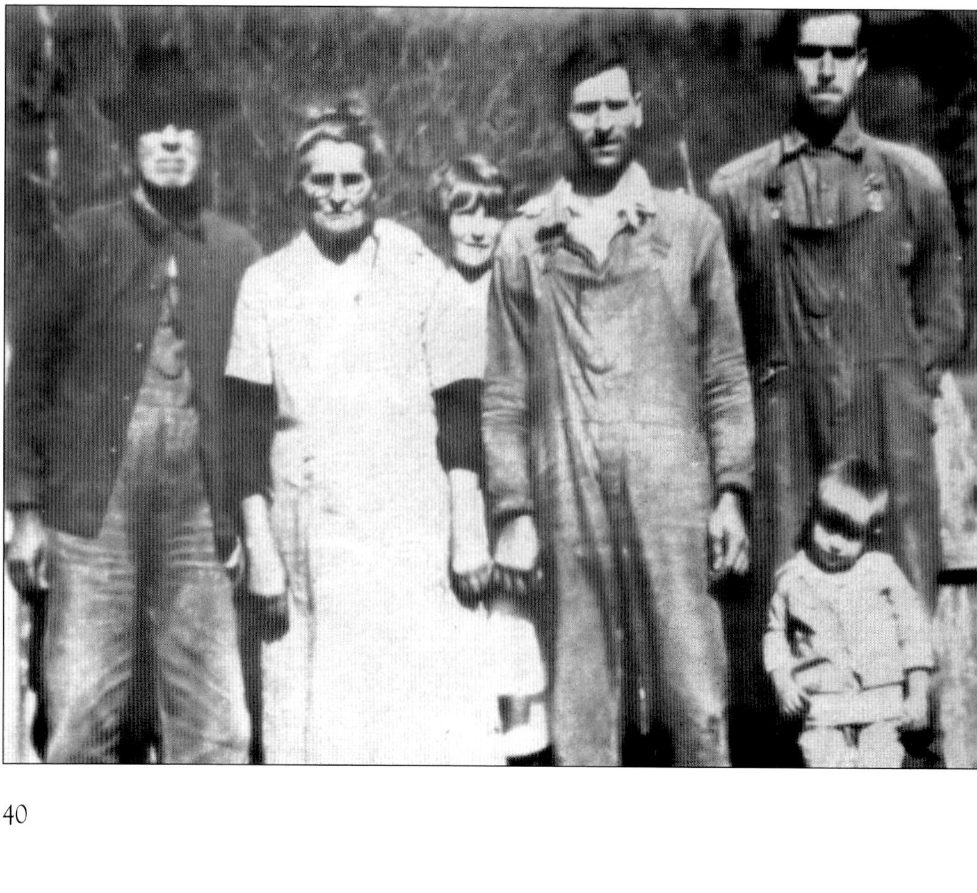

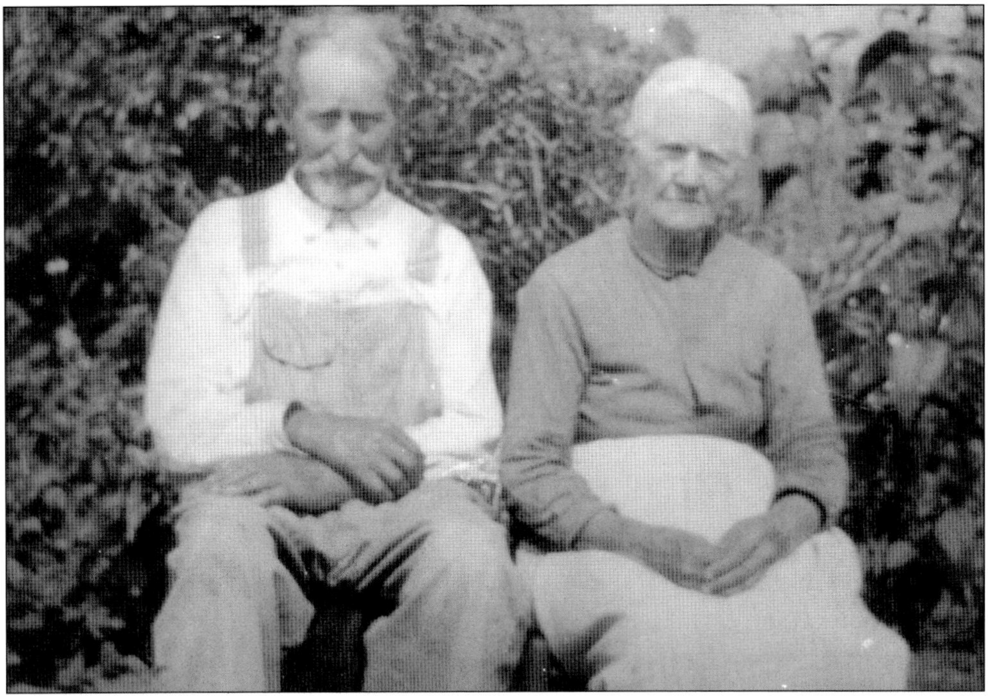

Noah Burchfield was born in Cades Cove in 1849 to Robert and Mary "Polly" Gregory Burchfield. In 1869, Noah married Sarah H. Brown, a daughter of Jesse Simeon and Mary Proctor Brown. Making their home on the property first settled by Noah's father, Noah and Sarah were well loved and respected by the cove community. Both were active in the Cades Cove Missionary Baptist Church, where Noah was the caretaker, which would often mean going to the church an hour early on Sundays to get a fire going in the stove before the members arrived. Having lived his entire life on the family property, Noah Burchfield died in 1934. (Both, courtesy of Margaret Oliver, John W. Oliver collection and NPS.)

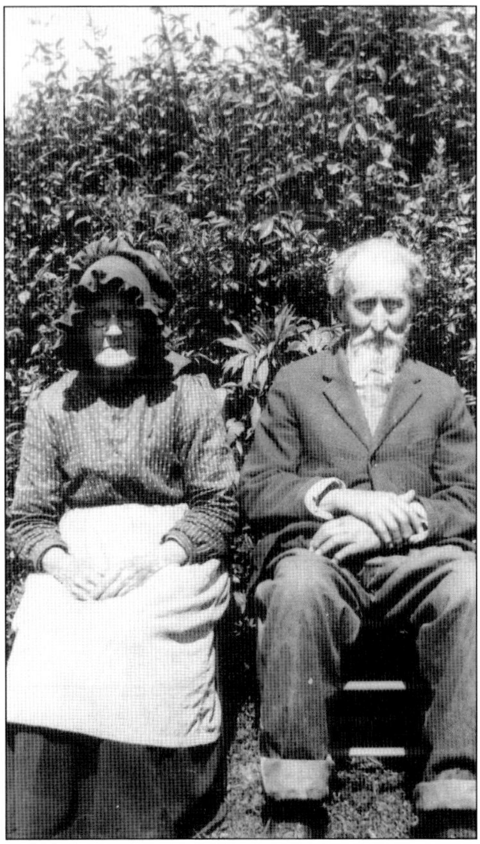

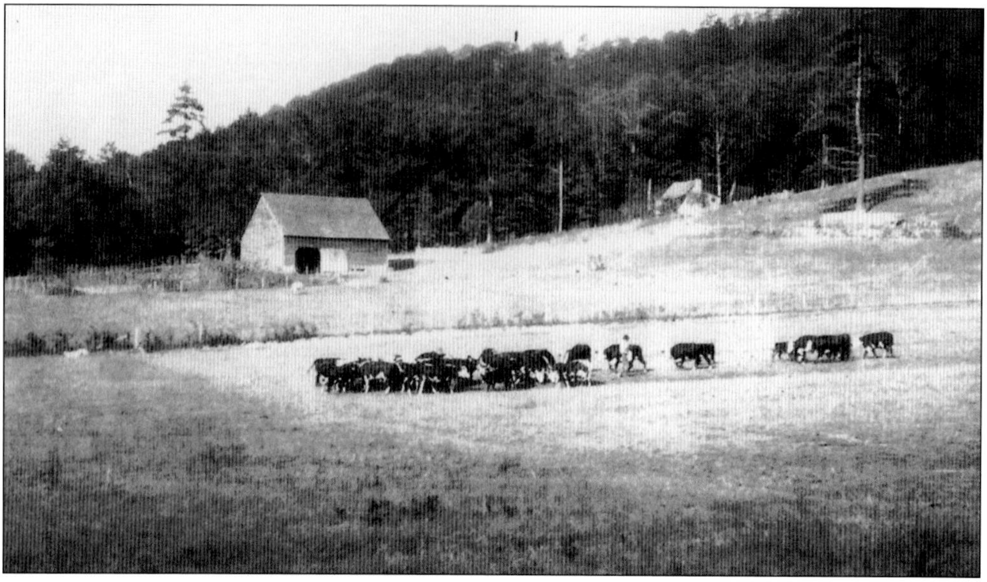

Charles "Charlie" Myers was born in Cades Cove and was the son of Peter Adam "Pete" Myers and Margaret "Maggie" Shields Myers. Charlie was born in 1892 and married Mae Shuler, a daughter of Henry and Mary Fisher Shuler. They had six children born while they lived in Cades Cove. A comment on permittees on May 3, 1946, by the National Park Service, says this about Charlie Myers: "He is a conservationist, practical and proud of his land operations. Has good quality of cattle and desires cattle barn so that steers may be fed and manure returned to the land. One of the best farmers and friends of the Service." Above is the Charlie Myers farm. The photograph below shows the Charlie and Mae Myers family while they lived in Cades Cove. (Both, courtesy of Margaret Oliver, John W. Oliver collection.)

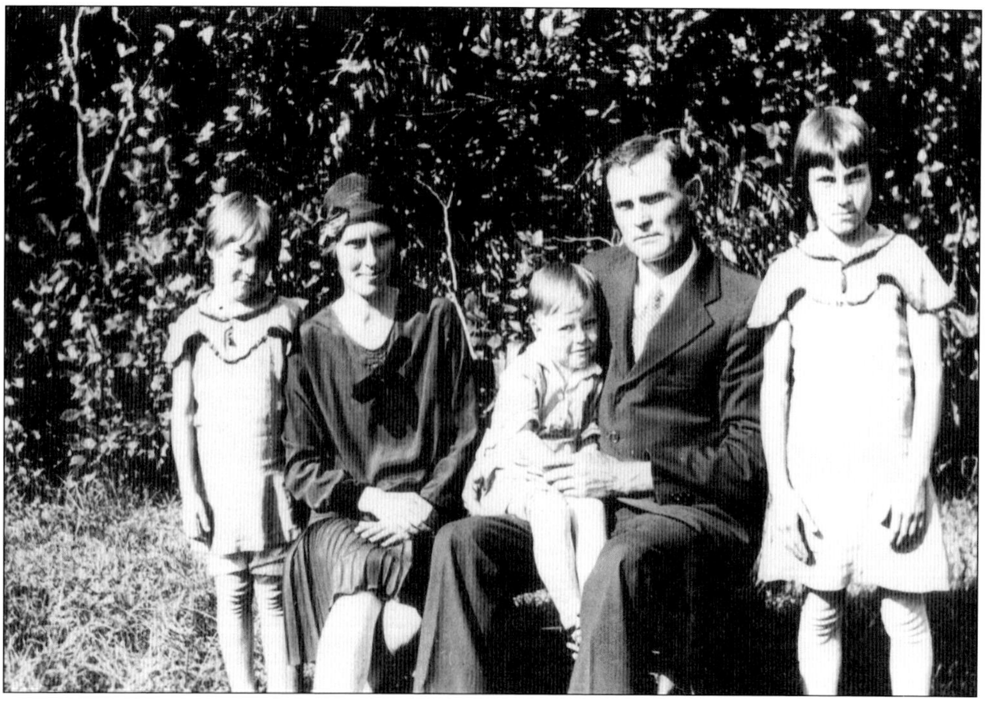

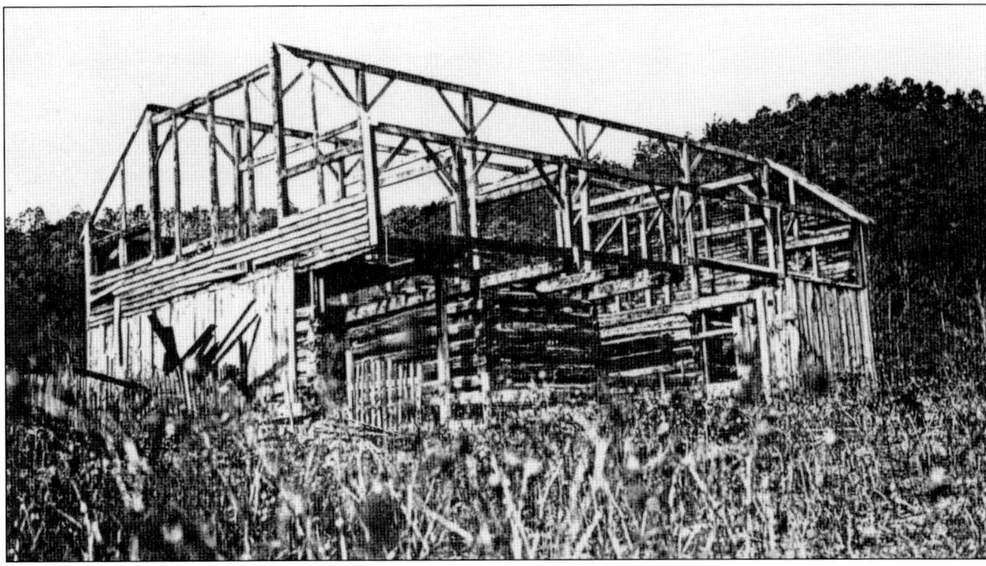

Golman Myers, also a son of Pete and Maggie Myers, was born in 1894. In 1920, he married Viola Burchfield, a daughter of John and Tennie Tipton Burchfield. With his brother Charlie, Golman ran a large farm in the cove. Construction of the barn, seen above, was very typical for the barns built in Cades Cove. Large lofts were needed to store hay for the cattle in the cold winters. The family home sat atop a ridge that overlooked Cades Cove. At right, the Golman and Viola Myers' children are, from left to right, (first row) Wayne and Bonnie; (second row) Thee and Clee. (Both, courtesy of NPS.)

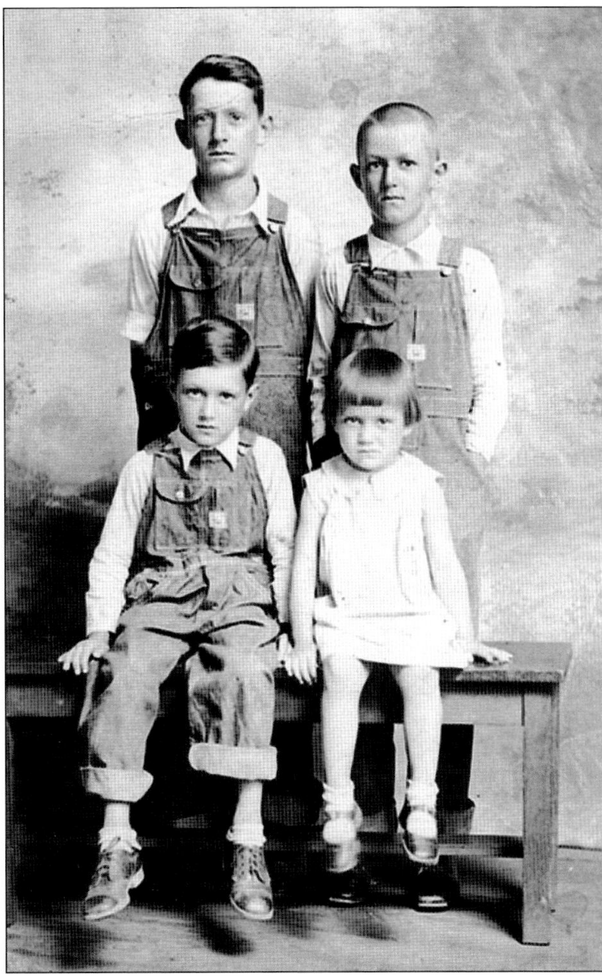

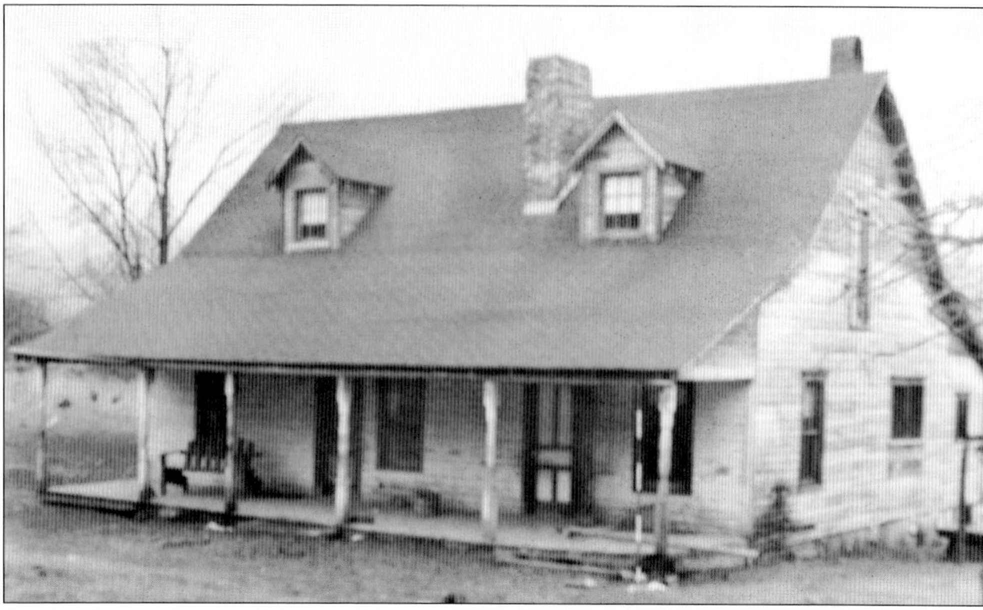

Asa Sparks was the son of Tom and Hannah Whitehead Sparks and was born and raised in Cades Cove. He married Amy Burchfield, a daughter of John and Tennie Tipton Sparks. The above house was built by Asa's brother Bob and was located on Sparks Lane. In later years, Asa moved the house onto the Cades Cove Loop Road. Asa and Amy Burchfield Sparks lived in this house from 1946 until 1960 with their 12 children. Pictured below are, from left to right, (first row) Larry, Lois Kay, Luke, and Linda Sparks; (second row) Leslie and Leland; (third row) Lennis, LaVerne, Lucille, Lenore, Leon, Asa, Lamon, and Amy Sparks. (Both, courtesy of Leon Sparks.)

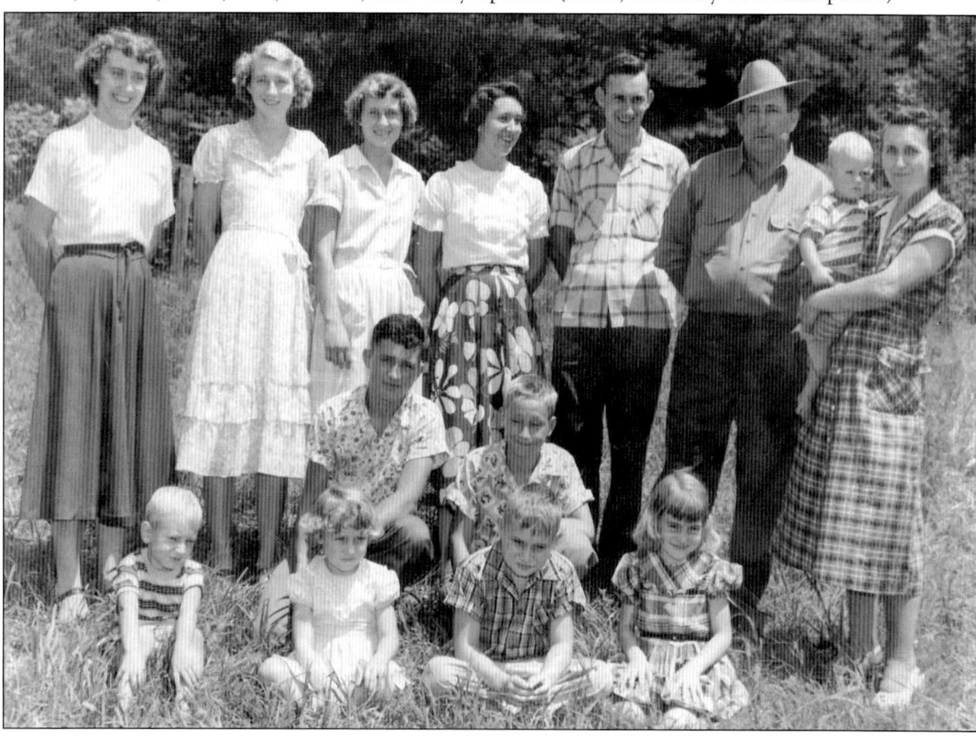

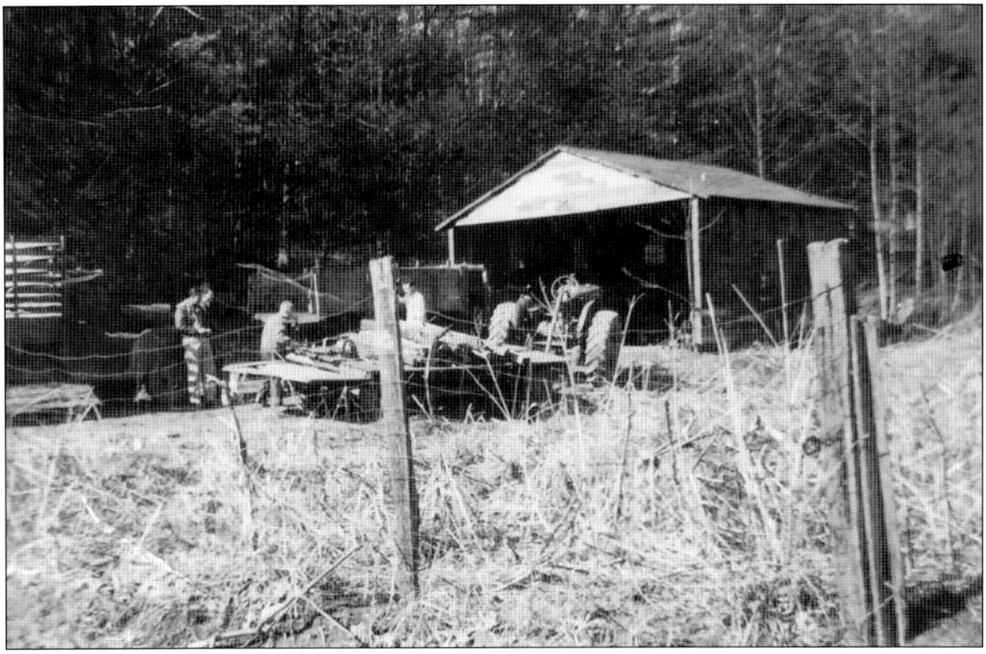

When the Civilian Conservation Corps (CCC) ended in Cades Cove, there were many buildings left. Many of the cove men thought of ways to recycle the wood; Asa Sparks built a garage at his house from wood from one of the buildings. Others built honey houses, and some used the wood to construct their own homes. (Courtesy of Lois Kaye Sparks Russell.)

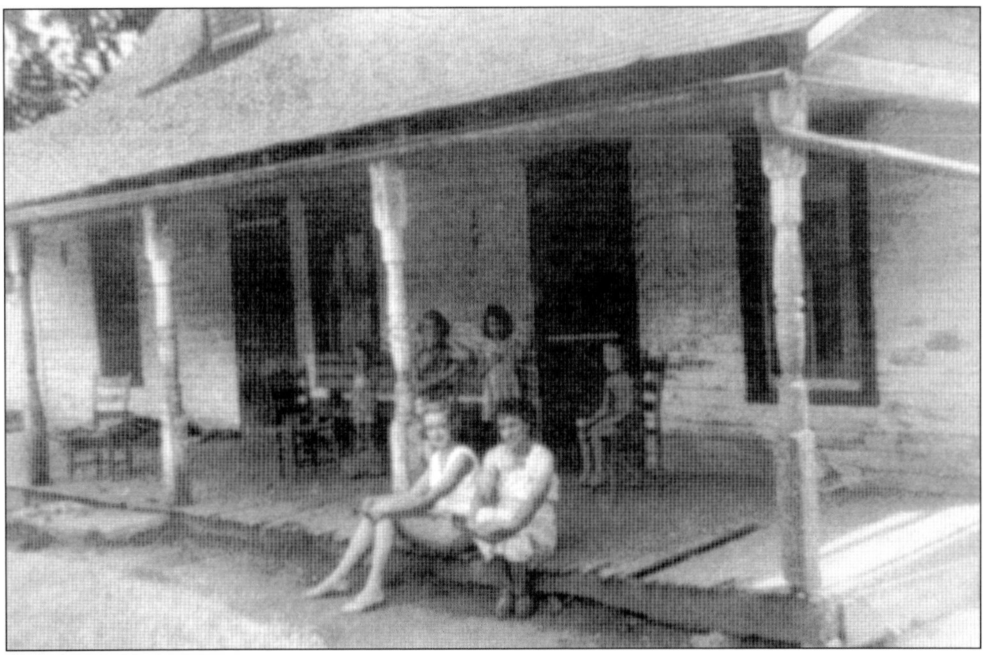

The children of Asa and Amy Sparks are seen here relaxing on the front porch. At the time the Sparkses lived in the cove, there was not many families residing there, so finding other to children to play with was not easy. There were plenty of chores to be done on the farm after a day at school, though. (Courtesy of Leon Sparks.)

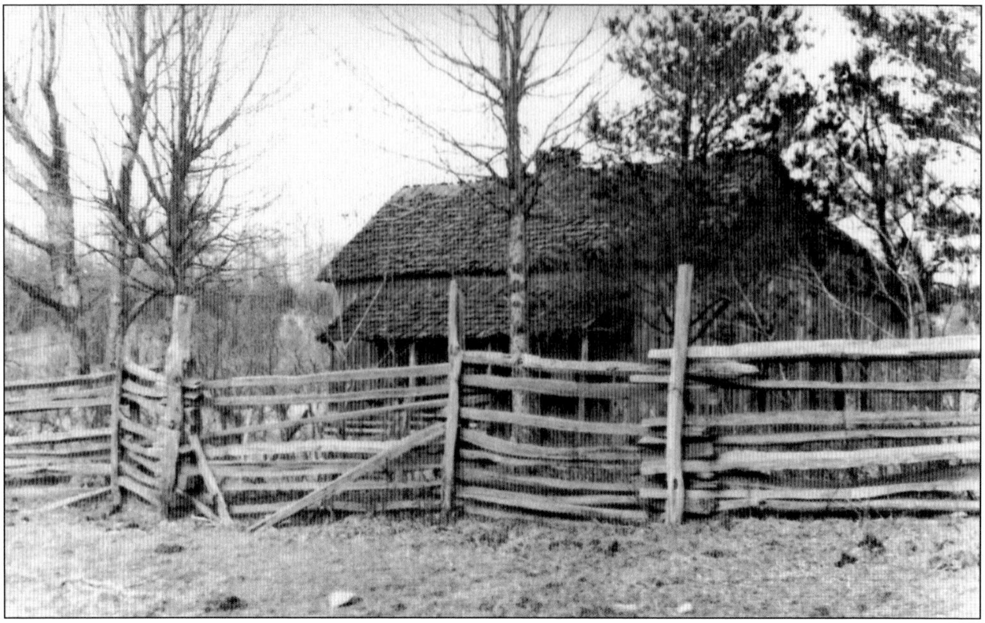

William "Barney" Cable, son of William Alfonzo "Fonz" and Lucinda Jane Sparks Cable, married Bertha Coada. Barney's farm had two different types of fences on it—above is a photograph of his house with a wooden fence around it, and below is his barn with a rock fence. Fields that needed to be turned into gardens had to be cleared out. The children and young adults had the chore of picking up rocks so fields could be plowed and crops planted. Then, these rocks were often used to construct a fence. (Both, courtesy of NPS.)

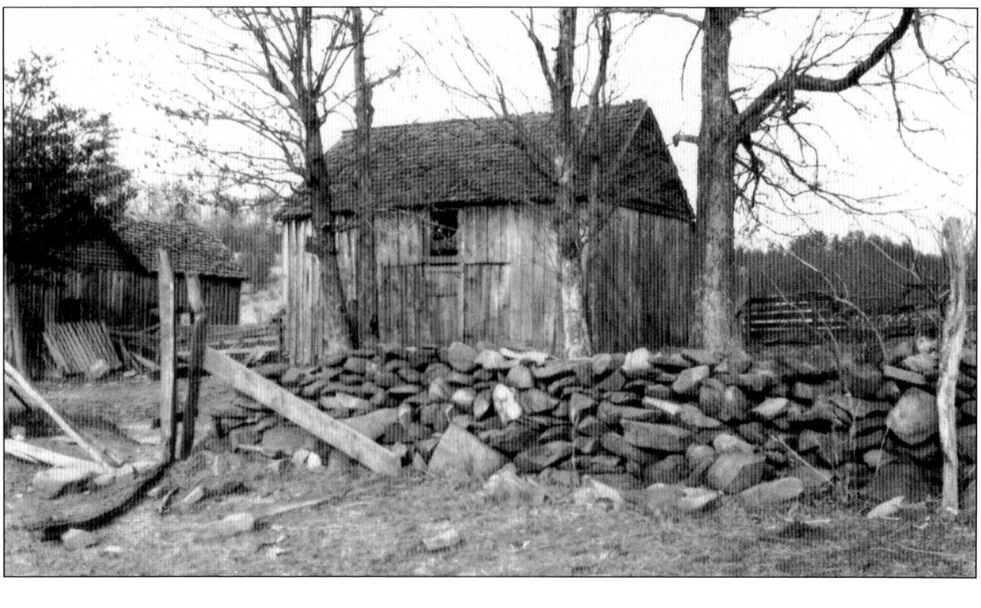

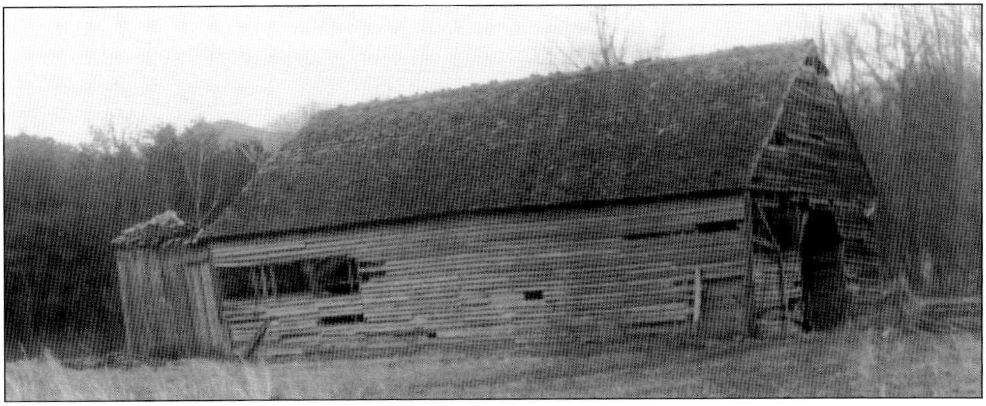

This barn and house barn belonged to Rebecca "Aunt Becky" Ann Cable, who was the second child born to John P. and Elizabeth Cable in Carter County, Tennessee. The family relocated to Cades Cove in 1868. Aunt Becky often said she did not have time for marriage and remained single her entire life. However, she was certainly never without family and always responded to the needs of her family, which extended well beyond genetic relationships. She was a lady of many talents, much industry, and considerable resiliency. She and one of her brothers, Dan, bought a two-story house of frame construction, which included a store on the first floor. It was located at the first ford of Mill Creek on Forge Creek Road. Aunt Becky is buried in the Cable Cemetery, adjacent to the field she formerly plowed and near the site of the Cable School, for which she gave the land. (Both, courtesy of NPS.)

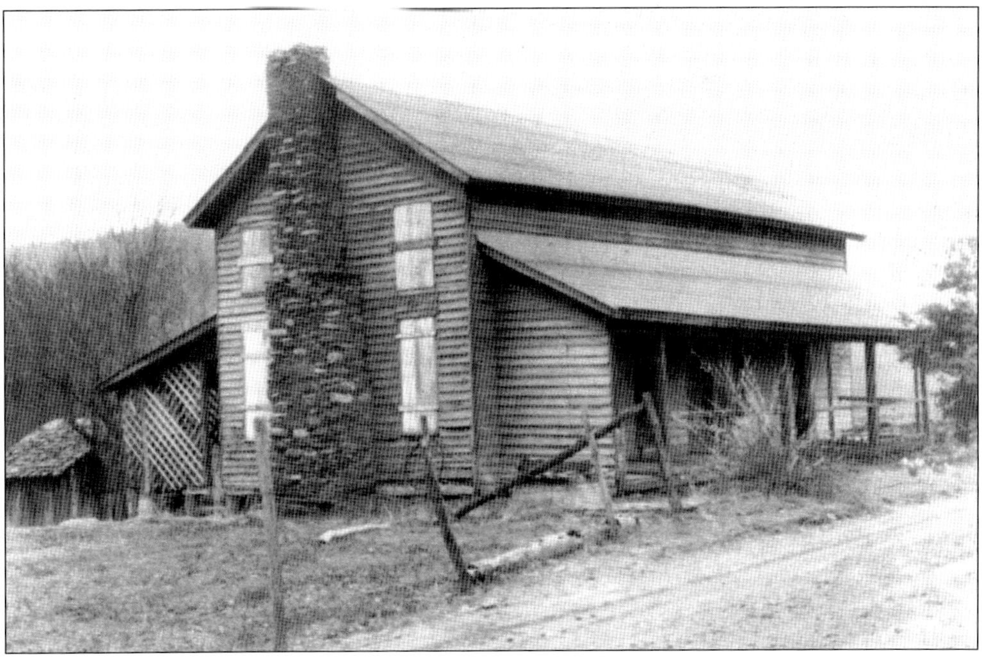

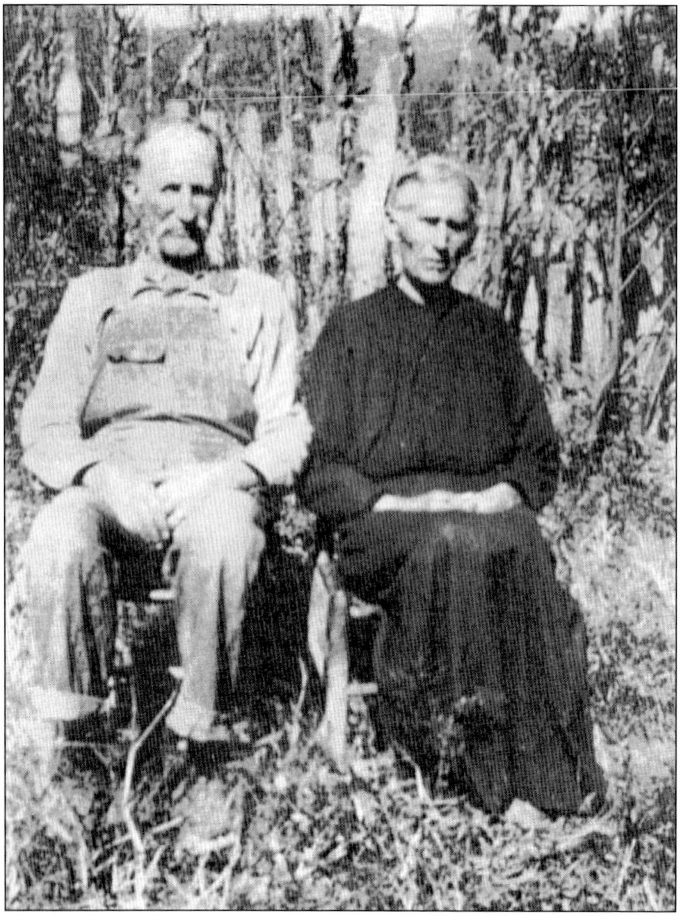

Pictured at left are John Case "Cassie" and Mary Ann "Sis" Gregory Myers. Below is a picture of their house, which was located in what was known as Myerstown because of the many Myerses who lived in this area. Myerstown was located close to the Cades Cove Missionary Baptist Church. Cassie was the son of John "Baldy" and Mary Ann Tipton Myers, who were first listed in the Cades Cove census in 1870. Baldy was a successful farmer and furniture maker and passed on his good traits to his son Cassie. Sis was the daughter of Walter and Rutha Oliver Gregory. Her maternal grandparents John and Luraney Oliver were the first white settlers in the cove. (Both, courtesy of Missy Tipton Green.)

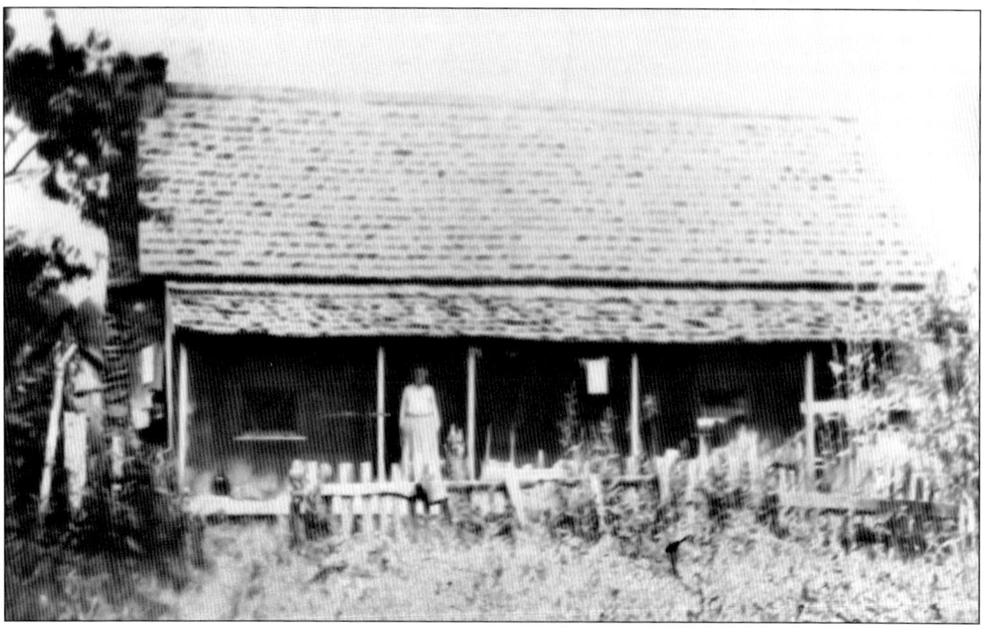

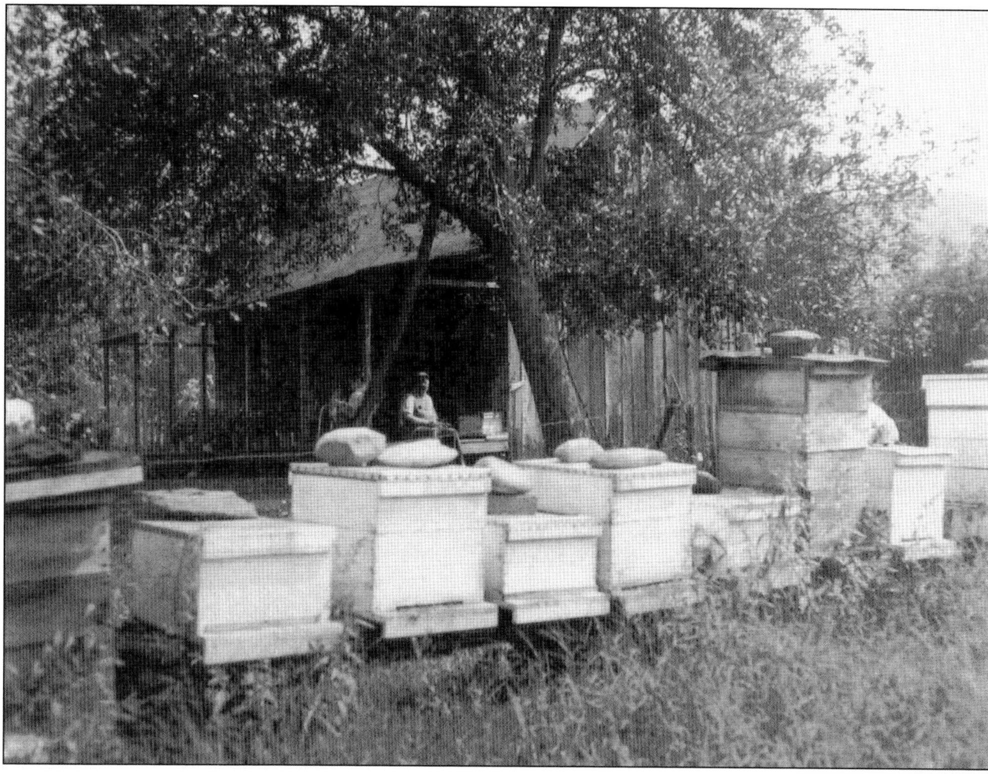

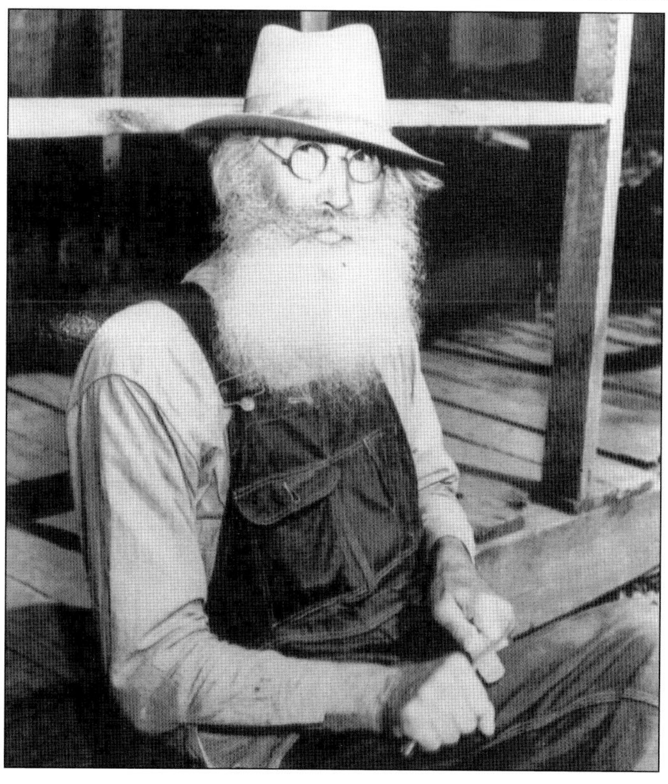

Daniel "Dan" H. Myers Jr. married Lurena Angelina "Babe" Gregory, a daughter of Walter and Rutha Oliver Gregory. Daniel's parents were Daniel H. Myers and Susan Matilda Cable Myers. Dan and Babe had eight children, all born in Cades Cove. Dan, or "Uncle Dan" as he was also known, was a well-known beekeeper and kept many hives, passing on his beekeeping skills to his son Labe. Dan was also a well-known herder. The cattle were driven to the peaks about April 15 every year. Then the livestock would be herded back to the warmer valley around September. The picture above shows the Dan Myers house and beehives. At right is Dan Myers whittling. (Both, courtesy of NPS.)

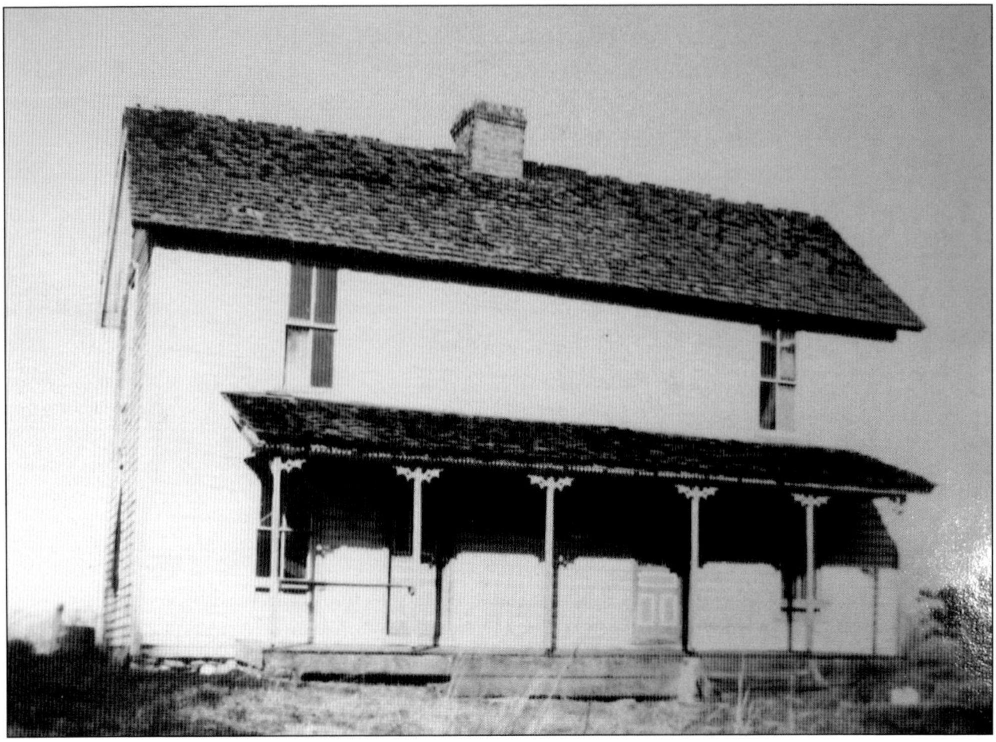

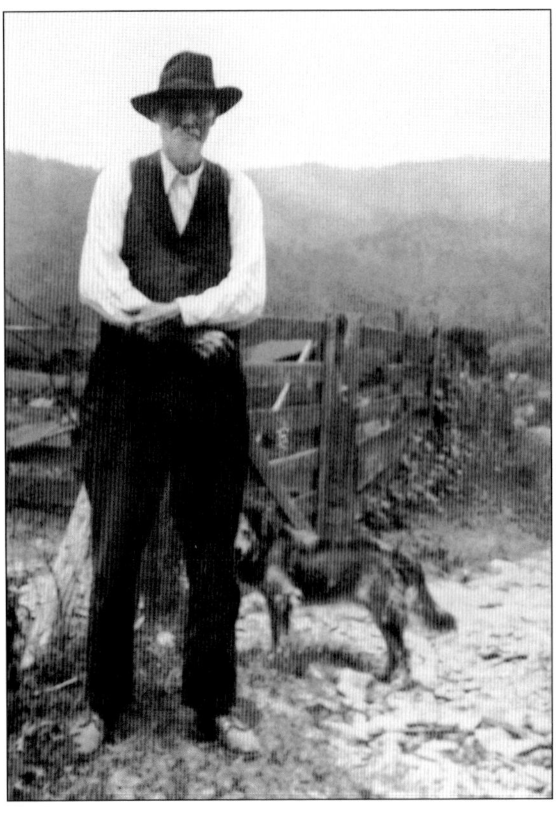

David W. "Dave" Sparks was the son of Nathan and Jane Potter Sparks. Nathan was a community leader, serving as justice of the peace for several terms, and he was active in the Cades Cove Home Guard during the Civil War. Dave married Mary L. Cameron and raised his children in their home located on Sparks Lane. There was no mowing of yards in those days; children of the house would have to sweep the yard with homemade brooms to get rid of weeds and grass. The above picture shows the front view of the house. At left is Dave, also a well-known herder in the area. His brothers Tom and Sam Sparks were herders. (Both, courtesy of NPS.)

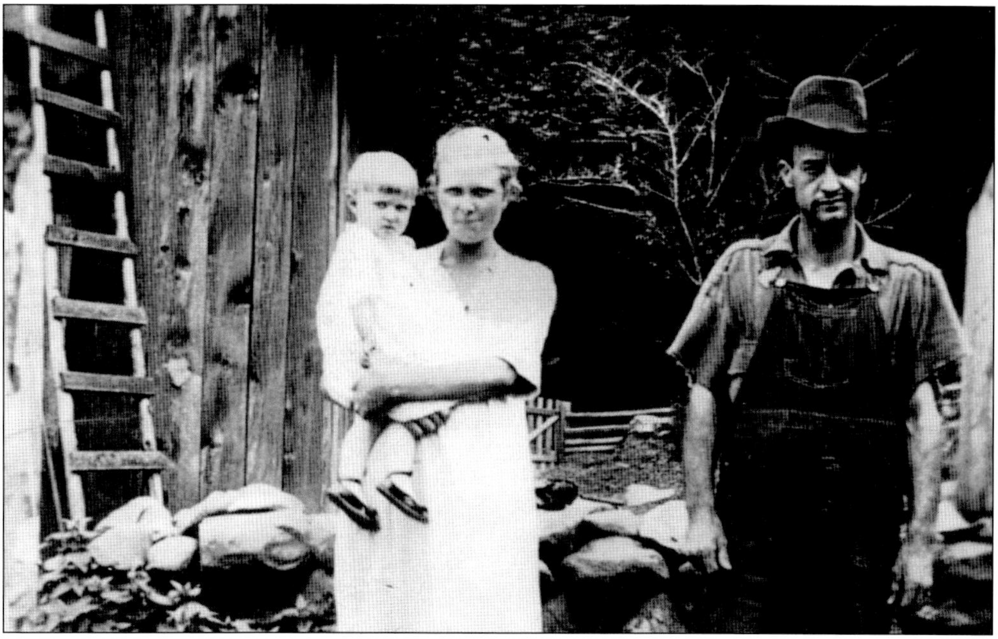

Henry R. Gibson Tipton and his wife, Bertha Proctor Tipton, are pictured above with their daughter Vina. Gibson was born in Cades Cove in 1898 to John Franklin "Chicken Eater" and Harriett Burchfield Tipton. Bertha was the daughter of Mary G. Proctor. The barn, seen below, was on 32 acres of land titled to Tipton on July 9, 1927. The location of his home and buildings was where the present Cades Cove Store sits. The builder of the house was said to be Samuel Roberts, who lived on the land in previous years. The people of Cades Cove had an unshakable faith in God. Their Bibles and hymnbooks were to them the greatest of all books. (Above, courtesy of Gibson Tipton family; below, courtesy of NPS.)

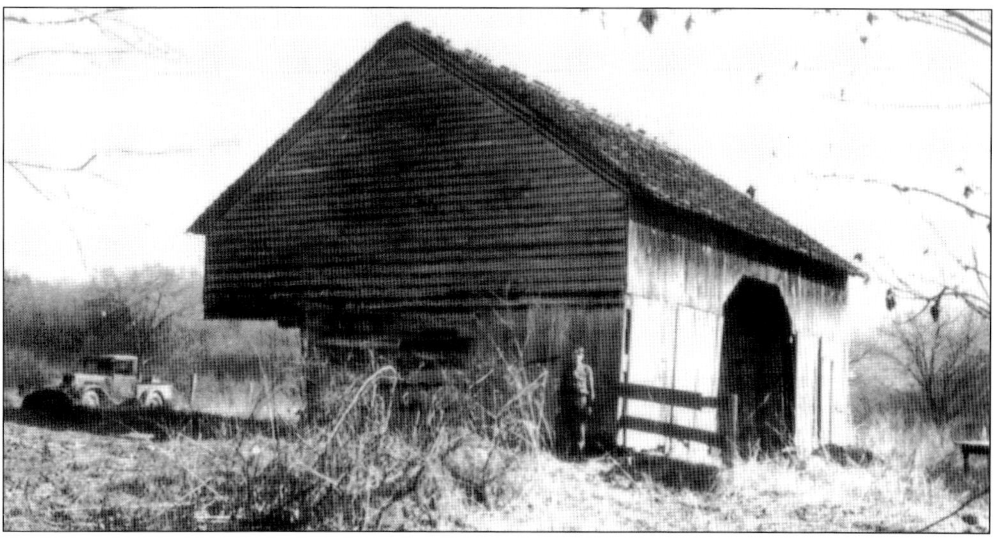

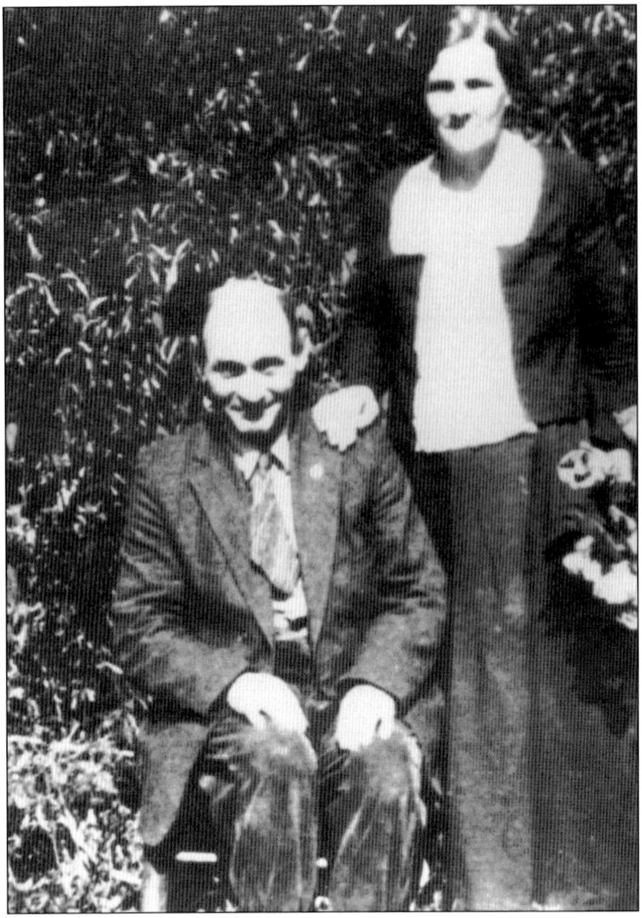

Born in Cades Cove in 1870 to Ebenezer and Matilda Shields Gregory, Josiah Jonathan "J.J." Gregory is descended from Russell and Susan Hill Gregory, pioneers of Cades Cove. Gregory Bald is said to have been named after Russell. J.J. married Elvira Feezell, the daughter of John Henry and Harriett Emily Feezell, and had 13 children born in Cades Cove. J.J. and Elvira are pictured at left. Their home is shown below. The property was near where the Gregory Cave is located and consisted of 114 acres, as registered in Book 103, page 578, of the Register's Office of Blount County, Tennessee. (Both, courtesy of NPS.)

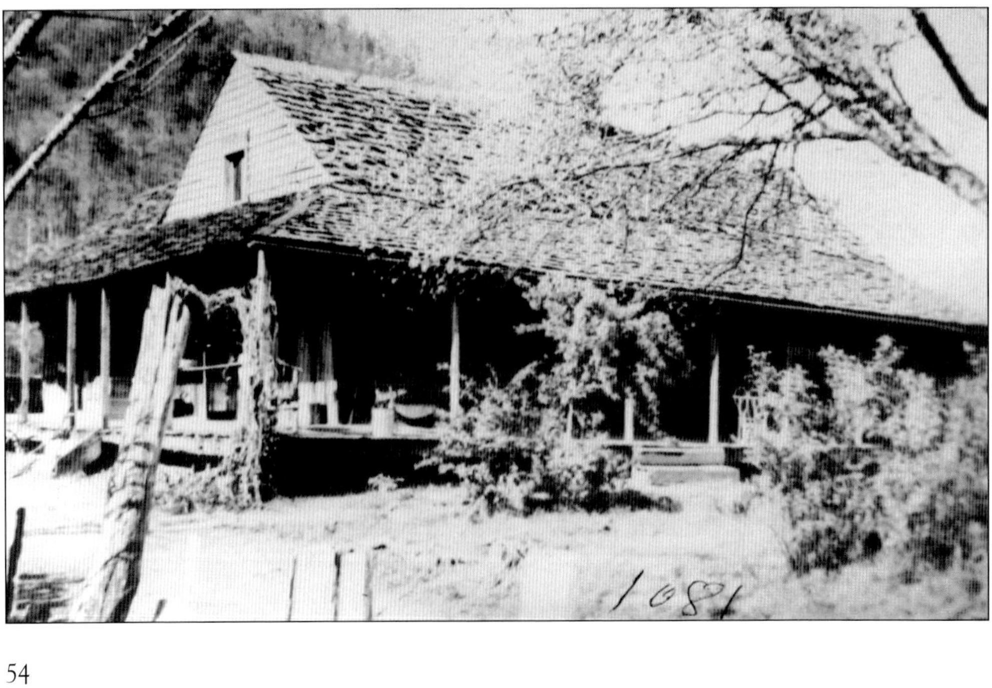

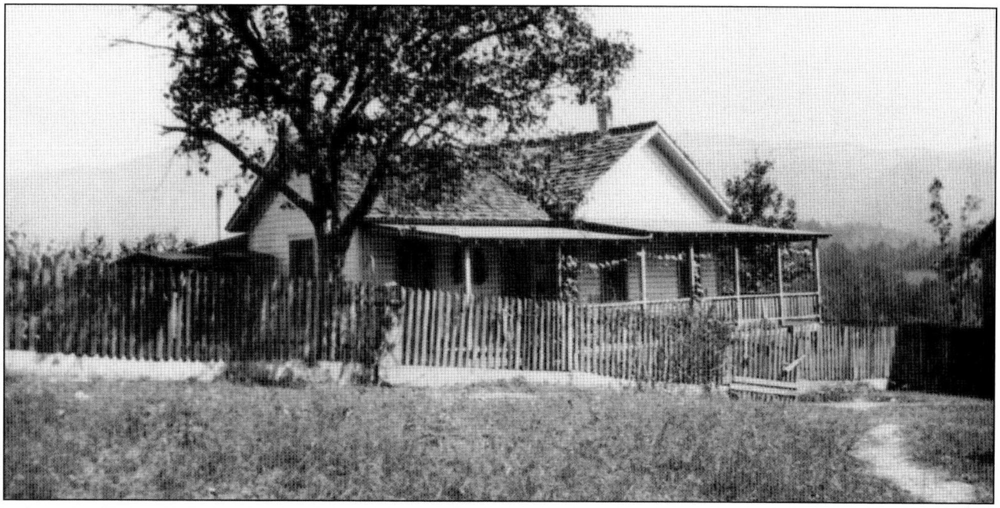

John Walter Oliver was born in Cades Cove in 1898 to William Howell and Elizabeth Jane Gregory Oliver. William Howell was the son of Elijah and Mary "Polly" Lawson Oliver and the grandson of the original settlers in the cove—John and Luraney Oliver. Elizabeth Jane Gregory Oliver was the daughter of Charles Garrison and Celia Carver Gregory. Both the Gregorys and Olivers were pioneer families in Cades Cove. John W. Oliver left Cades Cove at the age of 21 to attend Maryville College in Maryville, Tennessee. In 1901, he married Nancy Ann Whitehead, a daughter of Sarah Margaret Boring and Henry Whitehead. John was later appointed as rural letter carrier in Cades Cove. John and Nancy, along with their children, had a large farm to tend to in the cove with a large herd of Black Angus cattle; John also had many hives of bees. Seen above is the John W. Oliver house. Below are the granary and cellar. (Both, courtesy of Margaret Oliver, John W. Oliver collection.)

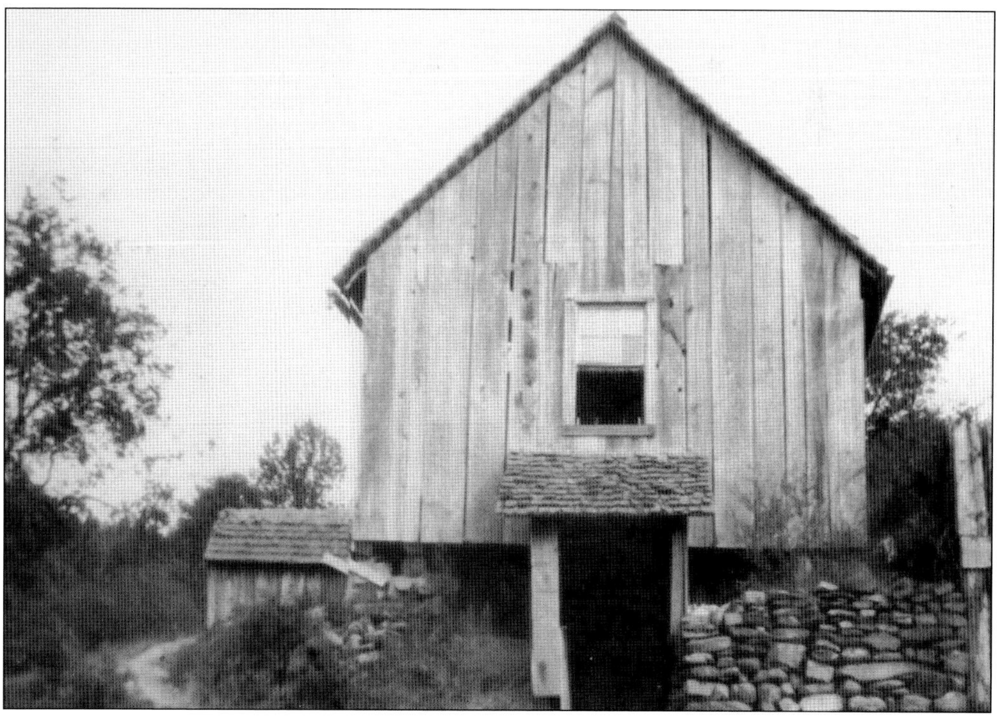

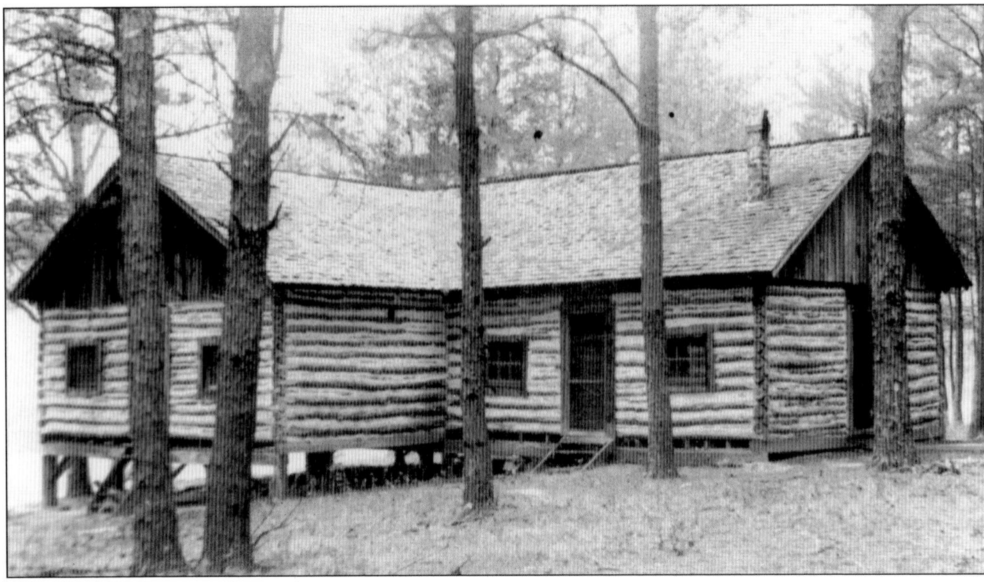

A God-fearing man and loyal member of his church, John W. Oliver was a deacon and a minister; he held many funerals for cove people. He was a man who was proud of his mountain heritage, his ancestry, and his country. John was also an avid photographer, and many of his wonderful pictures are used in this book. When talk started of forming a national park in the Cades Cove area, John fought with all his will to save his precious cove. John and Nancy had a tourist lodge on their property that was visited by many, especially the local hiking clubs. Nancy died in 1948, having been married for 47 years, and John died in 1966. Above is a picture of the Oliver Lodge. Below is a lodge advertisement. (Above, courtesy of Nancy Webber; below, courtesy of Margaret Oliver, John W. Oliver collection.)

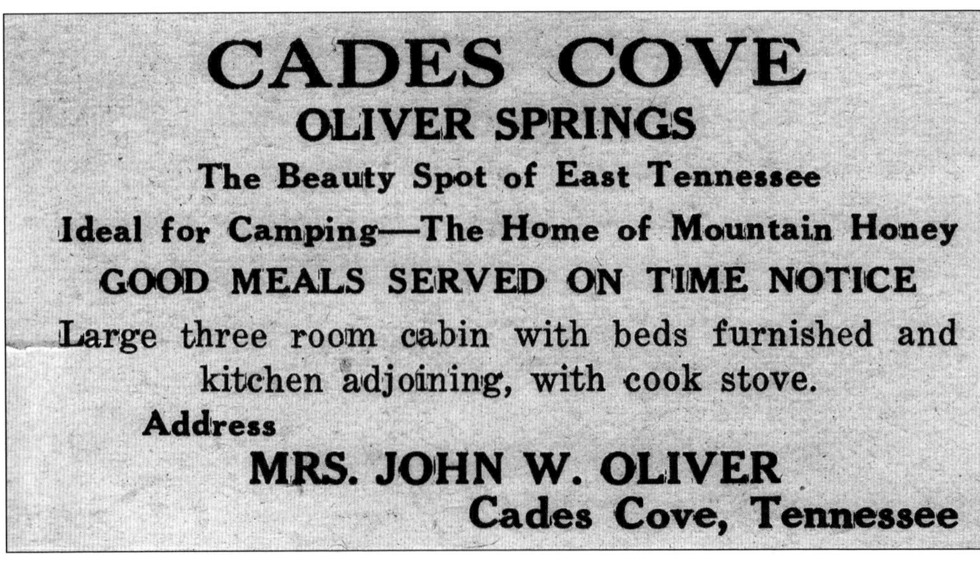

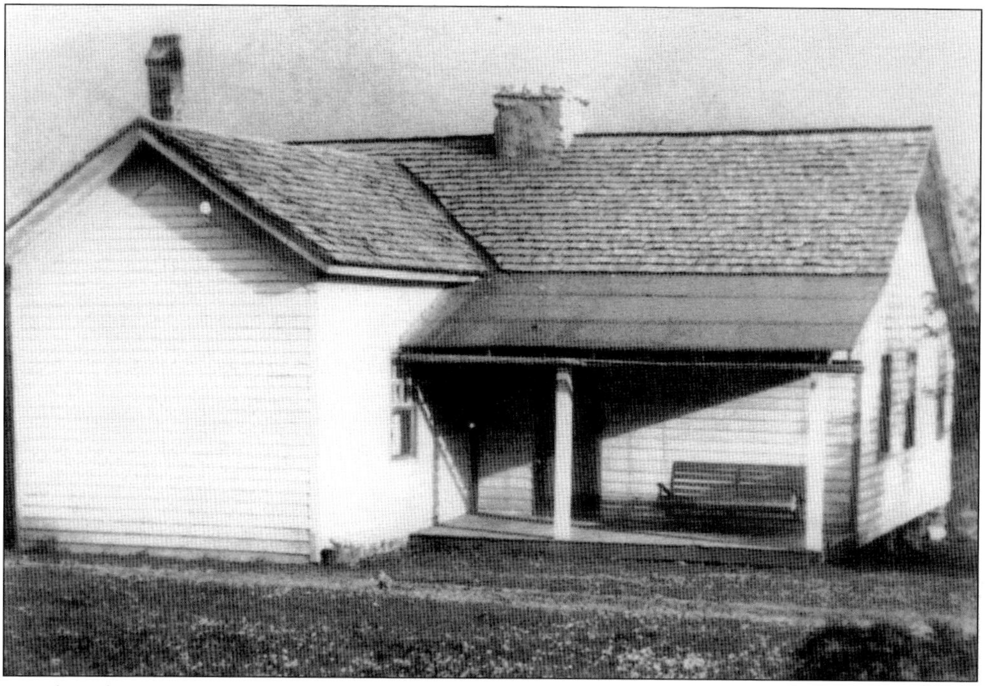

Joseph and Martha Womack LeQuire, along with six children, moved into Cades Cove from Swain County, North Carolina, during the Civil War. Joseph had two brothers and a sister cross over the mountains with him. Pictured in these John W. Oliver photographs is the Luther LeQuire house, the oldest frame house in the cove, located on the Joe LeQuire property. Luther would have been a grandson of Joseph "Joe" LeQuire. This land was located close to the current site of the John Oliver cabin. Each family that lived in the cove would have one or two dairy cows for milk and butter. And wild game was in abundance, so there was always meat for the table. (Both, courtesy of Margaret Oliver, John W. Oliver collection.)

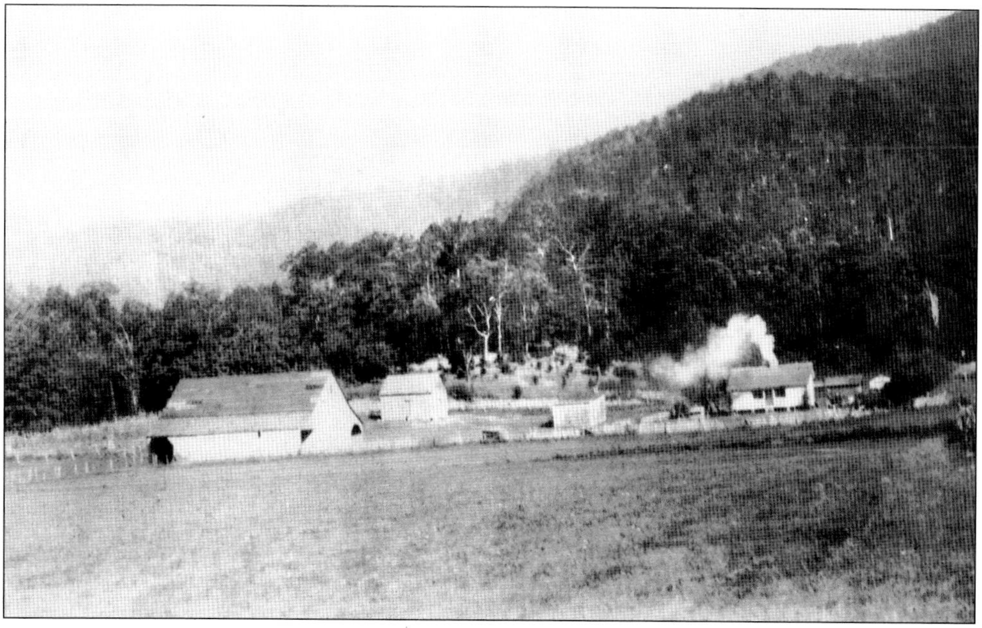

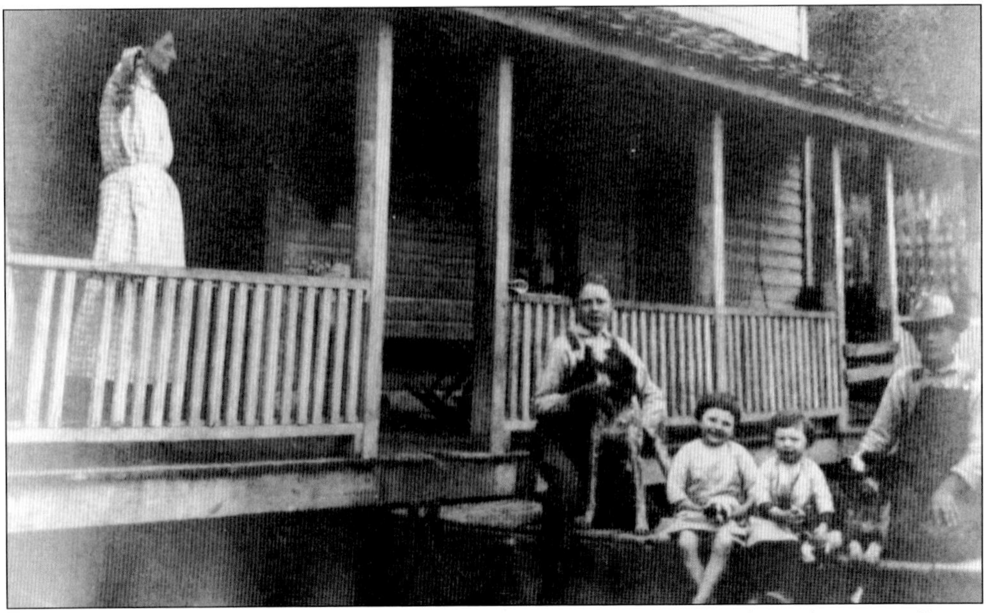

James Manuel "Mann" Ledbetter was the son of James Allan and Angeline Flowers. Ledbetter married Betty Jane Anthony. After her death, he married Louranie "Lurena" Shields, a daughter of Andrew "Witt" and Anna C. Walker Shields. Together, they had nine children, with eight of them being born in the house pictured above, which sat close to the present Cades Cove Riding Stables. Not far from their house was a tub mill, which was operated by the Ledbetter family. If present-day visitors looks closely in the springtime, they can see where this house sat, indicated by the daffodils in bloom. From left to right in photograph above are Witt, Rachel, and Katherine Ledbetter, and Elmer Myers. Pictured below are James Manuel "Mann" Ledbetter (left) and Louraine "Lurena" Ledbetter (right) with their children. (Both, courtesy of NPS.)

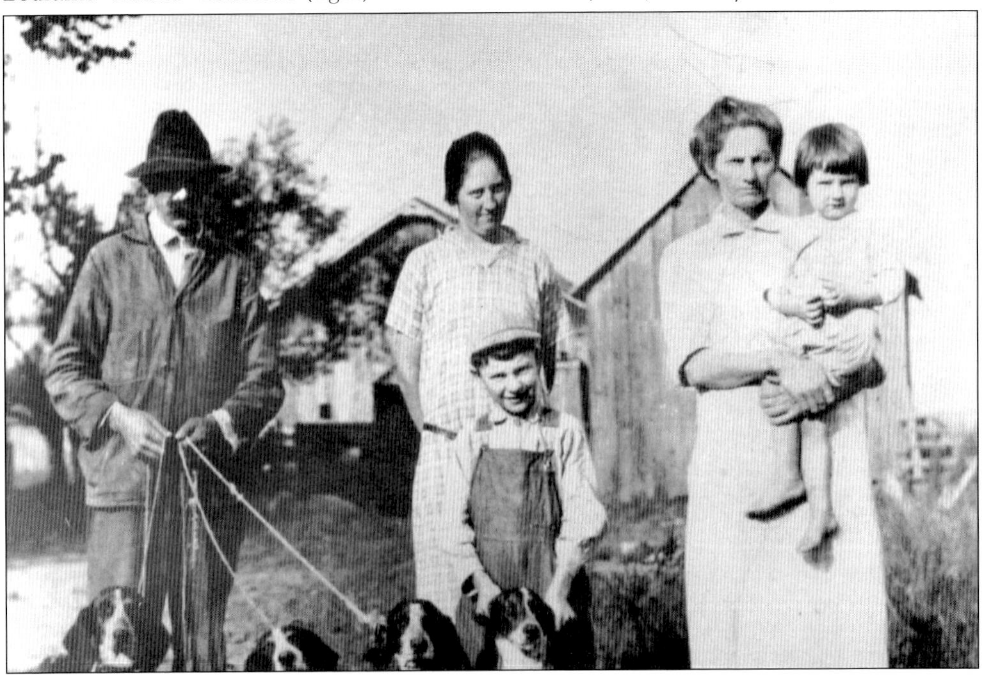

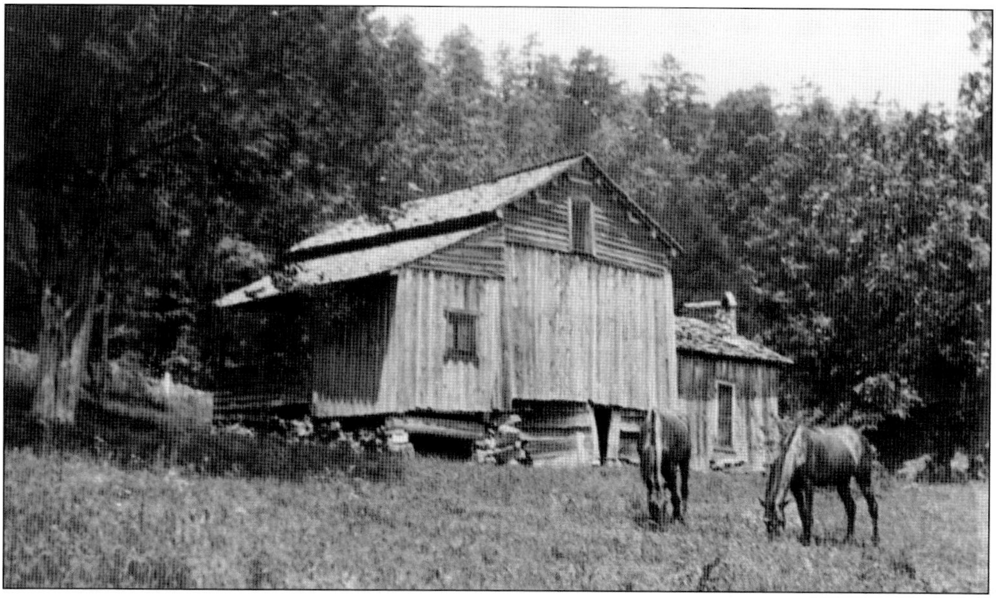

In 1849, John "Jack" Anthony purchased 98.5 acres of land, which included the site of what is known today as the Elijah Oliver House. The added-on kitchen shown in the above picture is said to have been built by Thomas Herron, who was married to Mariah Anthony, a daughter of Jack Anthony. In 1865, Elijah Oliver bought the property and moved back into Cades Cove from nearby Tuckaleechee Cove. Elijah was the second son born to John and Luraney Oliver. In 1852, he married Mary "Polly" Lawson, a daughter of Howell and Mary Bird Lawson. Elijah constructed many of the outbuildings on the property with the weatherboarding done with lumber that was sawn at Cable Mill. A small room was constructed on the front porch for people passing through with no place to spend the night. John W. Oliver, a grandson of Elijah Oliver, later purchased the house, and he rented the property and allowed the renters to live there as tenant farmers. (Both, courtesy of Margaret Oliver, John W. Oliver collection.)

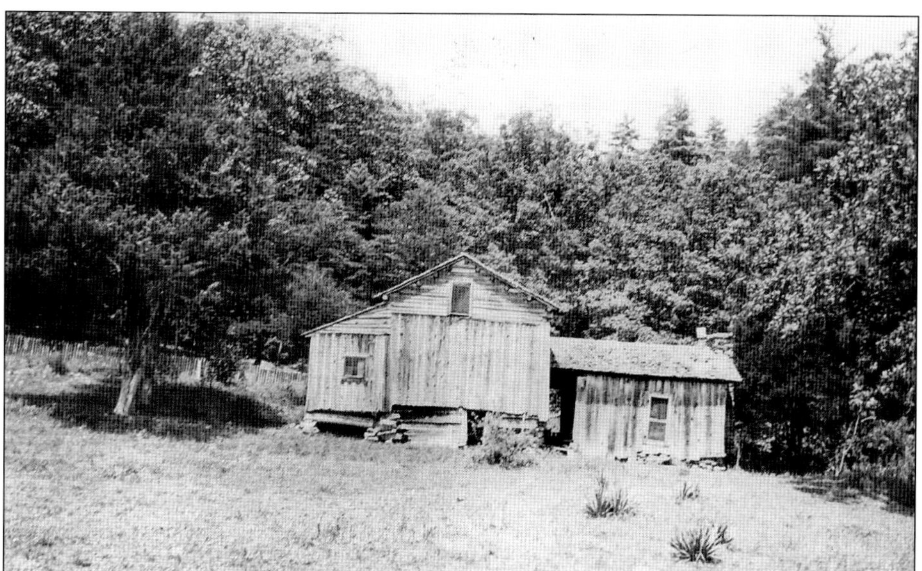

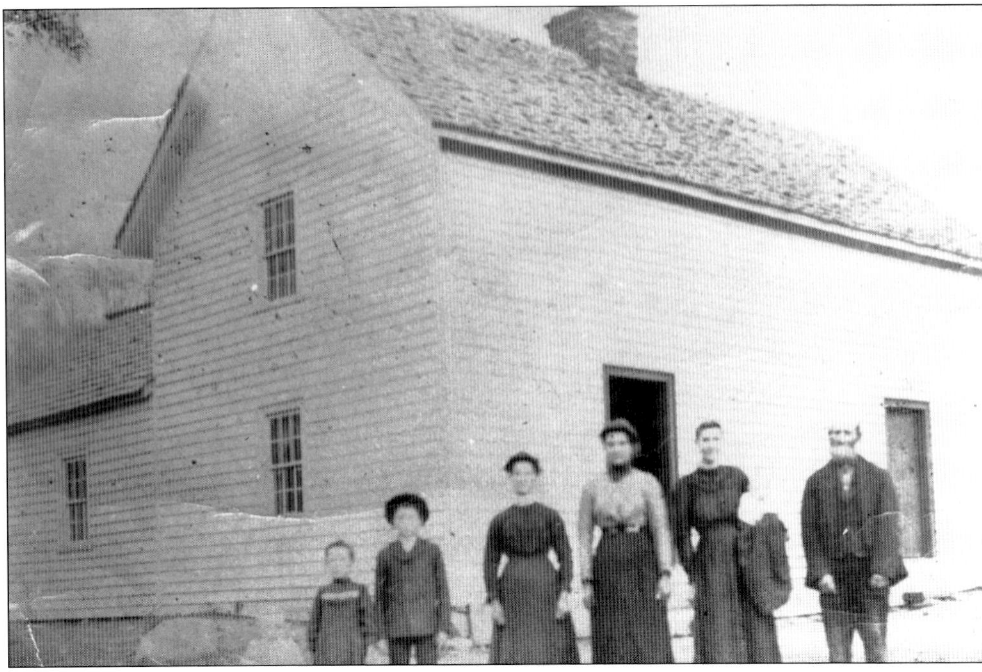

George S. Shields, son of Frederick and Mary Polly Oliver Shields, received land from his father's estate on what is now known as Mill Creek; in Frederick Shields's will, it was known as the Lyon's Field Farm. A two-story frame house was built by George in 1900 and stood until 1940. George, like many cove farmers, made a living as a beekeeper, with an apiary of 250 hives. George married Liza Jane Wilcox in 1884, and all of his children were born in Cades Cove. In 1910, George moved his family to Arkansas, and he sold his farm to Morton Butler Lumber in 1913. (Courtesy of Verna Lee Burchfield Myers.)

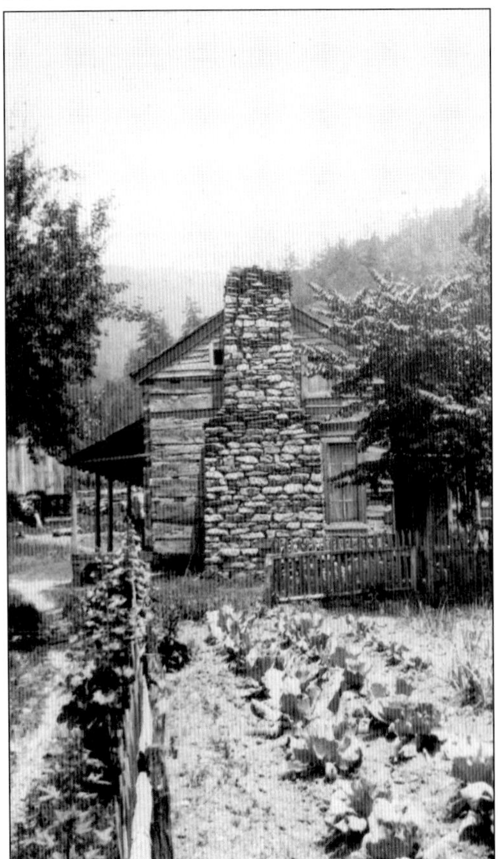

Pictured is the original home of the first white settlers into Cades Cove, John and Luraney Frazier Oliver. This was the second house they would live in; their first structure was described as only a lean-to. This photograph shows the Oliver garden, which was very close to the house. (Courtesy of Margaret Oliver, John W. Oliver collection.)

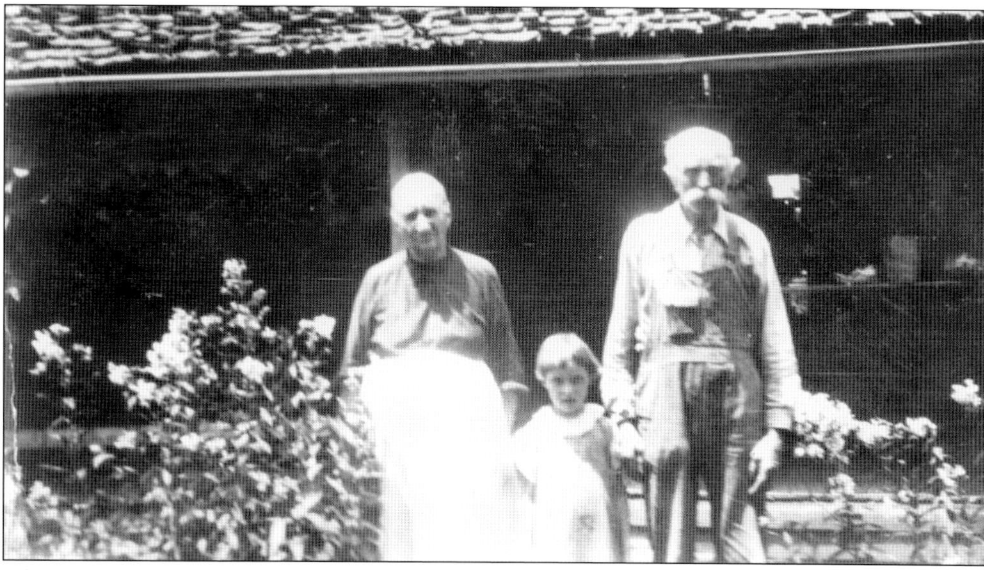

John Monroe LeQuire, son of Joseph and Martha Womack Le Quire, married Elizabeth "Bett" Cable, a daughter of John Primmer and Elizabeth Whitehead Cable. Monroe and Bett lived in close range to the Cable Mill, where Monroe was the miller. Cove inhabitants grew corn, wheat, rye, and a large variety of vegetables. They made their own clothing from their cotton and flax crops. Picture above are Bett (left), Laura Caughron (center), and Monroe LeQuire. In the photograph below are members of the LeQuire family in front of their home. (Both, courtesy of Verna Lee Burchfield Myers.)

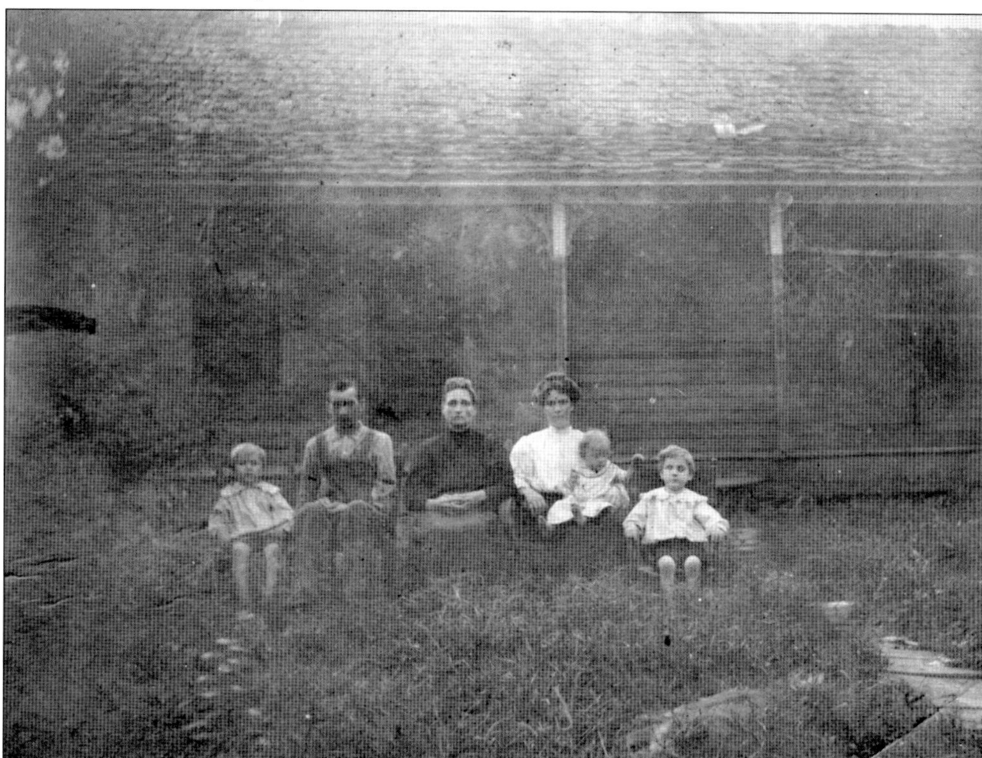

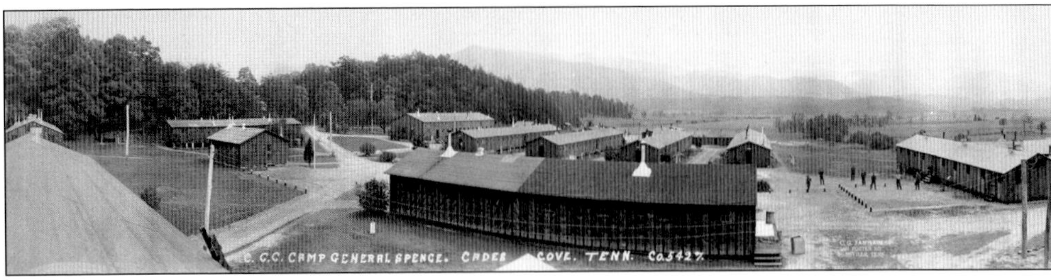

The Civilian Conservation Corps (CCC) in Cades Cove had its beginning in 1933; it was known as Company 5427, Camp General Spence, NP-11. The CCC was organized to help with maintaining trails and buildings in the cove as well as with firefighting. The camp had cannon that fired every day at retreat. The CCC employed many cove residents, and a large number of enrollees were provided an education. From their earnings at the camp, many of the members would only keep a small amount of their income and send the remainder home to their families. It was not always work for the corps; there was a baseball team that kept some of the men occupied playing other CCC teams. (Both, courtesy of NPS.)

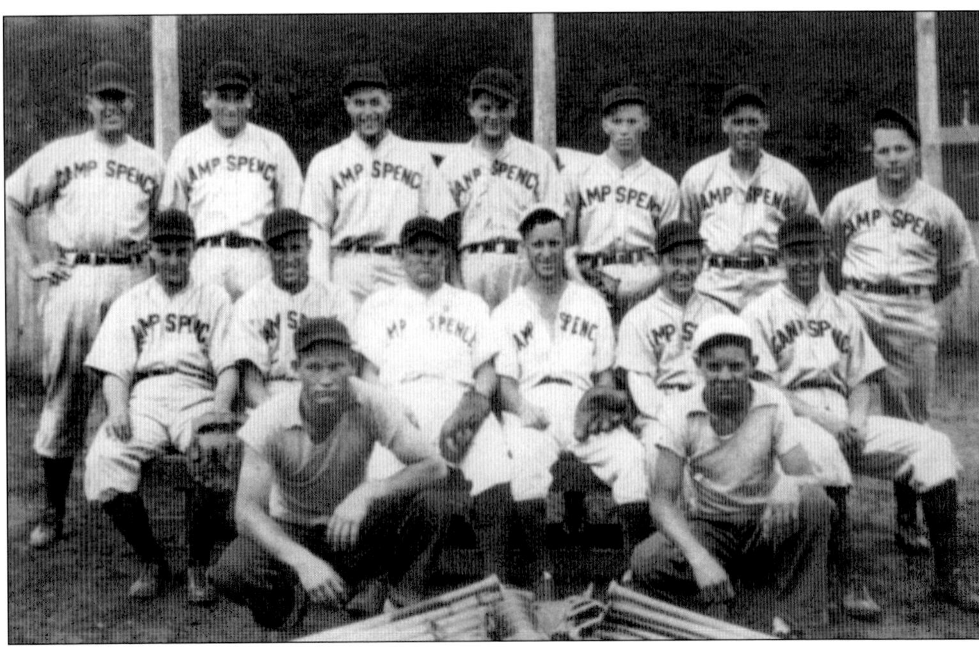

Four

Daily Life and People

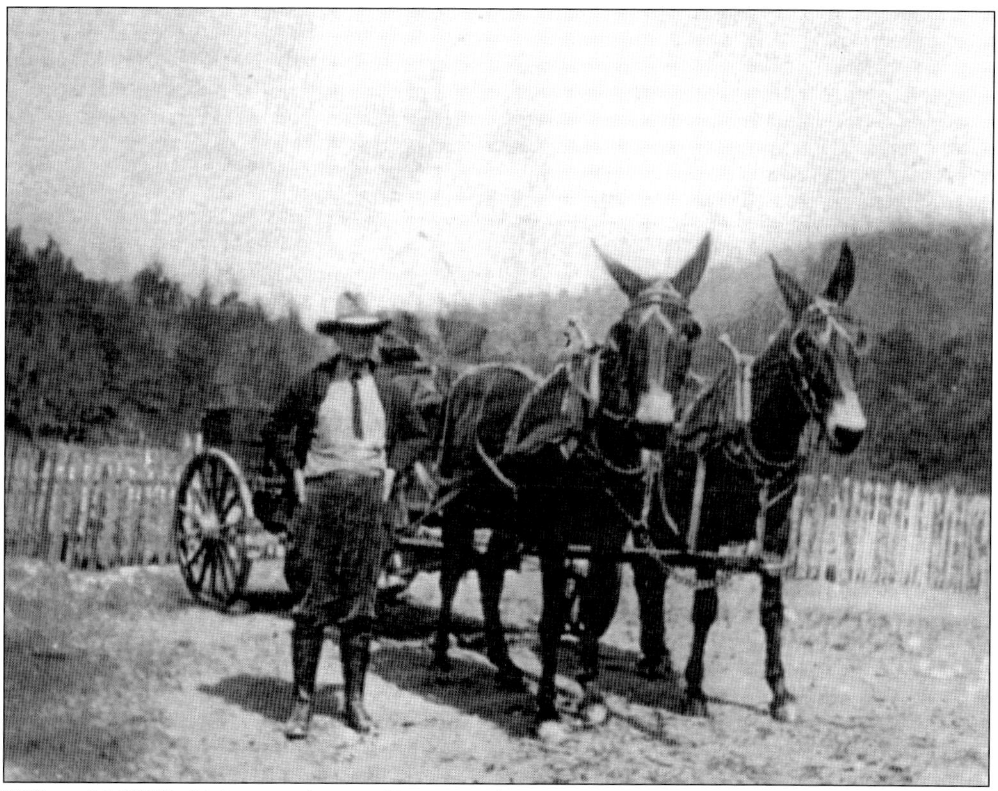

William H. "Willie" Myers was born to Henry Wade Hampton "Hamp" Myers and Susan Clementine Gregory Myers on November 11, 1888, in Cades Cove. He first married Eliza Hill and later married Harriett Ann "Hattie" Correll. Willie worked for the Civilian Conservation Corps in Cades Cove. Willie and Hattie operated the Ekaneetlee Lodge, located on Parson's Branch Road for many years until it was obtained by condemnation and acquired by the government in 1940. (Courtesy of NPS.)

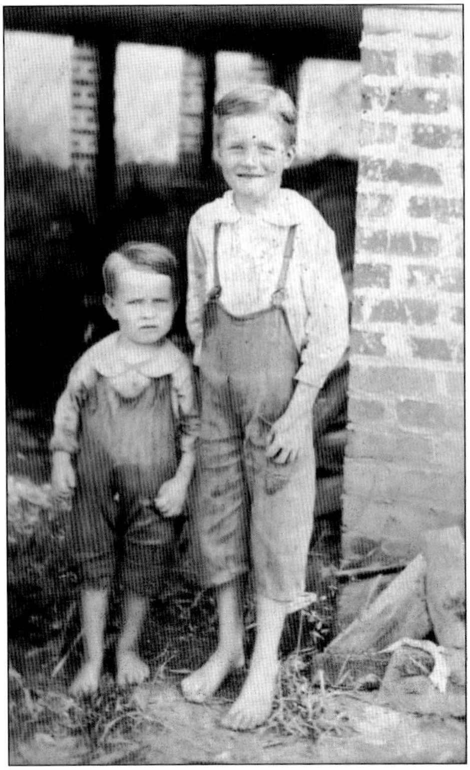

Willie (left) and Arthur Wright were children of Elmer and Mary Ann Myers Wright. Their grandparents were John Case "Cassie" and Mary Ann Gregory Myers. The Wrights lived in a house in the Tater Branch area, which is close to the Cades Cove Missionary Baptist Church. This picture, taken in the early 1930s in Cades Cove, shows the attire for children of this time and area. Most children went without shoes in the summer months and would get a new pair of shoes for the winter. (Courtesy of Margaret Oliver, John W. Oliver collection.)

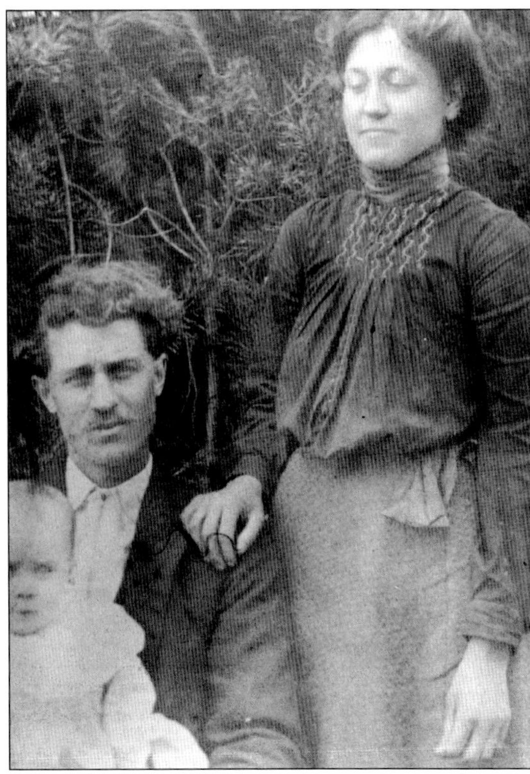

William Wade Myers, son of John Case "Cassie" and Mary Ann Gregory Myers, was born in Cades Cove September 25, 1879. On November 11, 1902, he married Martha "Matt" Wilson Myers, the daughter of Alexander "Alex" and Lucretia Whitehead Potter Wilson. Both Wade and Matt were born and raised in Cades Cove and made their home on Forge Creek Road. (Courtesy of Margaret Oliver, John W. Oliver collection.)

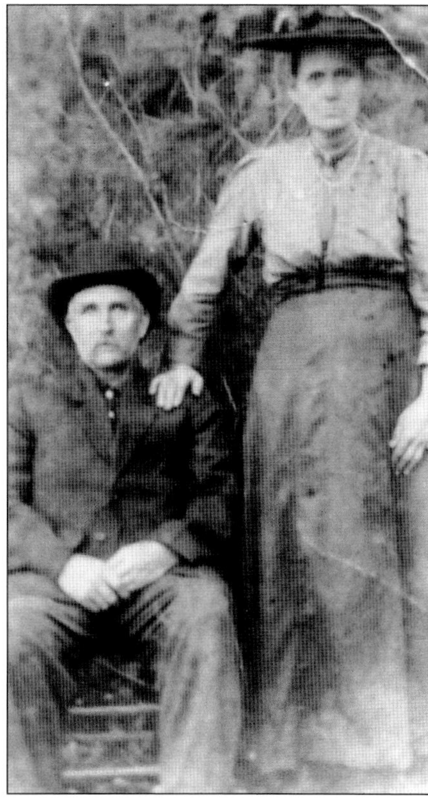

Charlie and Myria Miller Garland moved their family from North Carolina to Cades Cove in the early 1880s. They had 16 children and lived in the Bearded Cane area on Hesse Creek, near Miller's Cove, as well as in Cades Cove. Charlie was a man of many talents, including logging and farming. One story about Charlie that has been handed down for generations is that he had walked about 20 miles to the Crawford-Caldwell Hardware Store in Maryville to make a purchase of a step-stove. This stove weighed about 200 pounds, and the storekeeper wondered how Charlie was going to get it home because he had not brought a wagon or help with him. Charlie's response was that he was going to carry the stove on his back, 20 miles. The storekeeper thought this was unbelievable and challenged Charlie that if he could carry the stove back to Bearded Cane without putting the stove down for a rest, he would give the stove to him at no charge. One of the store workers is have said to have walked back with Charlie to make sure he went by the storekeeper's rule, and Charlie made it back without putting the stove down at all. Charlie Garland passed on in 1923, and Myria Miller Garland died in 1954. Below is the Charlie Garland family. (Both, courtesy of Sylvia Garland Galde.)

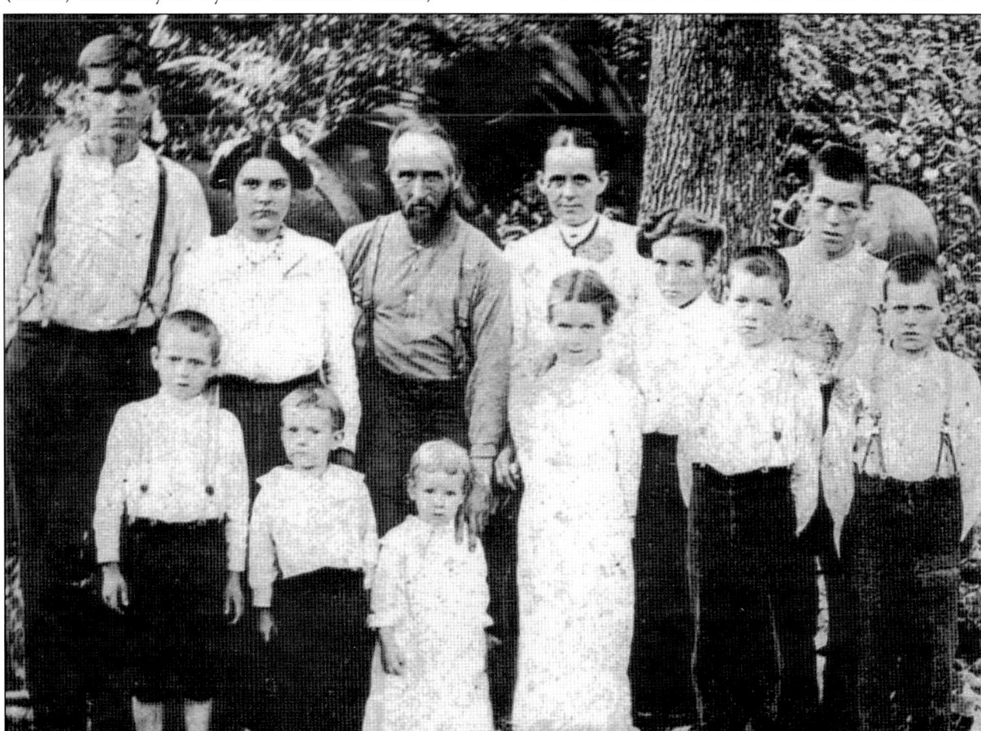

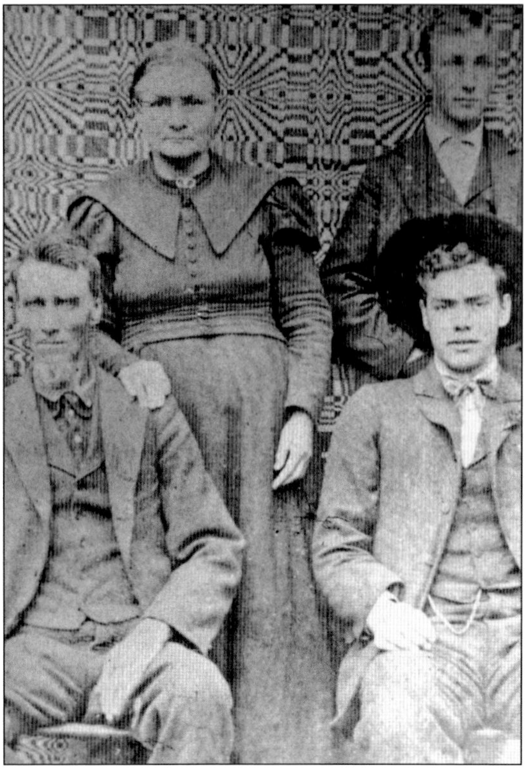

Pictured from left to right are (first row) William A. "Billie" Feezell and Wesley; (second row) Mary Shields Feezell and Lee Feezell. Billie, born in North Carolina, moved into Cades Cove as a young boy in the 1840s. He married Mary Shields, a daughter of Henry and Martha Oliver Shields, in 1861. After the death of their daughter Lydia in 1862, Mary died, and Billie married Modena McEldry Spradlin in 1865. They had eight children born in Cades Cove. Billie's family lived on land that was up behind Cades Cove Methodist Church and donated the property where the church is now located. The Feezell land was still in family possession when the park purchased it in 1935. (Courtesy of NPS.)

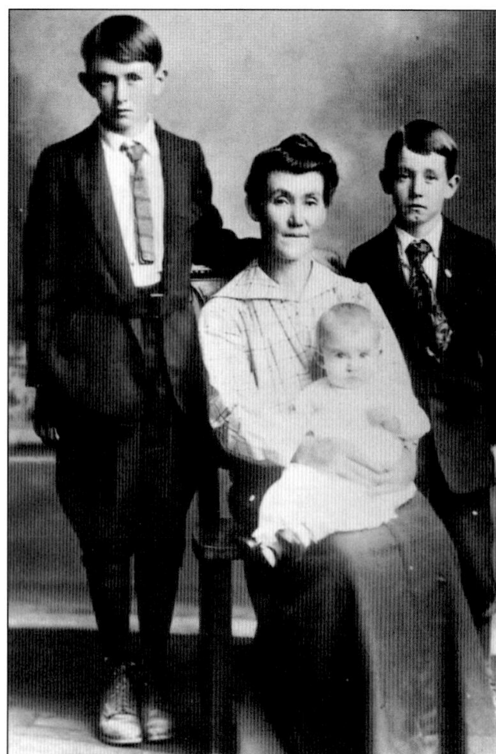

Susan Tipton Burchfield was born in 1882 to George and Tuckaleechee "Tuck" Burchfield Tipton. She married Jesse Young Burchfield, a son of Noah and Sarah Brown Burchfield. Together, they had three children born in Cades Cove, and Jesse died not long after the last child was born. The family lived close to the Noah Burchfield farm. Susan had to rear the children on her own as well as take care of a farm. This was common for many of the cove women who lost their husbands early in life. (Courtesy of NPS.)

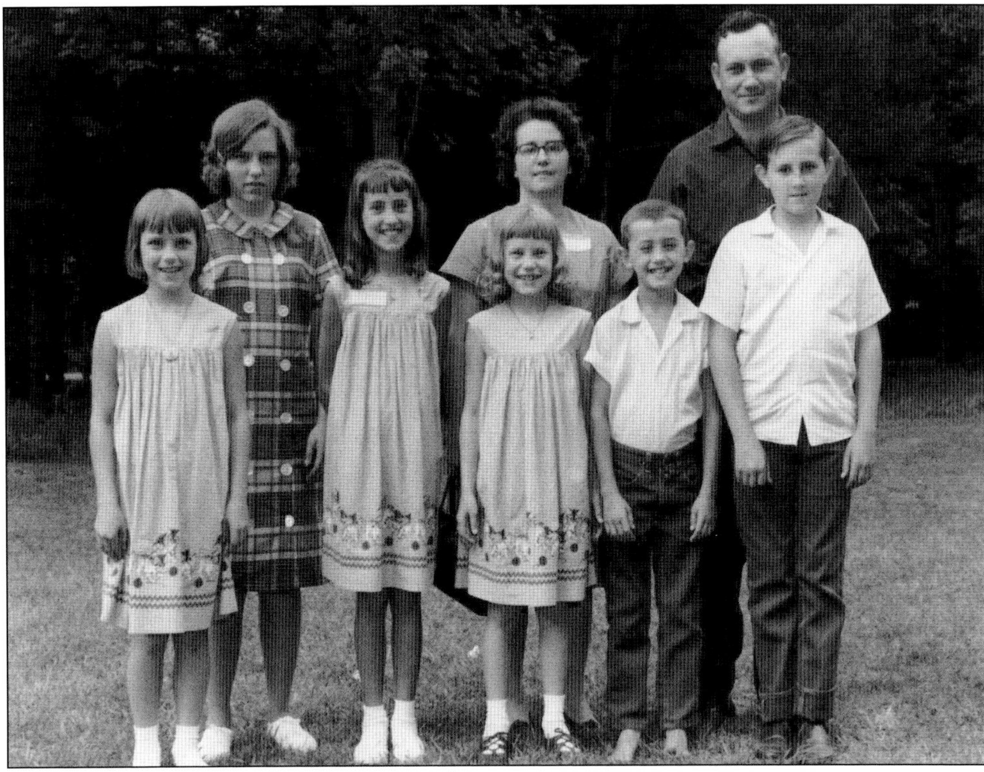

Leon Sparks was born July 29, 1929, in Cades Cove, Tennessee, to Asa and Amy Burchfield Sparks. In 1951, he married Johnnie Bryant, born December 30, 1928, to John Andrew and Ruthie Angeline Ledbetter Bryant in Dry Valley, near Cades Cove. When Leon and Johnnie married, they moved into his parents' household, which included Leon's 11 younger brothers and sisters. Four of Leon and Johnnie's six children were born while they lived in the cove. In 1956, the Sparks family moved out of Cades Cove, but they cherish the memories of the years they spent there. (Leon and Johnnie Sparks photograph.)

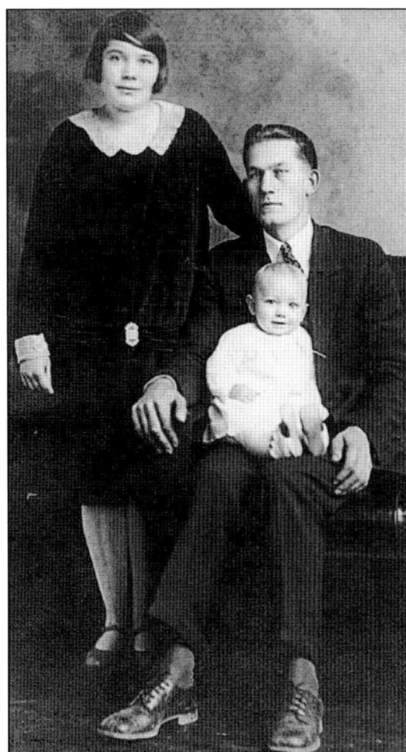

Vernie R. Burchfield and Nora Mae Myers Burchfield are pictured with one of their children. He was born in 1905 to Tennessee "Tennie" Tipton and John Burchfield. Nora, born in 1910, was the daughter of Jonathan and Martha LeQuire Myers. Vernie and Nora had three children—two boys and one girl. Vernie was employed by Kitchen Lumber Company, a logging company in Cades Cove, as a young man. He then worked on dairy farms before becoming an employee of the Aluminum Company of America, where he stayed until retirement. (Courtesy of Verna Lee Burchfield Myers.)

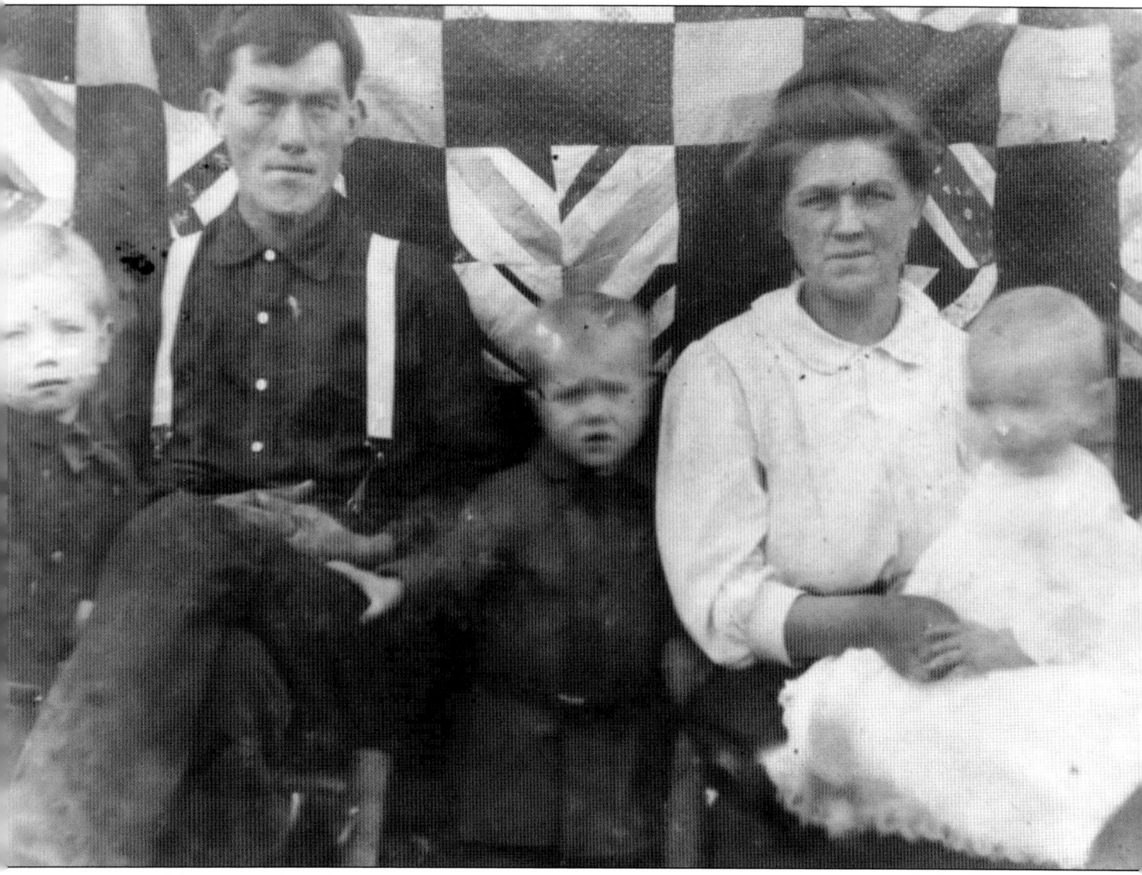

Pictured here are, from left to right, Vernie, Jonathan Caswell "Preacher Johnnie" Tipton, Roy, Louisa Myers Tipton, and Ruth Tipton. Johnnie was born in 1887 to George and Tuckaleechee "Tuck" Burchfield Tipton in Cades Cove, probably on Rowan's Creek, where the family lived at the time. Louisa, the daughter of John Case "Cassie" and Mary Ann Gregory Myers, was also born in Cades Cove. Johnnie was a farmer and a molasses maker. The family belonged to the Cades Cove Missionary Baptist Church, where Johnnie and Louisa were very active. Some of their children were born in the cove; others were born after they moved to the Forest Hill Community in Maryville. In 1929, Johnnie and Louisa Tipton sold 156 acres to the park service and moved out of the cove. William Tipton, Johnnie's great-great-grandfather and the first land grant holder in Cades Cove, originally owned this land. (Courtesy of Missy Tipton Green.)

Pictured in 1907, the children of John H. and Tennessee "Tennie" Tipton Burchfield are, from left to right, Vernie, France, Amy, and Viola. One can tell in the photograph that the clothing of the children is homemade, probably made from cloth that was spun out of cotton or flax by their mother. (Courtesy of Verna Lee Burchfield Myers.)

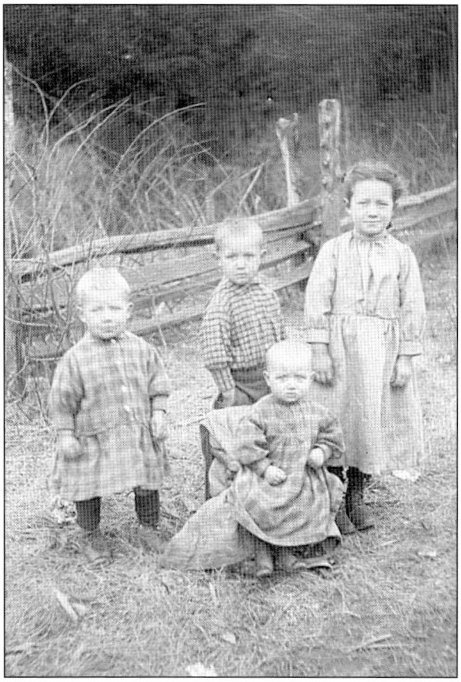

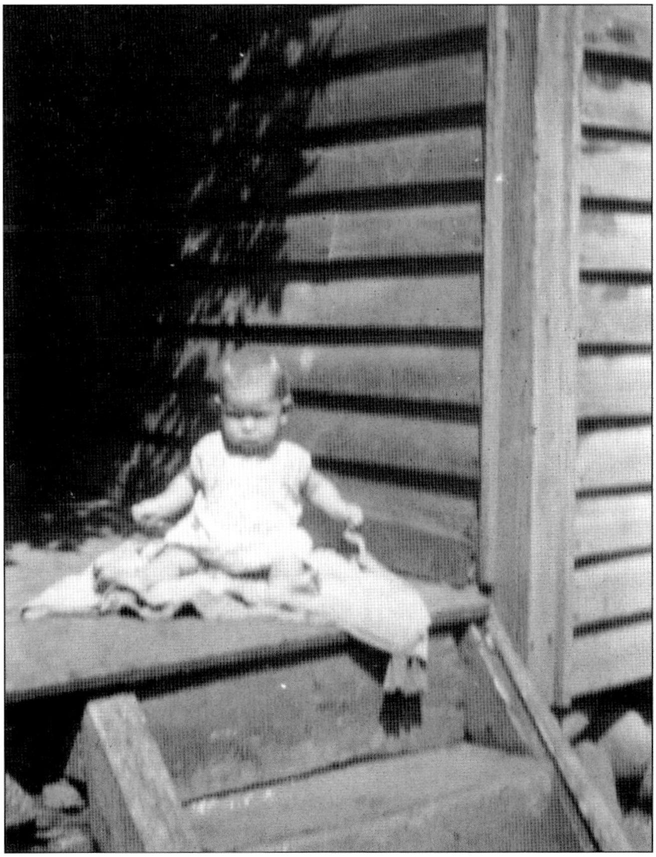

Verna Lee Burchfield was the second child born in Cades Cove to Vernie and Nora Mae Myers Burchfield. In 1928, Verna married Hugh Myers, the son of Charles and Mae Shuler Myers. Hugh and Verna Lee had four children and resided in Cades Cove until 1976 as lessees. They operated the Cades Cove Riding Stables until 2008. Verna Lee is pictured at the George Shields house on Mill Creek. (Courtesy of Verna Lee Burchfield Myers.)

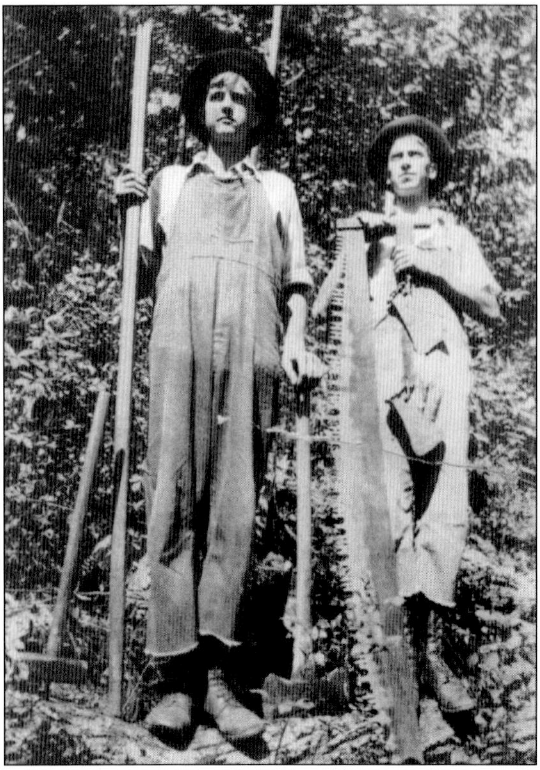

Houston Chambers (left) and Alex Gregory are shown here with tools, including an ax, crosscut saw, and other implements, that were required for a young man to do a day's work in Cades Cove. They were clearing some trees, possibly to construct a building or to clear out for fields. (Courtesy of NPS.)

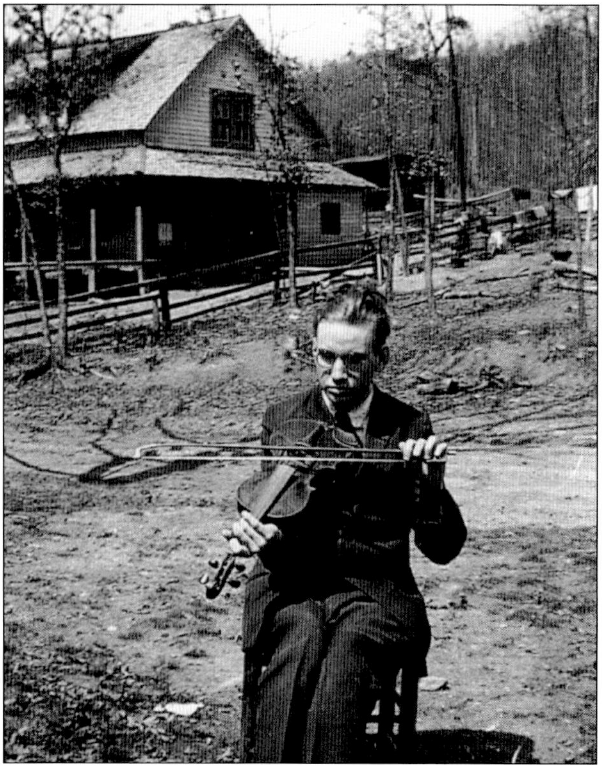

Ollie Myers enjoyed playing all types of instruments and was very talented. Ollie was born blind and never got to see the beauty of Cades Cove, but he could make beautiful music about the area. He was the son of Jonathan Wade Hampton and Martha "Sis" LeQuire Myers. Ollie is pictured in front of his home, which was located in proximity to the Cades Cove Missionary Baptist Church. (Courtesy of Verna Lee Burchfield Myers.)

Martha Elizabeth "Sis" LeQuire Myers Burchfield, the daughter of John Monroe and Elizabeth "Bett" Cable LeQuire, is pictured sitting on the porch at the Noah Burchfield house. The women of the cove were most always seen wearing aprons. Sis was married to Jonathan Myers. After his death, she married John Burchfield. John and Sis lived in the Noah Burchfield house after the death of Noah. (Courtesy of Verna Lee Burchfield Myers.)

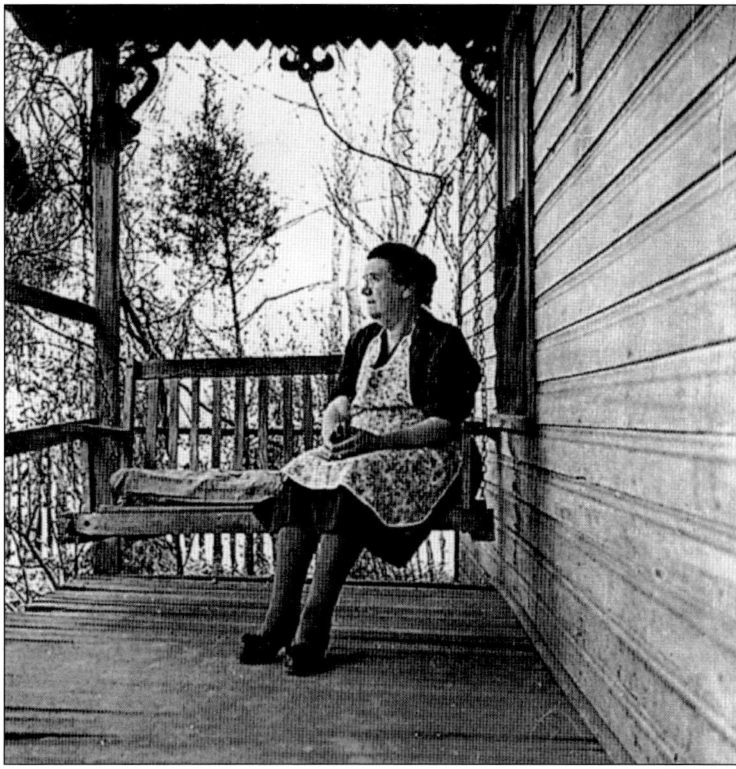

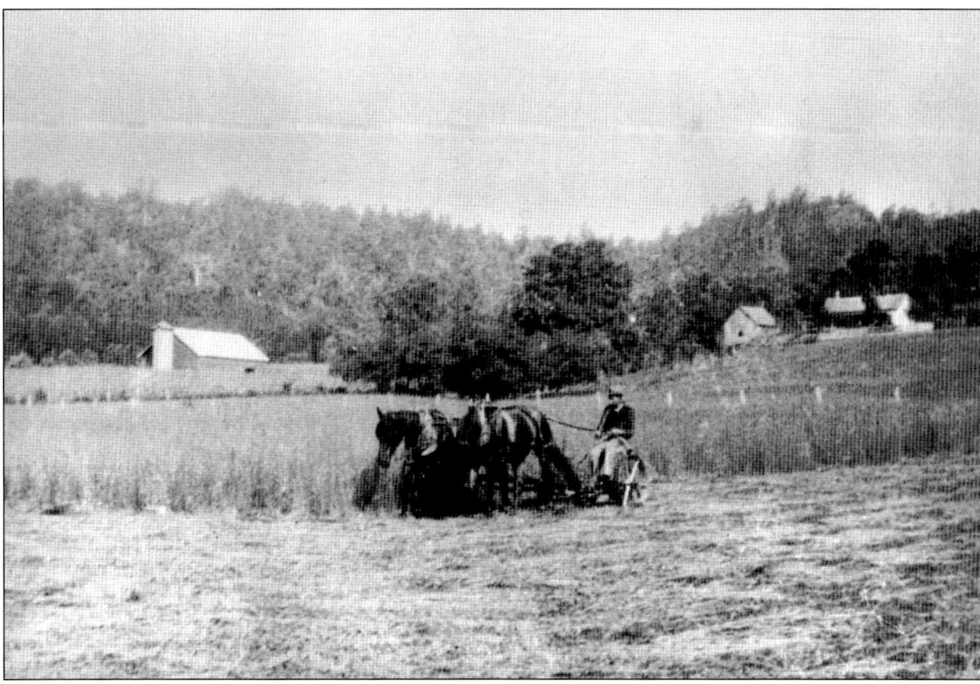

Mowing the fields was a very hard job and took days to complete. When it was time to cut the hay, some farmers hired people to do it for them. Pictured is the John W. Oliver field as John Burchfield cuts with a horse-drawn mower. (Courtesy of Verna Lee Burchfield Myers.)

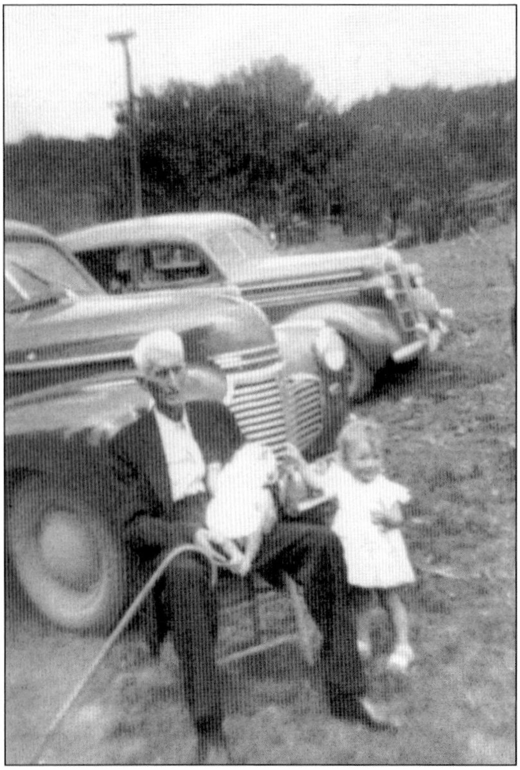

John Burchfield is proud of his great-grandchildren Judy (in his lap) and Shirley, children of Lee Roy Burchfield, whose father was France Burchfield. This picture was taken at a family reunion in Cades Cove. (Courtesy of Verna Lee Burchfield Myers.)

At most mill sites, there was a millpond. This one, located at Shields Mill, was a wonderful place to go swimming. The Shields children look to be having lots of fun cooling off in the water. Cove children had to find their own activities to do, and swimming was one of the favorites in the summer. (Courtesy of NPS.)

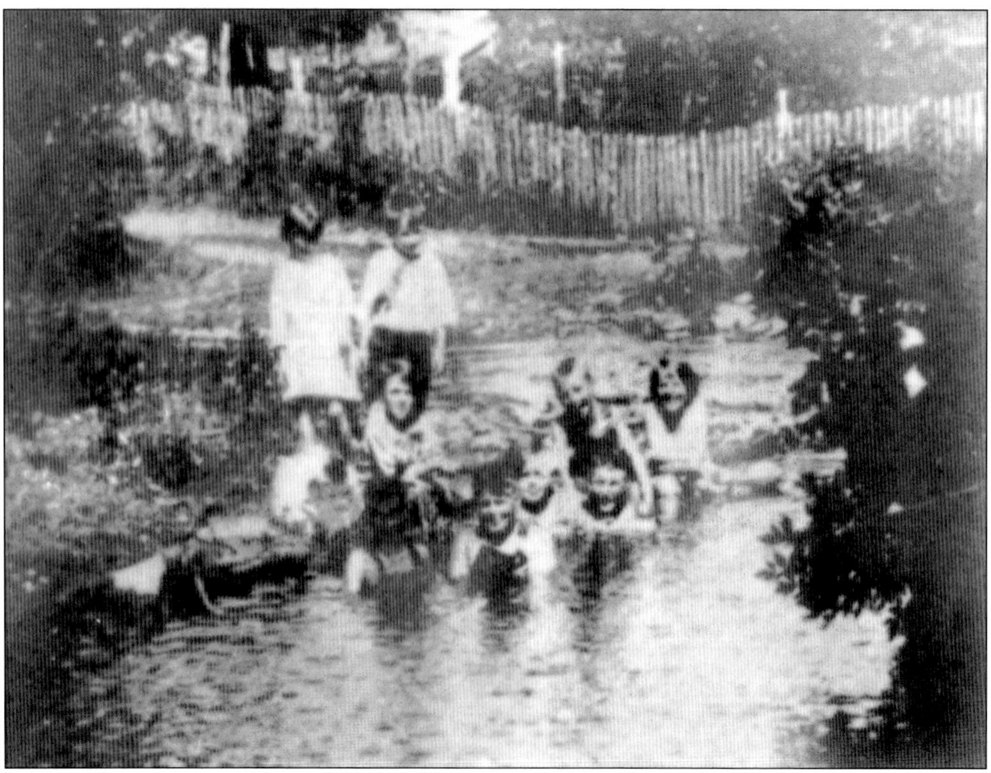

Pictured is the Payne family, who resided in the area close to the Dan Lawson/Peter Cable house. From left to right are (first row) Hazel and Moda Payne; (second row) Sherman, Carlos, and Hattie Wilcox Payne, daughter of Caleb Wilcox Jr. and Mary Ann Burchfield Wilcox. The Wilcox family arrived in Cades Cove in the early 1870s. (Courtesy of NPS.)

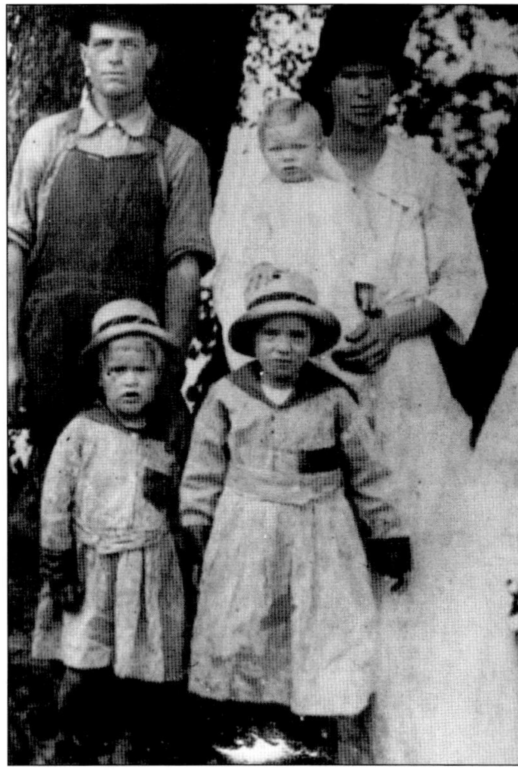

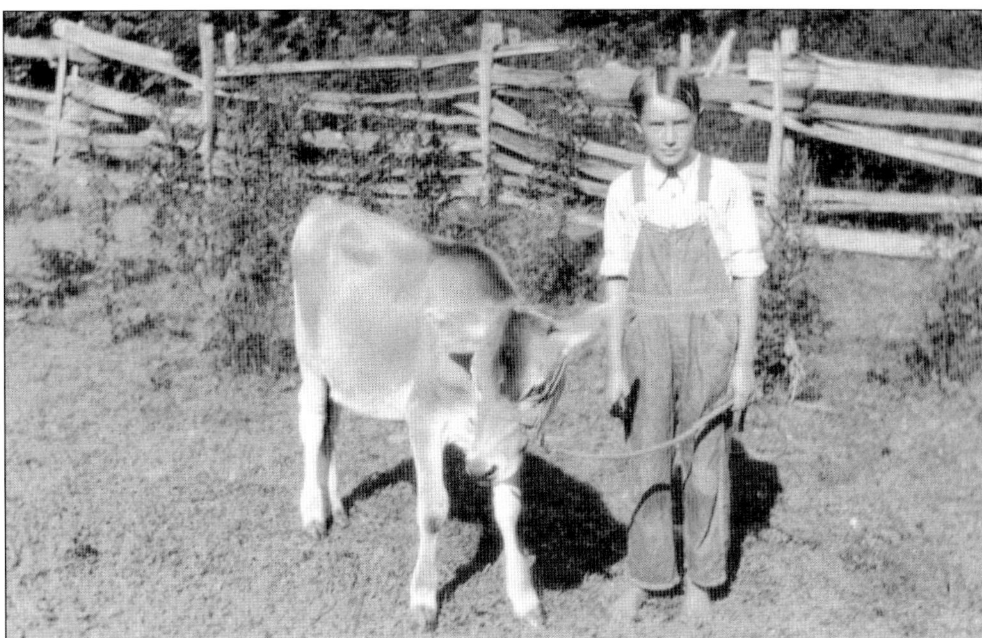

Those living on farms could become attached to farm animals. It seems that Otis Tipton has taken this calf as his pet. Otis was born in Cades Cove to George and Lula Burchfield Tipton. It was typical for children in the cove to play and romp the fields and mountains without shoes. (Courtesy of Margaret Oliver, John W. Oliver collection.)

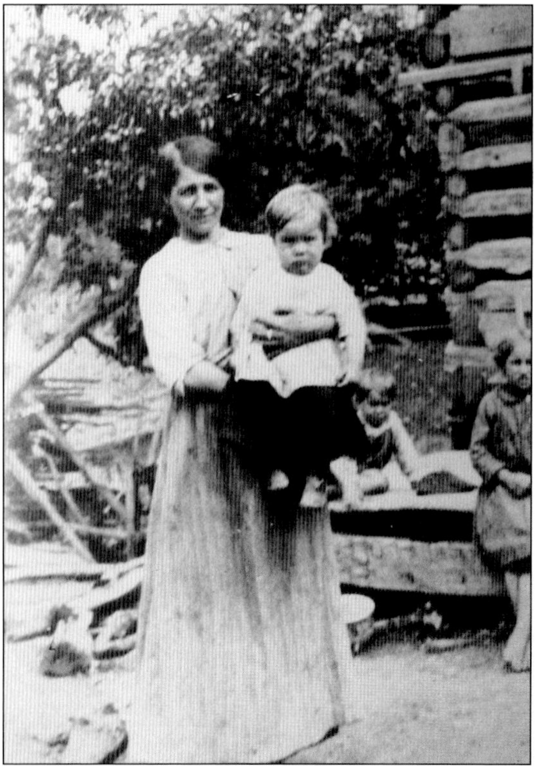

Rutha Angeline Myers McCaulley is pictured with daughter Anna Lee. Rutha was married to John Thomas McCaulley and lived up Forge Creek Road on a large farm where John also tended to many beehives. Rutha was the daughter of John Case "Cassie" and Mary Ann Gregory Myers. (Courtesy of NPS.)

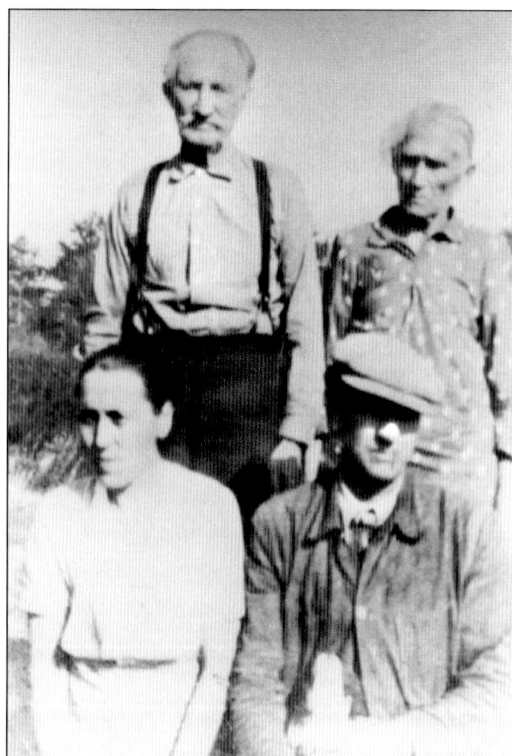

John "Cassie" and Mary Ann Gregory Myers are pictured with daughter-in-law "Matt" Wilson Myers and son Wade Myers in Cades Cove. There was not much time to stop for a family photograph, as there were so many chores that had to be done each day. (Courtesy of Dale Sparks.)

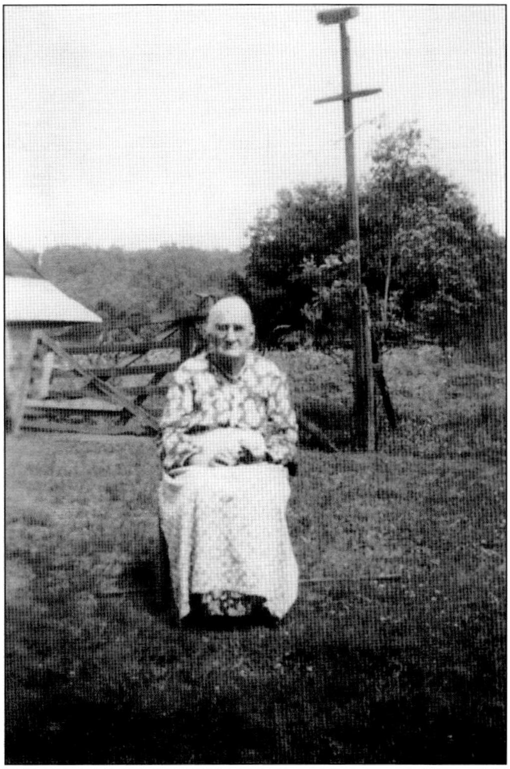

Elizabeth "Bett" Cable LeQuire, daughter of John Primmer and Elizabeth Whitehead Cable, married James Monroe LeQuire. Bett and Monroe lived close to the Cable Mill, where Monroe was employed as a miller. John P. Cable had moved his family into Cades Cove in 1868 from Carter County, Tennessee. (Courtesy of Margaret Oliver, John W. Oliver collection.)

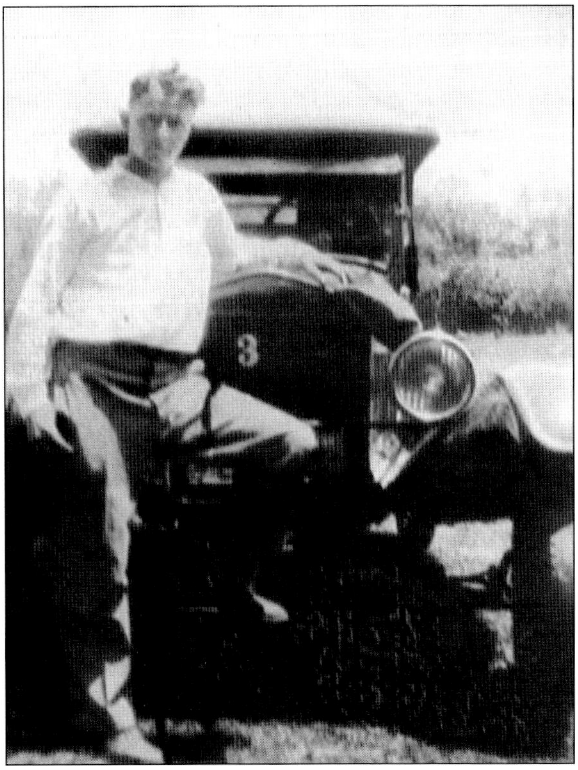

Charles Bluford Sparks is pictured here showing off his ride in Cades Cove. Many cove residents had vehicles, although rain made it hard to travel on the muddy cove roads. Bluford, the son of Sam and Texana Gregory Sparks, married Pearl Myers. (Courtesy of Dale Sparks.)

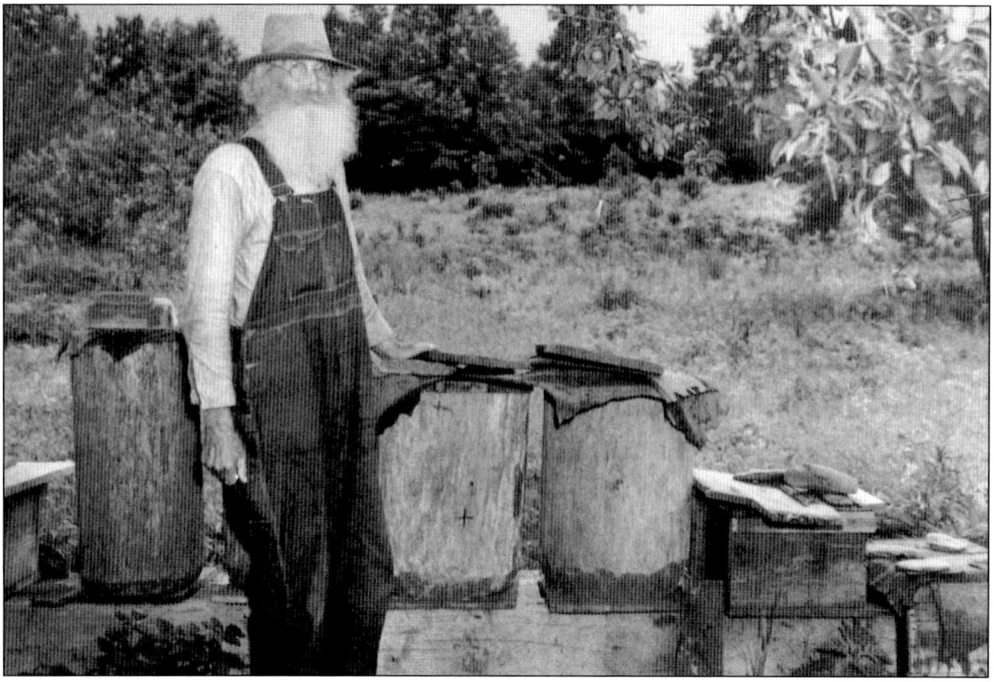

Daniel H. Myers Jr. was well known for both his knowledge of beekeeping as well as his herding of cattle on the balds. Here, he is shown with his hives, which were made from tree stumps. If one was driving through the cove in the days before the national park, beehives could be seen on almost every farm. The art of beekeeping was handed down from generation to generation, and many keepers had different kinds of hives. (Both, courtesy of NPS.)

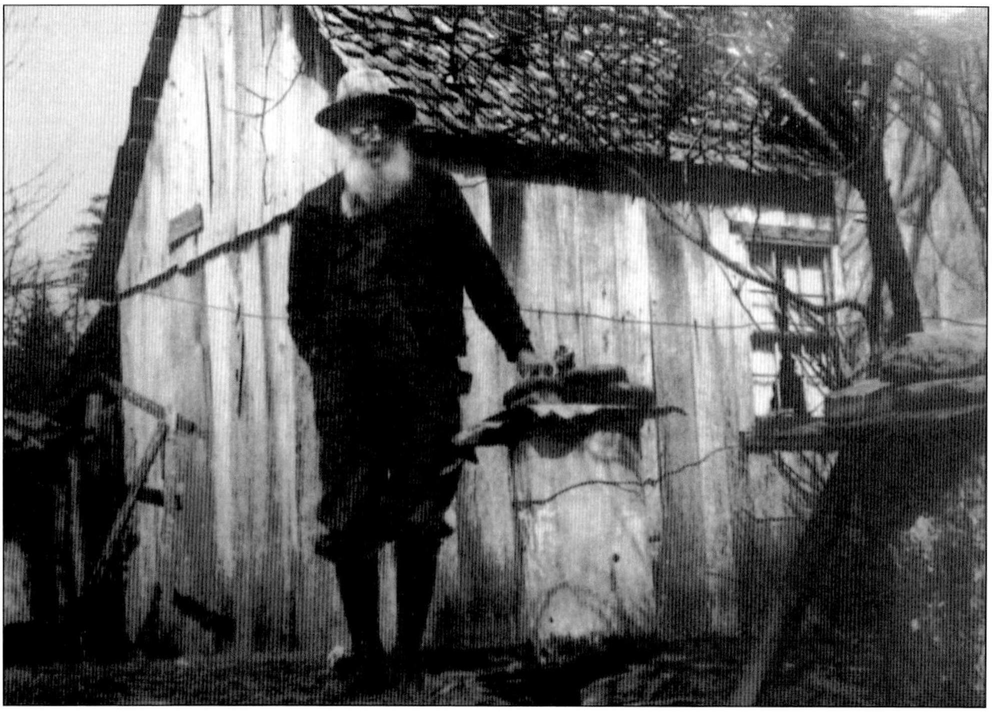

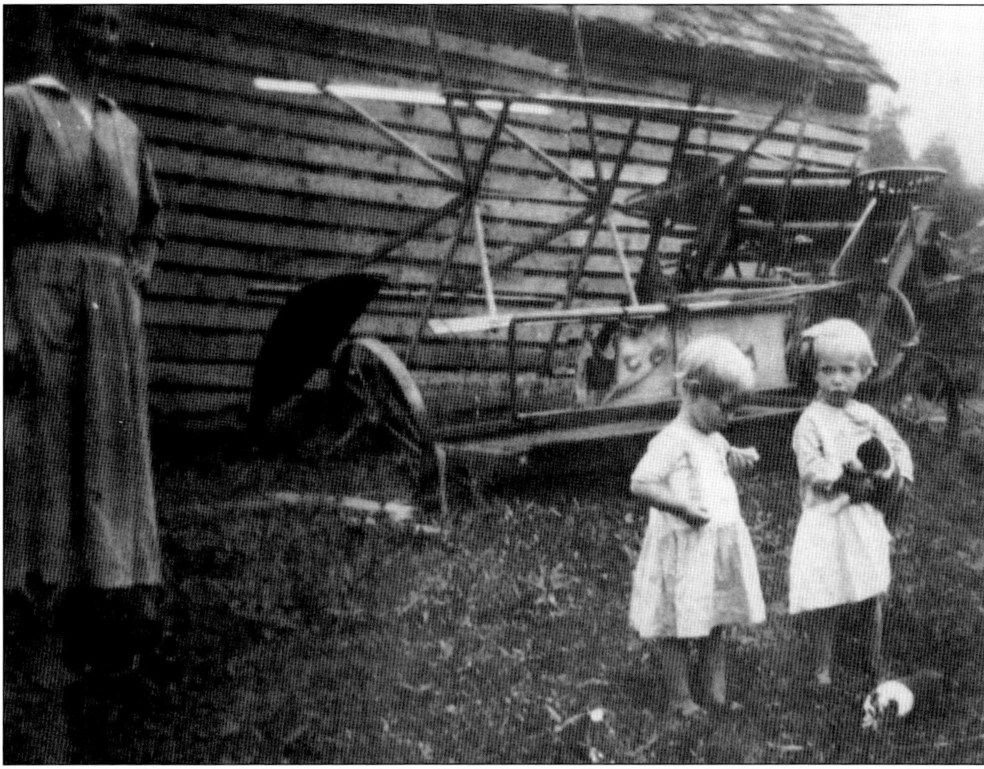

Edna Abbott and Mildred Tipton are having fun with what appears to be puppies or kittens. They are standing in front of an old threshing machine. Many children in the cove would take remedies from their mothers that were passed down from their grandmothers: tea from the bark of wild cherry trees for measles and colds; honey and alum for sore throats; ragweed for stings; heavily salted cornmeal poultice for sprains; and tea made of ground ivy for the croup. (Courtesy of NPS.)

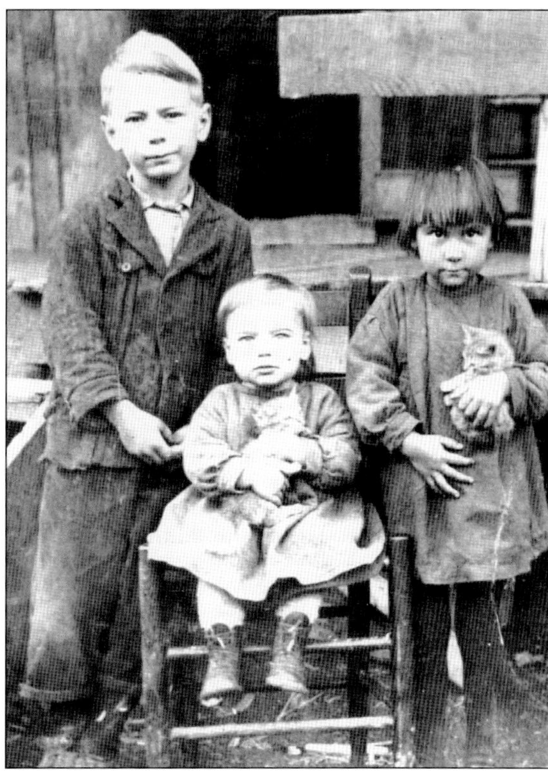

Elmer (left), Clemmie (center), and Mary Myers hold their kittens. Children living in the cove would occupy themselves with whatever they could find to play with. Parents made most of the toys, whether it was a corn shuck doll or a truck. Some of the games played by the youngsters were marbles, hide-and-seek, and tag. (Courtesy of NPS.)

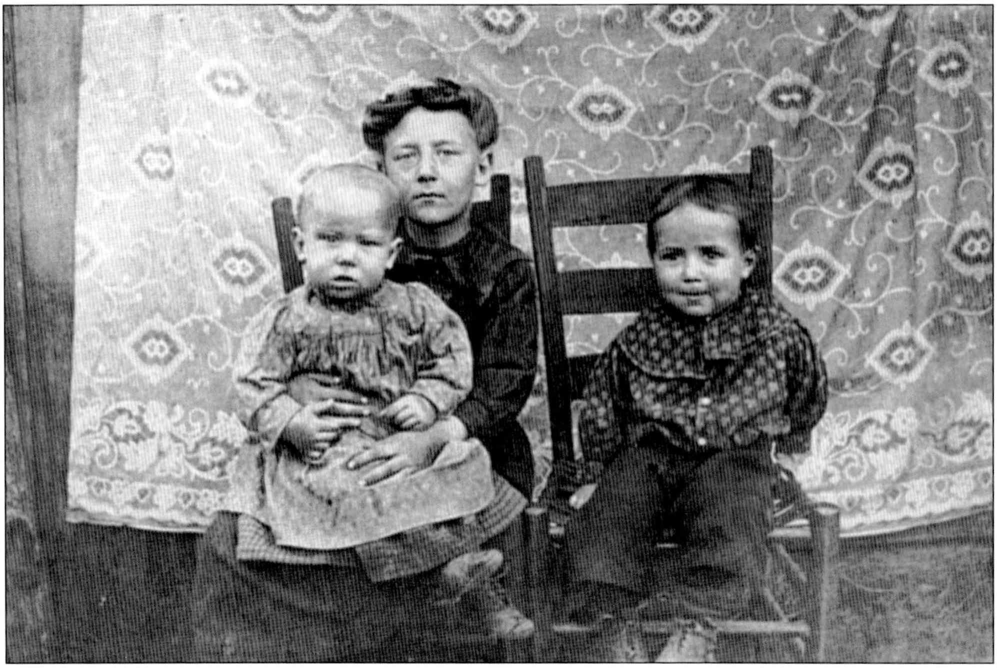

From left to right are Ella Tipton, Huse Gregory, and Henry Gregory. The different photographers of the cove would use various backgrounds for pictures; some used quilts, coverlets, or pine boughs. They would also develop their own pictures in darkrooms at their homes. (Courtesy of NPS.)

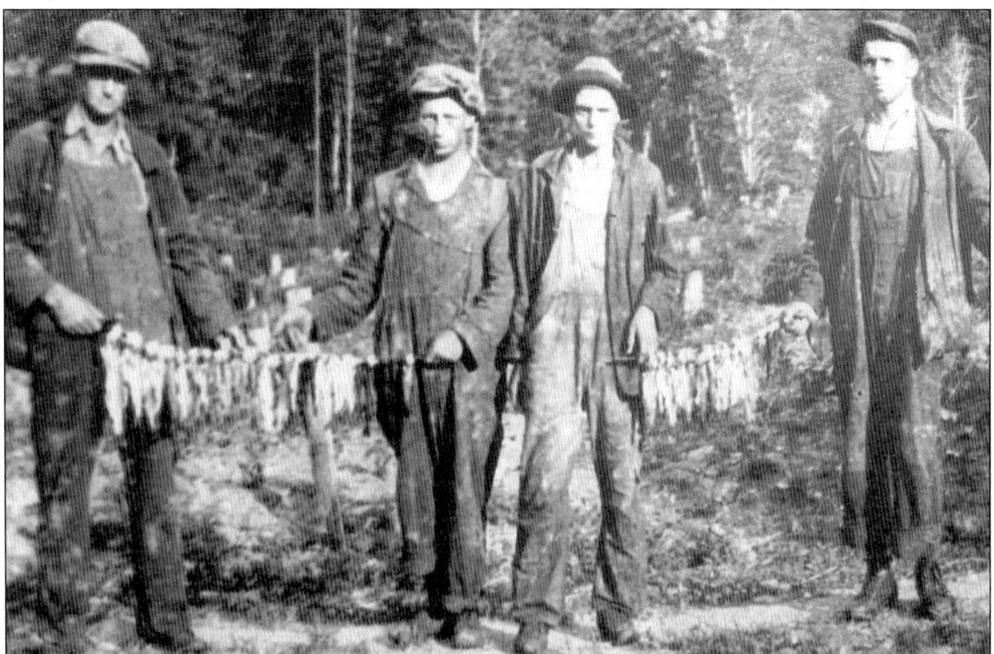

Fishing was something that was enjoyed by young and old. From left to right, Ernest, Floyd, and Luther Abbott and an unidentified man look like they have the catch of the day. There were many great fishing holes in the cove. Whether by fishing or hunting, meat was supplied by the men. (Courtesy of NPS.)

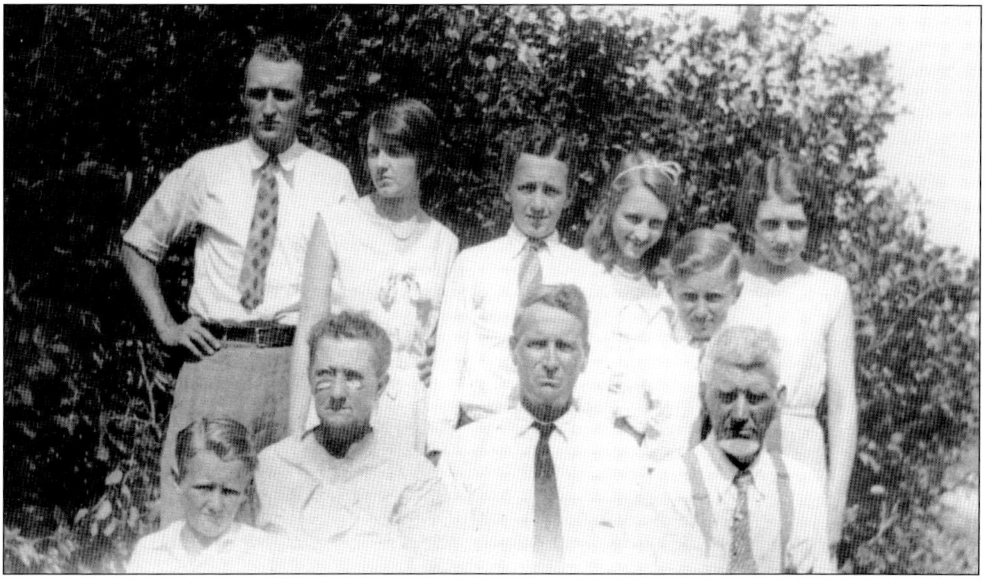

John W. Oliver was an avid photographer in Cades Cove. In this 1929 picture, he has taken his family to Cherry Branch for a family portrait. He would have the children carry chairs until he found the right spot for the photograph, which caused the youngsters to complain if they had to carry them too far. This photograph includes (first row) Nancy Ann Whitehead Oliver (second from left), John W. (third from left), and his father, William Howell Oliver (right); the rest are the children of Nancy Ann and John W. (Courtesy Nancy Webber, John W. Oliver collection.)

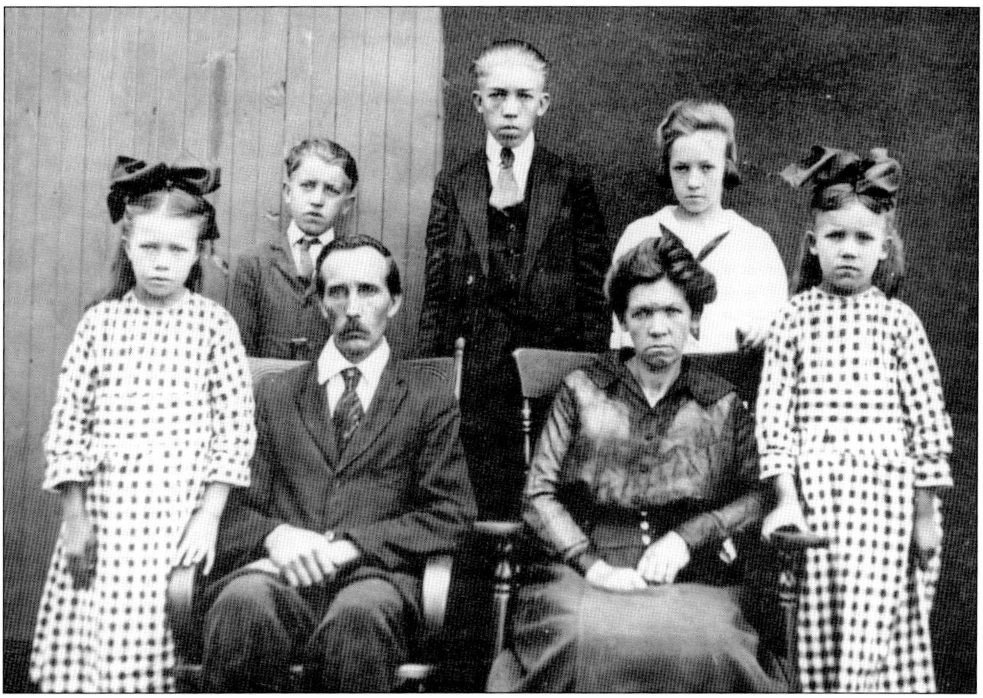

The George and Samantha Farr Oliver family is pictured here. George was the son of William Howell and Elizabeth Jane Gregory Oliver and a brother to John W. Oliver, who took this photograph. (Courtesy of Margaret Oliver, John W. Oliver collection.)

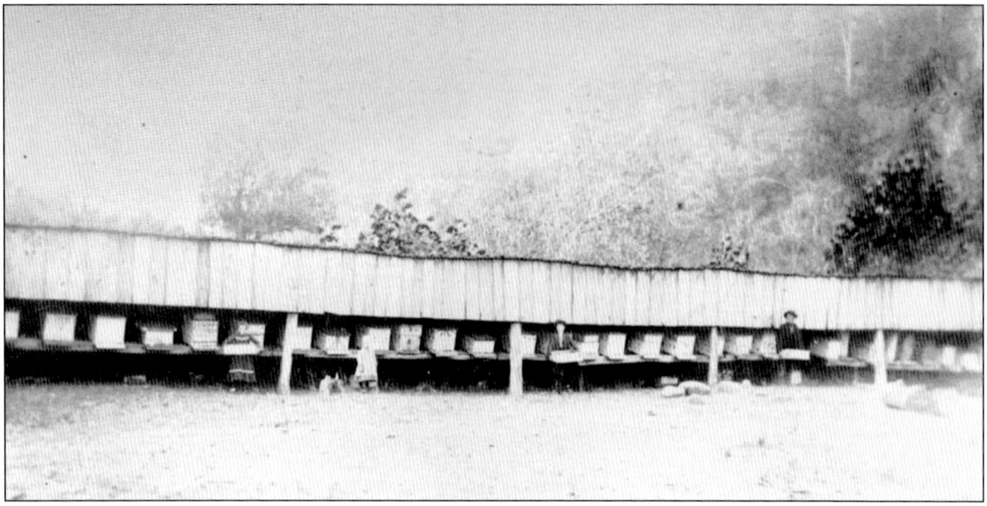

The family of George Shields is shown working the bees in this 1912 photograph. This apiary protected the bees from bad weather. The children were involved in all of the hard work that took place with collecting the honey. (Courtesy of NPS.)

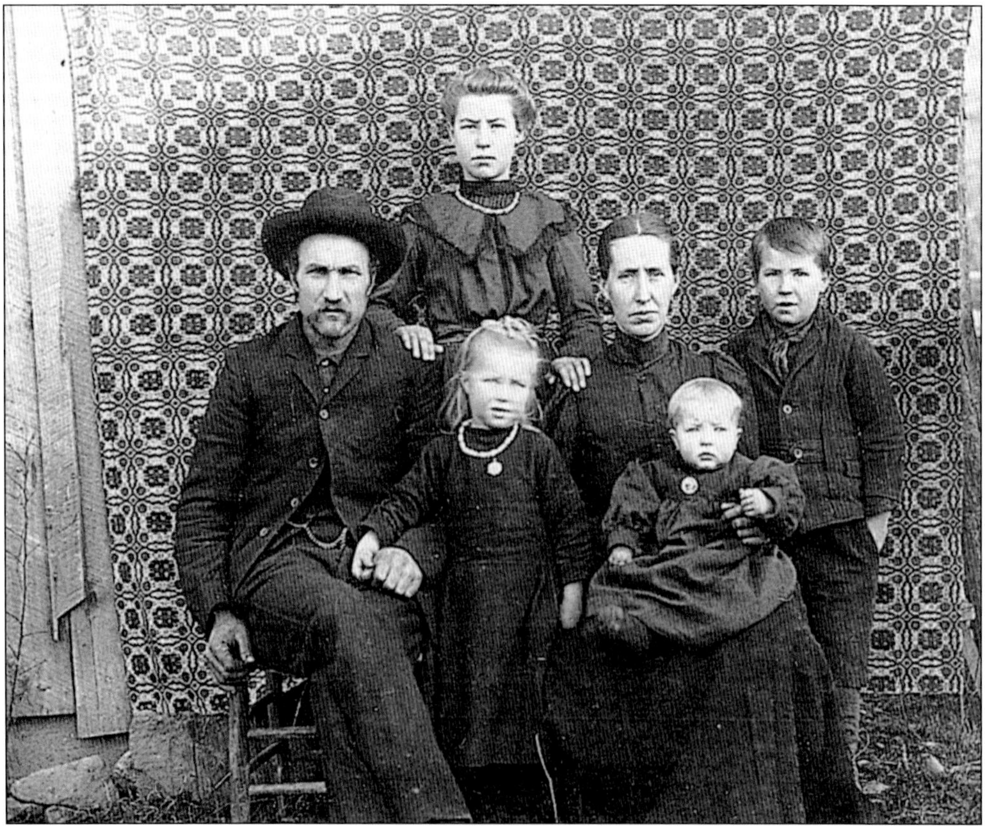

The family of George Houston, son of John "Baldy" and Mary Ann Tipton Myers, and Elizabeth Burchfield Myers, daughter of Noah and Sarah Brown Burchfield, poses for a portrait. From left to right are (first row) George, Lillie, Mary Ann holding France, and Russell; (second row) Zeni. (Courtesy of Verna Lee Burchfield Myers.)

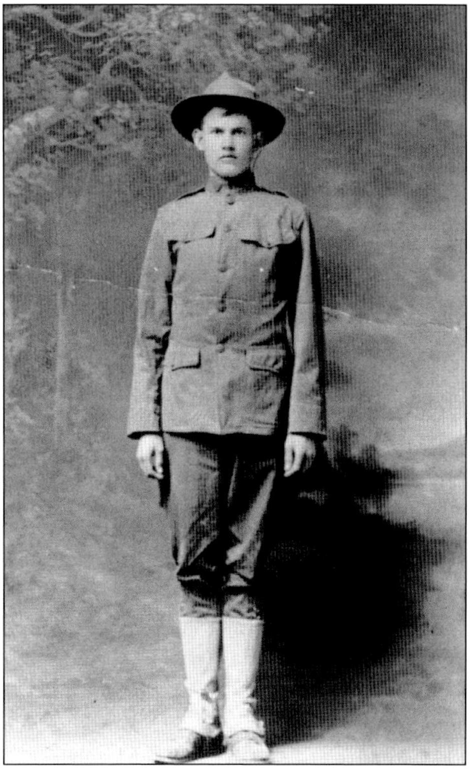

Gilbert Sands, son of Henry Anderson and Laura Texanna Burchfield Sands, is shown in his World War I uniform. Pictured below is his sister Iva Texanna Sands, who married Shade Tipton. The Sands family lived on land near the headwaters of Laurel Creek. (Both, courtesy of NPS.)

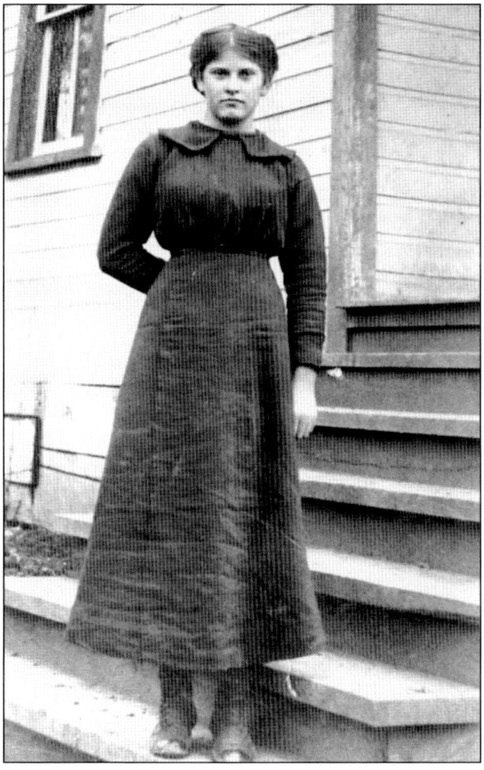

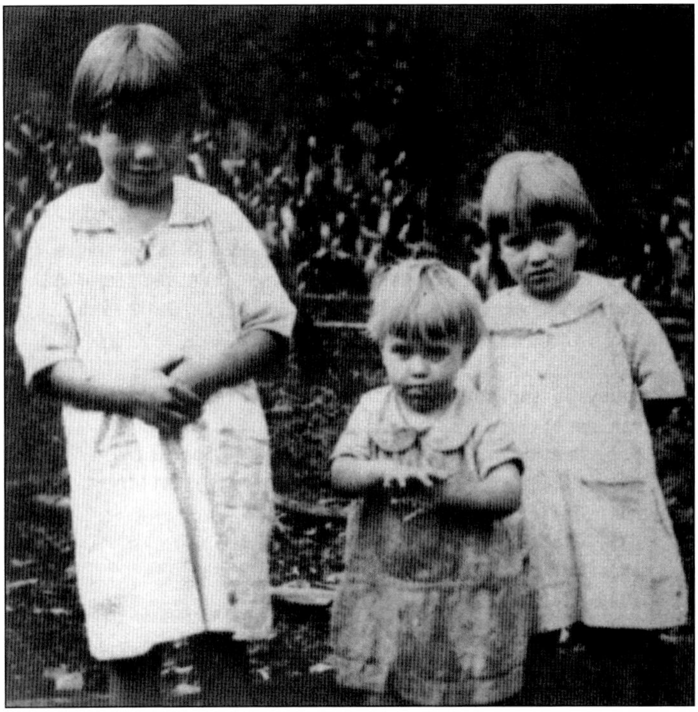

Pictured are Dorothy (left), Julia (center), and Lois Shuler, children of William T. "Will" and Laura Anthony Shuler. Gardens had to be tended daily, so when mothers would go to the fields or gardens to work, they took their children with them. The older ones would help with the work, and the smaller ones found things to occupy them. (Courtesy of NPS.)

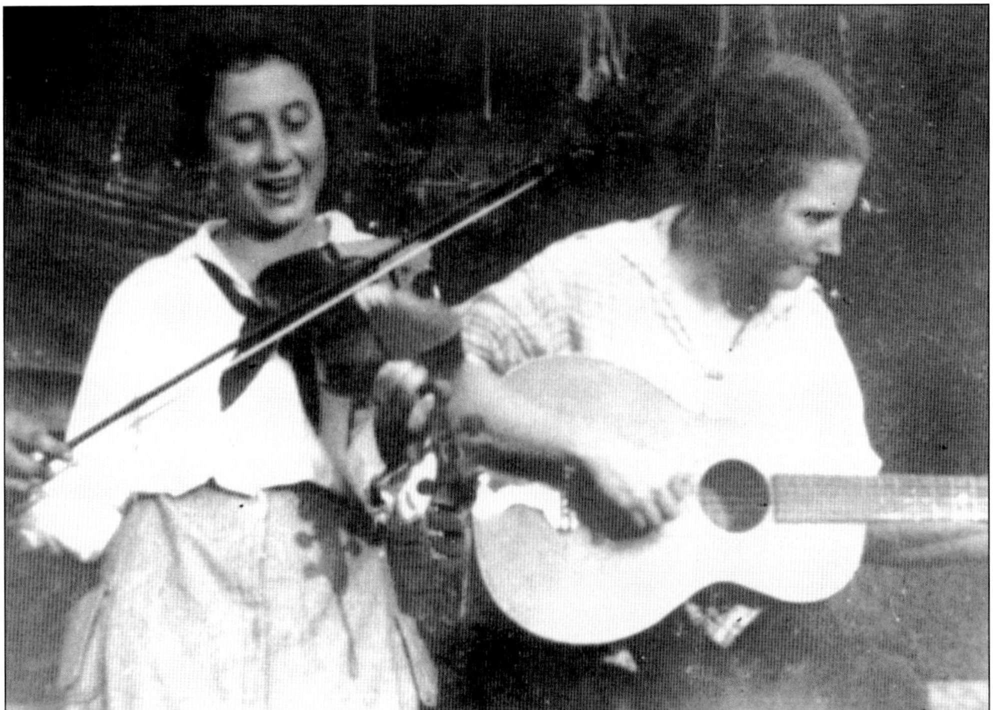

Frances Whitehead Brown (left) and Loma Brown are surely enjoying themselves by making music. Many of the cove residents were talented in the fact they could play musical instruments. Folks would gather together in the evenings and enjoy singing and music. (Courtesy of NPS.)

Hunting dogs were a necessity in the cove, and most every household had a few of them. In this photograph, George (left), Wade (center), and John Tipton seem to be taking off for a hunting trip, and the dogs look ready to go, too. (Courtesy of NPS.)

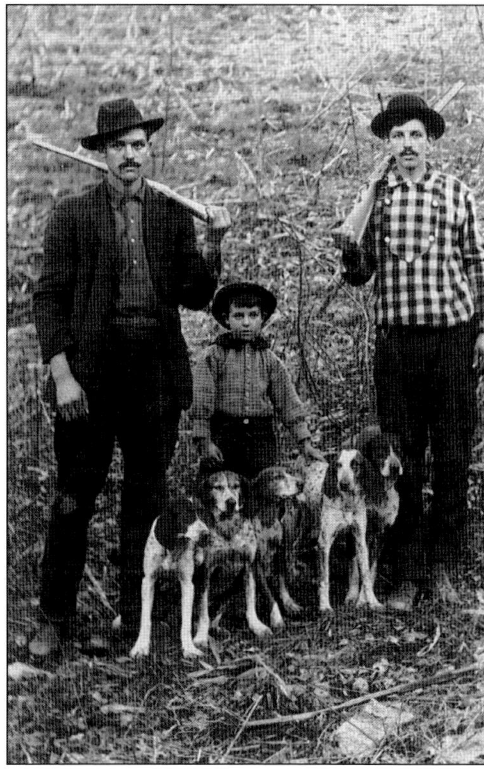

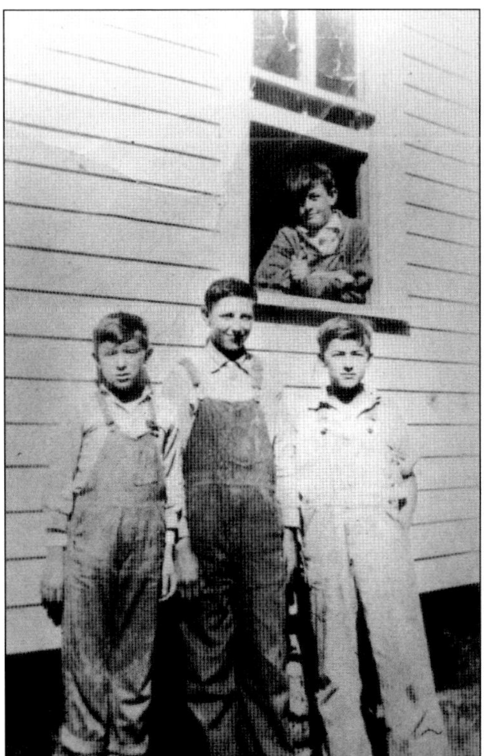

From left to right, Henry Burchfield, Maynard Ledbetter, Granville Chambers, and an unidentified boy in the window are possibly standing outside of a school or church building waiting for class or Sunday school to begin. (Courtesy of NPS.)

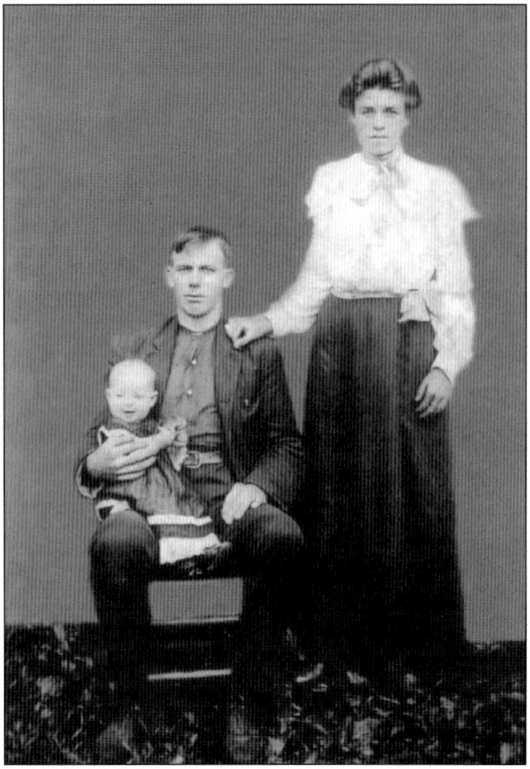

Jacob "Jake" and Sarah Davis Franklin Garland are pictured with daughter Angie. Jake, the son of Charlie and Myria Miller Garland, and Sarah had seven children. The Garland family first settled in what was known as the Bearded Cane on the headwaters of Hesse Creek. Later, they moved into the Cades Cove area, where Jake purchased land near the Cooper Road area. (Courtesy of Sylvia Garland Galde.)

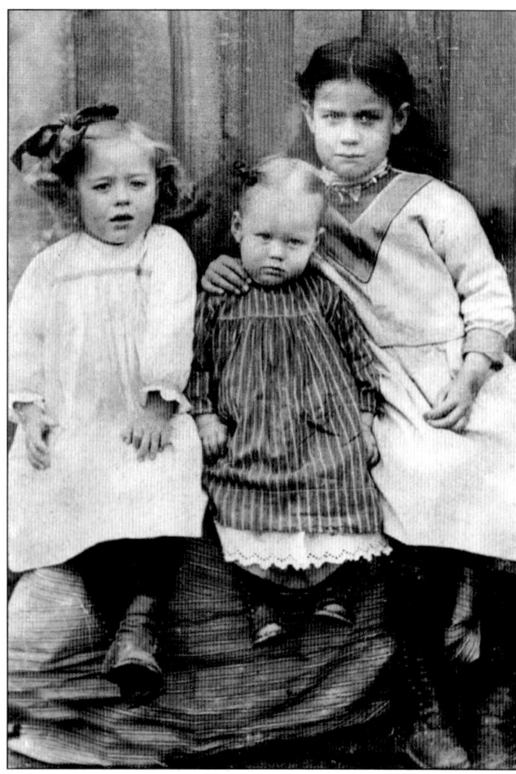

Leona, Angie, and Nancy Garland, three of Jake and Sarah Garland's children, pose for a picture in 1914. These girls, like most cove residents, slept on featherbeds or straw ticks. Featherbeds were filled with the feathers of geese that were raised on the farm. When straw ticks became worn, new straw would be changed out for the old to make the tick more comfortable. (Courtesy of Sylvia Garland Galde.)

Zena Millie Garland (left) and Nancy Garland are pictured in Cades Cove. After the death of Jake's wife, Sarah, he married Zena Millie Proctor, daughter of James N. and Mary Moore Proctor. Jake and Zena had 12 children born to them. In addition to taking care of children, a few of the daily activities for cove women included rising early in the morning to get breakfast going, milking the cows, gathering the eggs, waking the children, fixing school lunches, working in the garden, washing clothes and hanging them on the clothesline, and preparing dinner. (Courtesy of Sylvia Garland Galde.)

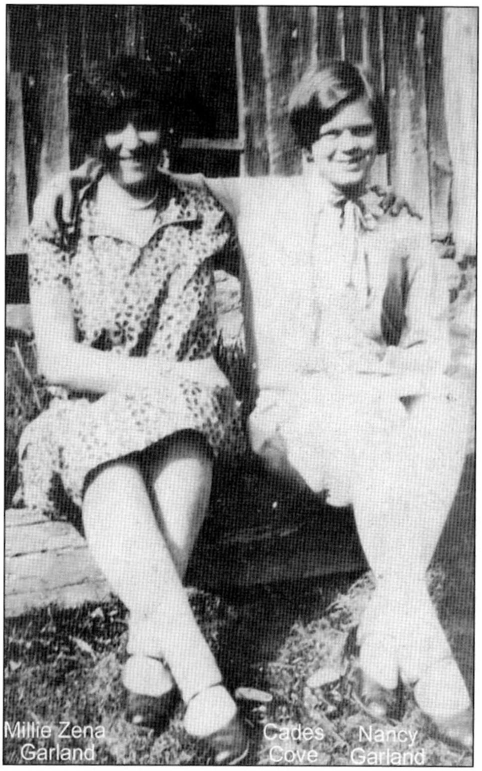

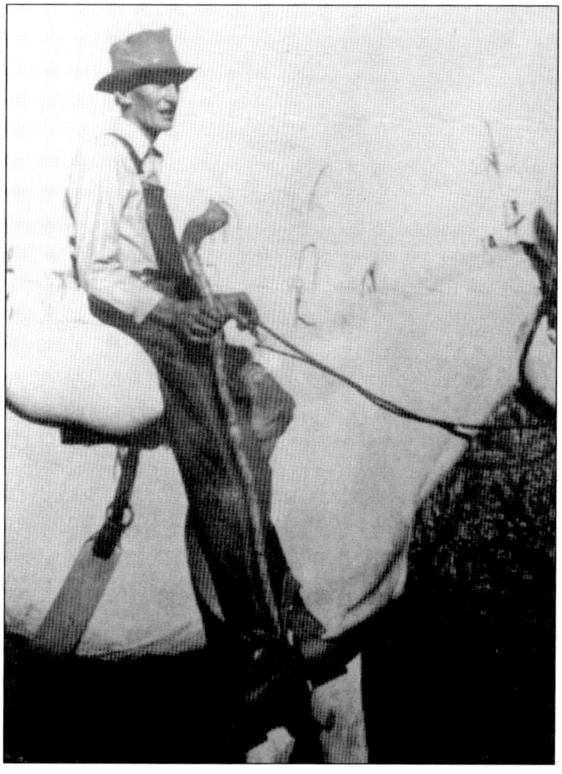

John Burchfield is on his way to or from the gristmill in this image. The corn would be carried in meal sacks to the mill to be ground and then put back into the same sacks. It would often take about two hours for the meal to be ground, and while waiting, people would take advantage of fishing in Forge Creek. (Courtesy of NPS.)

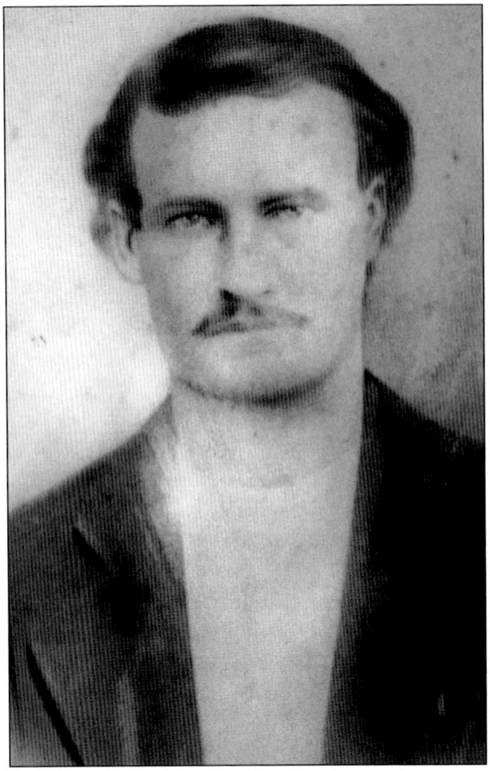

John Franklin "Chicken Eater" Tipton, son of John Jacob and Naomi Abbott Tipton, married Harriett L. Burchfield, daughter of Robert "Bob" and Amanda Battles Burchfield. Because so many of the cove individuals had the same names, they were often given a nickname to distinguish who people were talking about. There were several John Tipton's in the cove: Chicken Eater, John "Gull," and Preacher Johnnie. (Courtesy of Robert Tipton.)

John McCaulley stands atop the hay wagon while members of his family pose alongside. It took many hours to get the hay loaded on a wagon like this and then put into the hayloft. (Courtesy of NPS.)

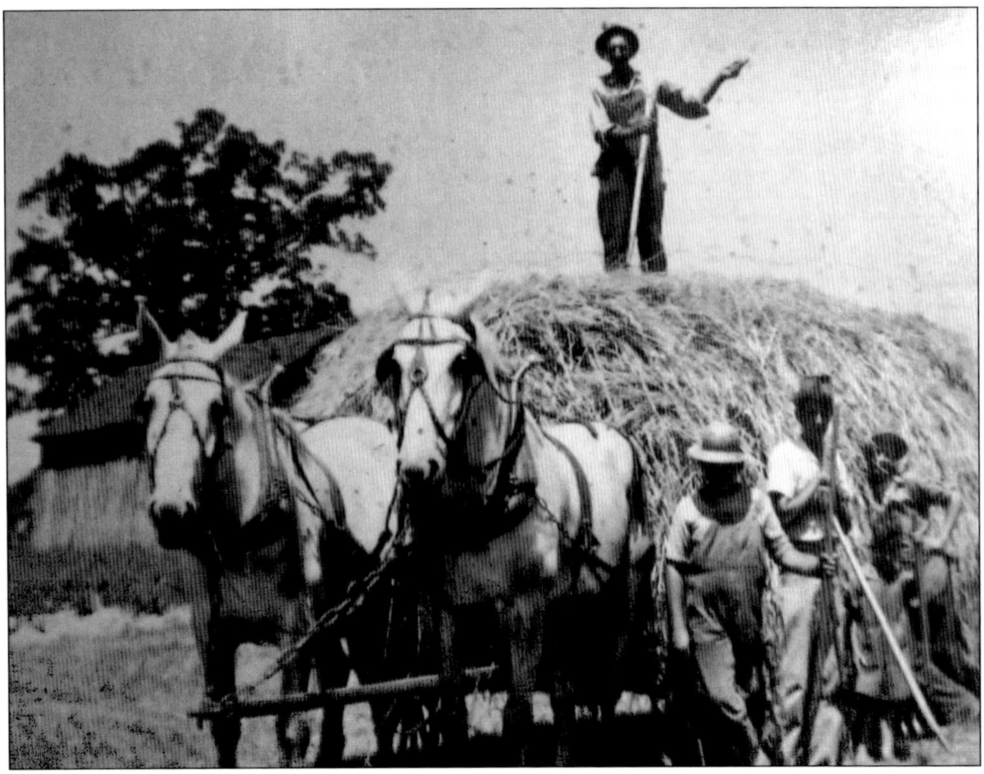

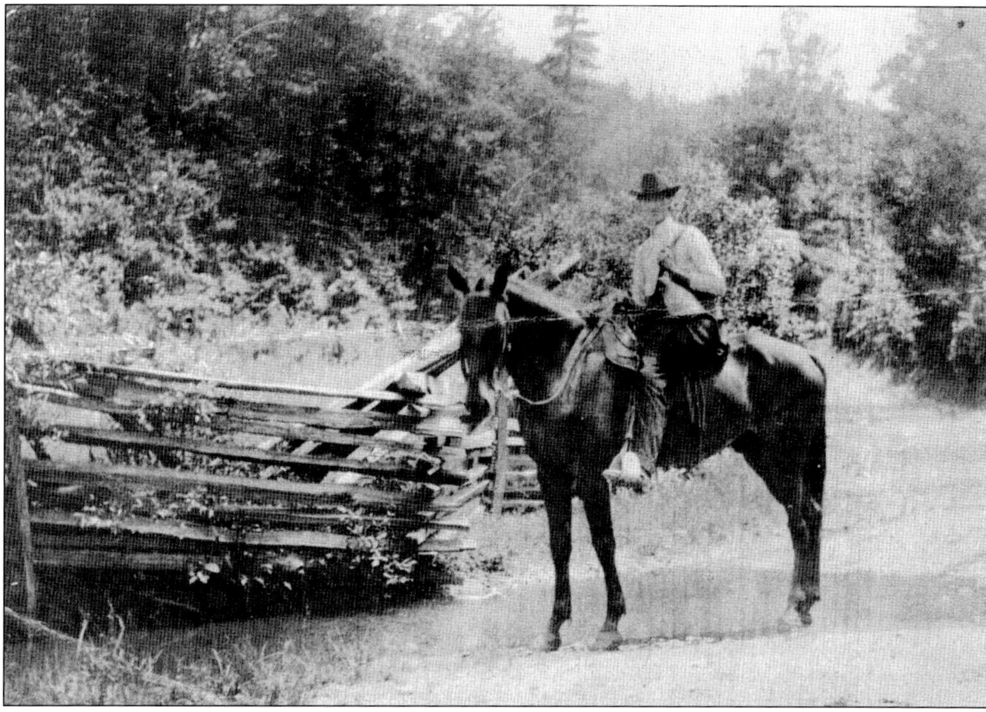

John W. Oliver was the mail carrier in the cove for many years. In this c. 1908 photograph, he is delivering mail by horseback. Later, he purchased a vehicle that he used to deliver the mail, if the weather permitted. (Both, courtesy of Margaret Oliver, John W. Oliver collection.)

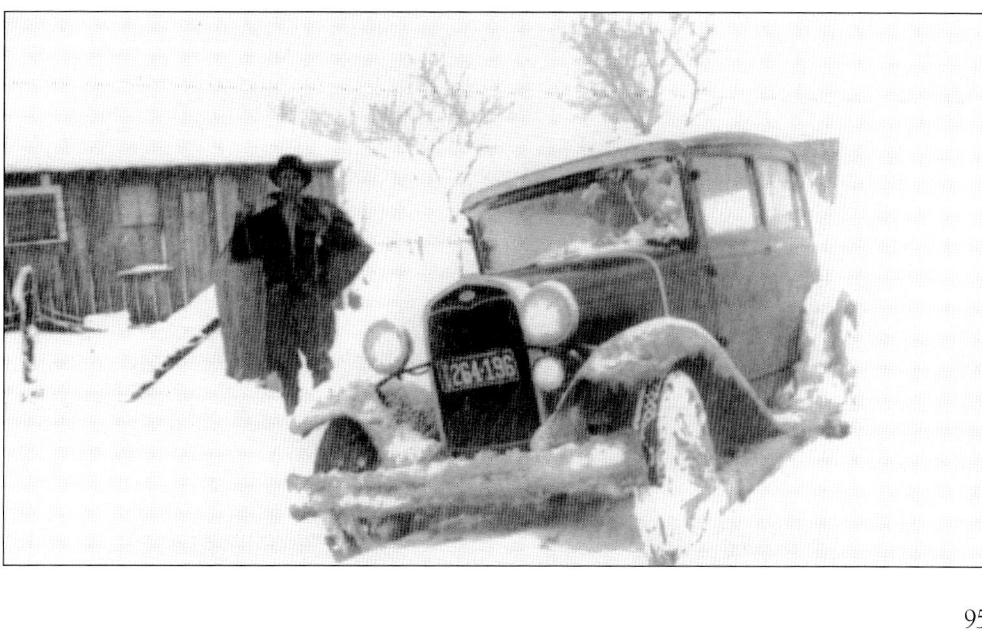

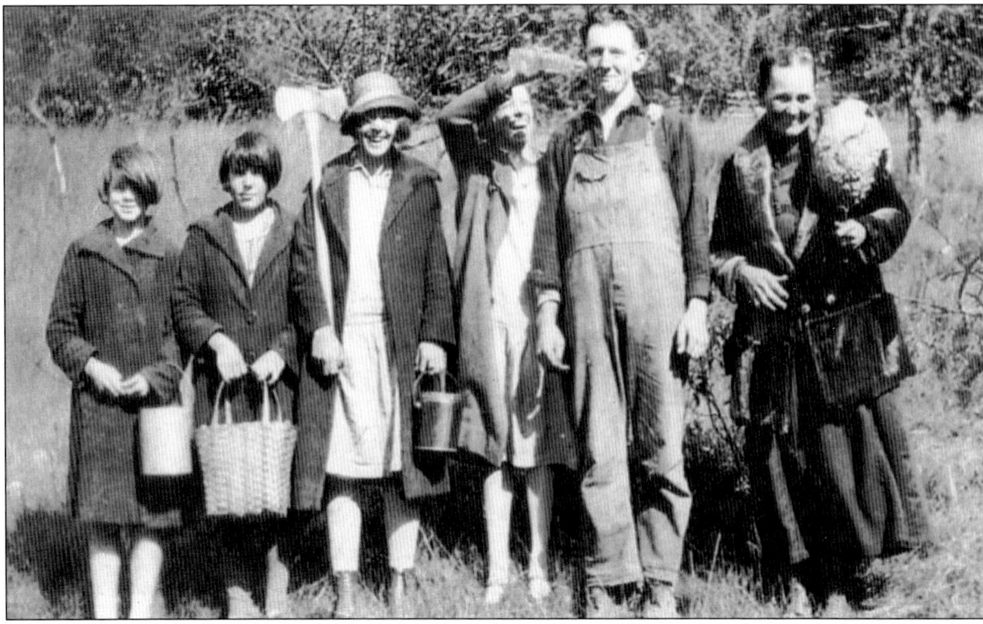

The Garland family is off to gather chestnuts. From left to right are Nancy Garland, Mamie Harmon, Leona Garland (with ax), Lillie Buchanan, Townsend Garland, and Myria Garland. Chestnuts could be gathered and then sold in nearby Maryville, Tennessee. These outings would be enjoyable for the family. (Courtesy of Sylvia Garland Galde.)

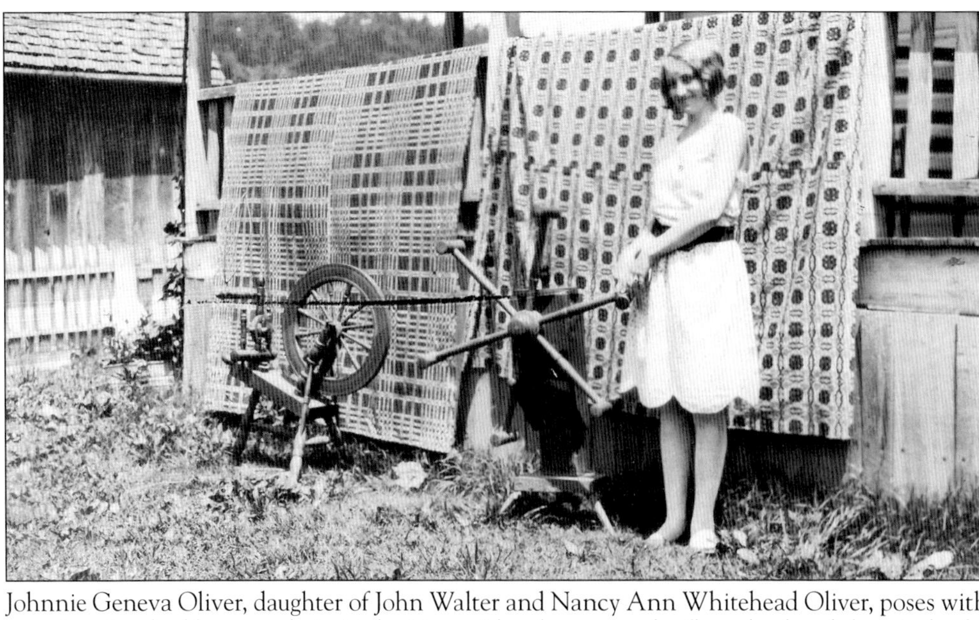

Johnnie Geneva Oliver, daughter of John Walter and Nancy Ann Whitehead Oliver, poses with coverlets that had been made in Cades Cove. Also shown are the flax wheel and the winder for the thread. Many cove homes had items like these, used for making various items for the family. (Courtesy of Margaret Oliver, John W. Oliver collection.)

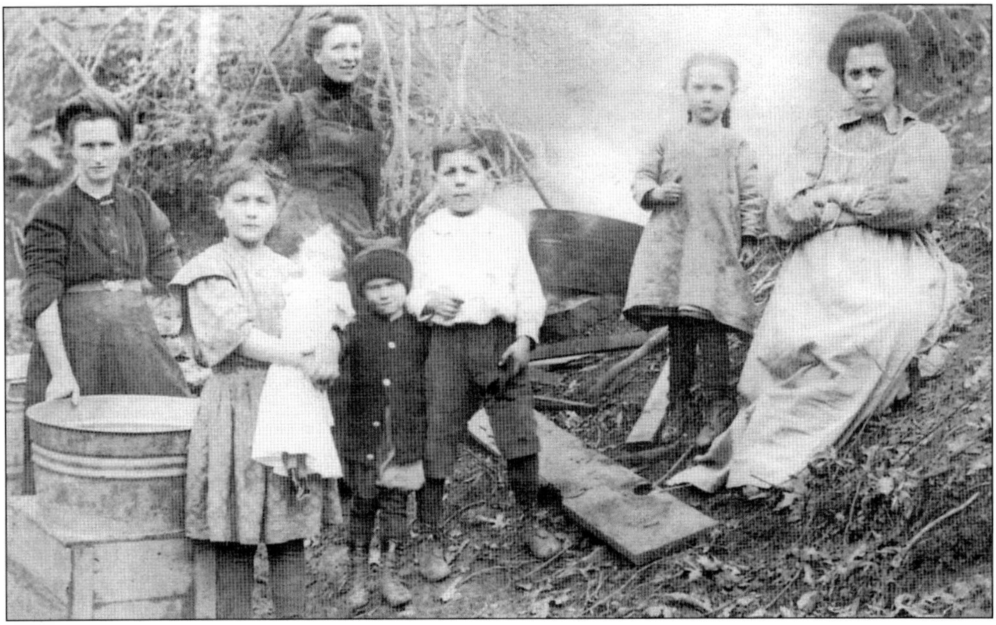

Wash day was usually on Monday and would take all day to finish. It would take place close to a creek, so the water would not have to be carried. Large washtubs would be placed over a fire to get boiling water. Scrubbing would commence on a scrub board with soap added, probably lye made by the women. Rinsing would be done either in the creek or another large tub, and the clothes would be put out to dry. (Courtesy of Missy Tipton Green.)

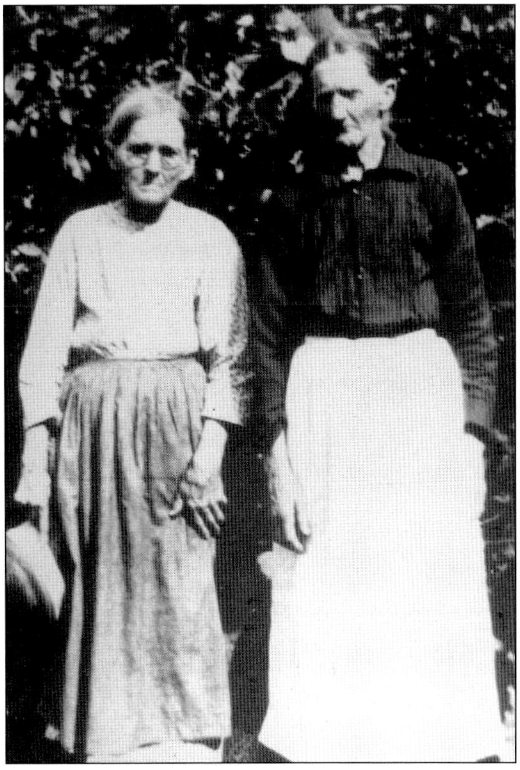

Rhoda Lawson Abbott (left) and her sister Kate Lawson would spin their own cloth to make clothing for the children. They would shear their own sheep, card the wool, and then spin it into thread. They were also well known for making beautiful coverlets. (Courtesy of NPS.)

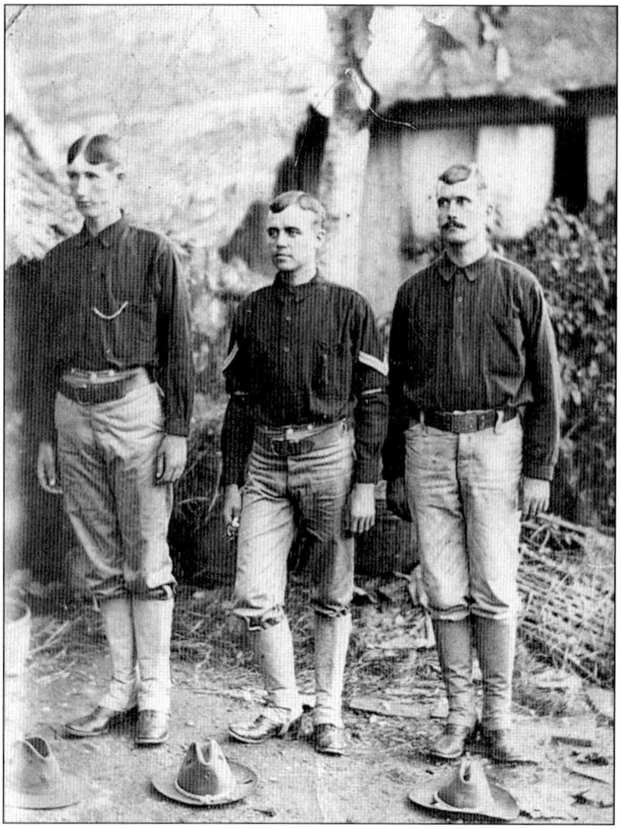

The men of the cove were always willing to answer the call to serve their country. At left are soldiers from the Spanish-American War of 1898. From left to right are Ed Sparks, Eagle Rose, and Tom Jenkins. Below is Lee Gregory in his World War I uniform. Many of the cove men were not able to serve in the military, so they formed the Cades Cove Home Guard, which guarded the livestock, homes, and ammunition of the cove residents. Renegades would come into the cove and take livestock and garden vegetables and harass the community. (Left, courtesy of Verna Lee Burchfield Myers; below, courtesy of NPS.)

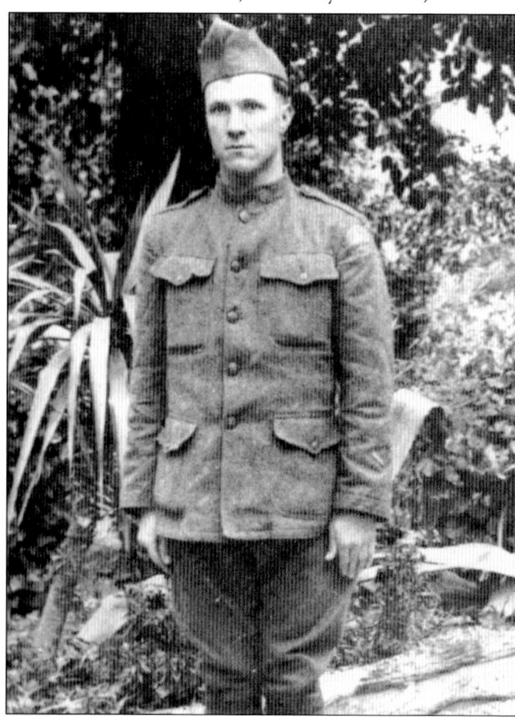

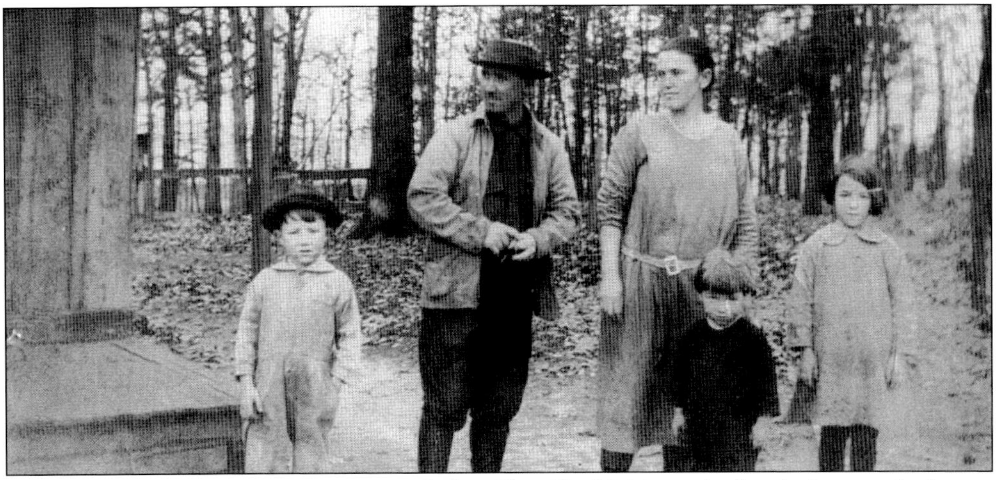

The family of William Martin "Mart" and Flora Elsie Shields Tipton look to be leaving the house. Pictured from left to right are Lamar, Mart, Elsie, Chester, and Audraine Tipton. Mart was the son of George and Tuckaleechee "Tuck" Burchfield Tipton. Elsie was the daughter of William Henry and Jane McCaulley Shields. (Courtesy of NPS.)

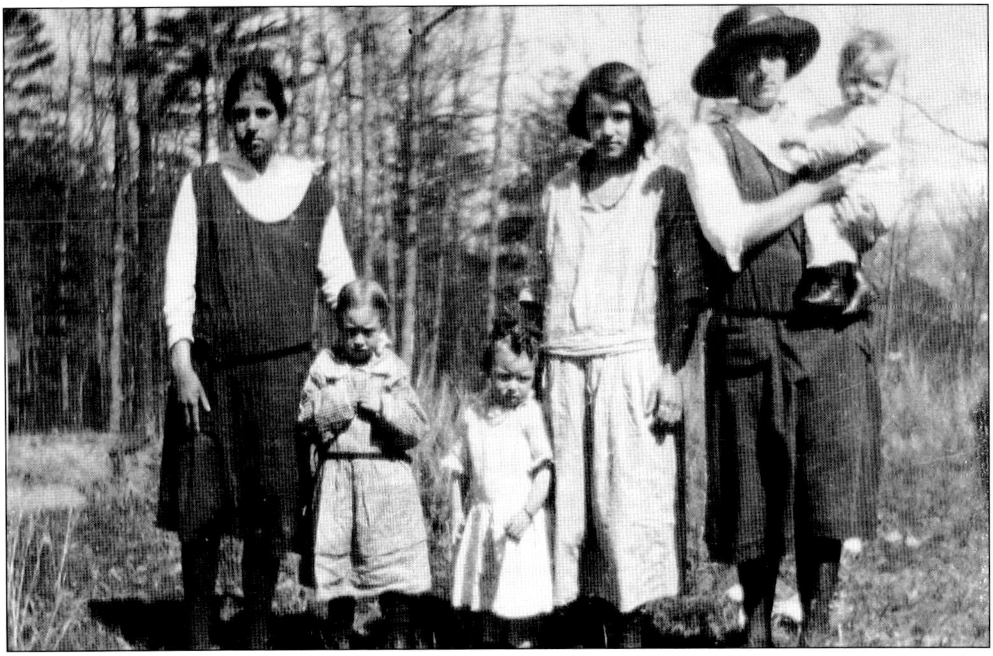

Minnie Proctor Harmon (left) is pictured here with other family members. Minnie was married to Austin Hale Harmon, the son of Samuel "Sam" Patterson Harmon and Polly Ann Davis Hagaman Harmon. Around 1912, Sam and Polly moved their family into Cades Cove and purchased land on Cooper Road, where Sam built their home. Polly was one of the first midwives in Cades Cove and was well respected and very knowledgeable in the birthing of babies. After the babies would arrive, she would help the family in daily chores to give the mother some rest. The Harmons were members of the Church of Jesus Christ of Latter-day Saints, also known as Mormons. Since there was no church of this faith in the cove, they obtained permission to use Hopewell Methodist Church for their worship services. The Harmon family was also well known for ballad singing. (Courtesy of NPS.)

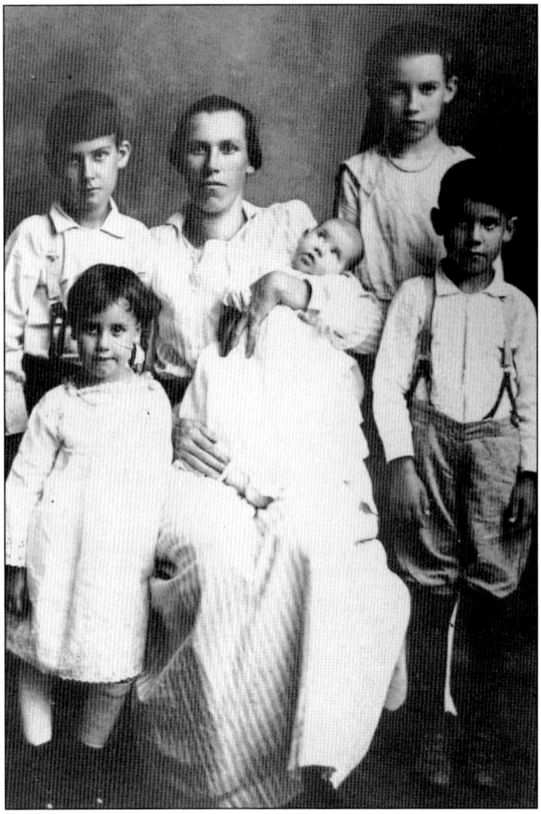

Louraine Angeline "Babe" Gregory Myers is shown with her children. Babe, the daughter of Walter and Rutha Oliver Gregory, was married to Daniel "Dan" H. Myers Jr., the son of Dan and Susan Matilda Cable Myers. Dan and Babe lived on the north side of the Cades Cove Loop Road, midway from the entrance gate and Sparks Lane. (Courtesy of NPS.)

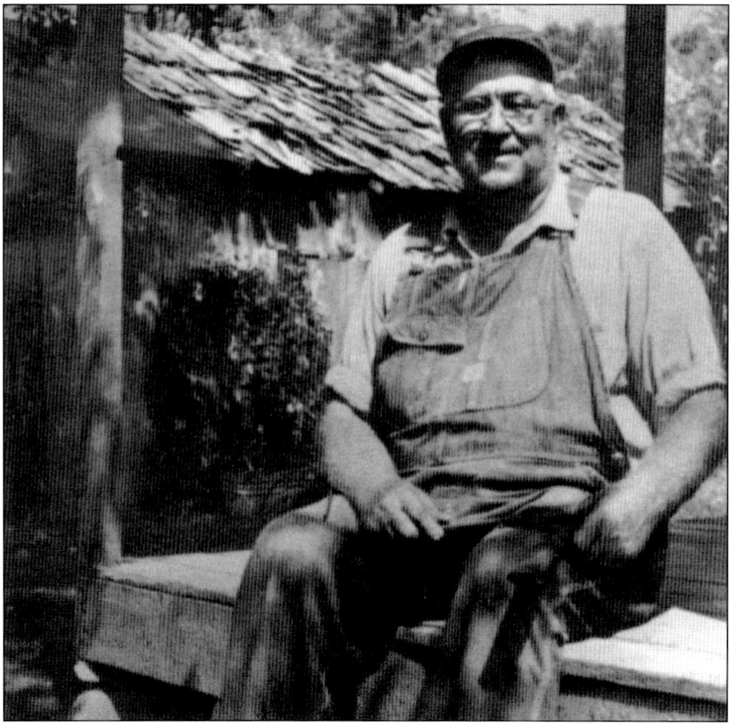

Labe Myers learned his beekeeping skills from his father, Dan Myers Jr. Beehives were made from the stumps of gum trees or handmade by the beekeeper. A good country breakfast was not complete without homemade cathead biscuits and sourwood honey from one's own beehives. (Courtesy of NPS.)

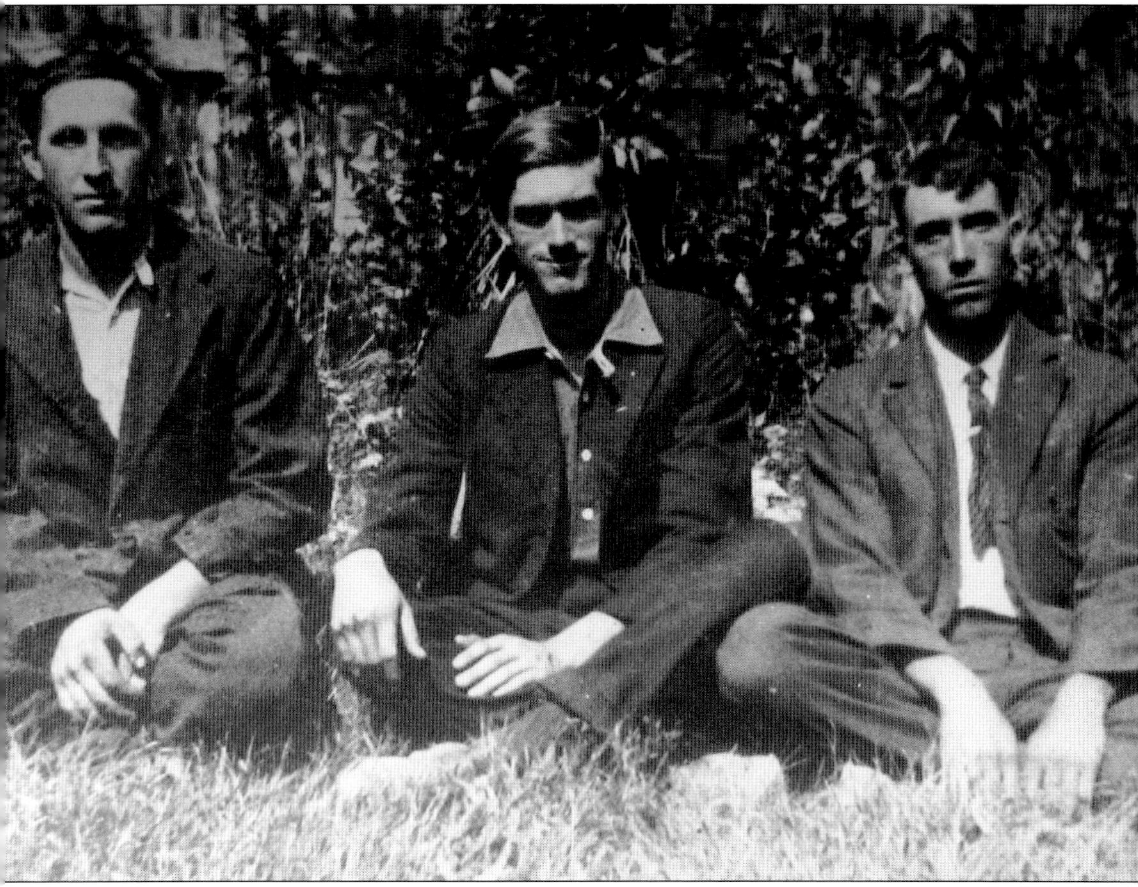

Christmas Eve brought on a different type of socializing by the young men of the cove. They would gang up on horseback or go walking from house to house serenading, which consisted of parading around the house ringing cowbells, shooting guns, and making loud noises. It was the custom for the host to come out and visit with the serenaders and partake in some liquid Christmastime refreshment. The serenaders would then move on to the next house and repeat the same entertainment. Pictured above are three young men of the cove—Russell Myers (left), Horace Myers (center), and George Brown. (Courtesy of NPS.)

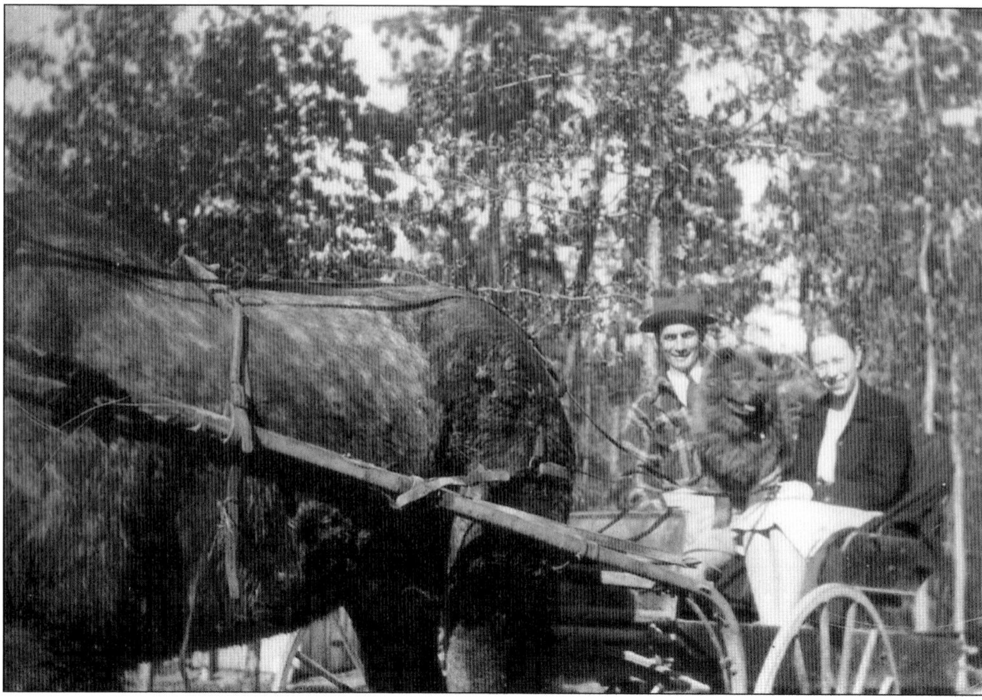

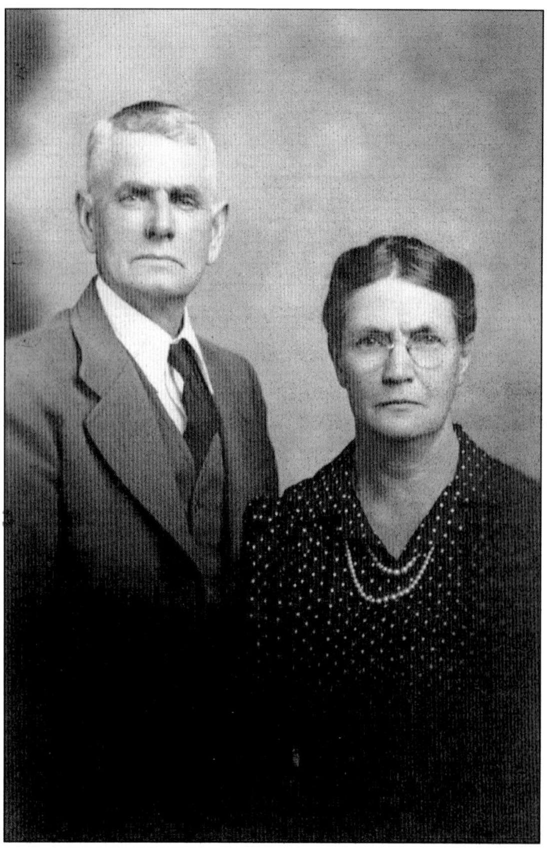

Out for a ride are John Lester and Claudia Erwin Shields. Sunday was usually a day of visiting with family and friends to catch up on news of the cove. Men would gather together and talk about how their crops were doing, while the women would trade recipes or work on quilts. (Courtesy of George Shields.)

George Henry and Polly Ann Gregory Shields lived in the Witt Shields house. George was the son of Andrew Witt and Anna Walker Shields. Polly was the daughter of Calvin and Emmaline Headrick Gregory. George and Polly lived in the large 2.5-story house that his father had built. Water was piped into the kitchen of the house; it flowed by gravity. (Courtesy of George Shields.)

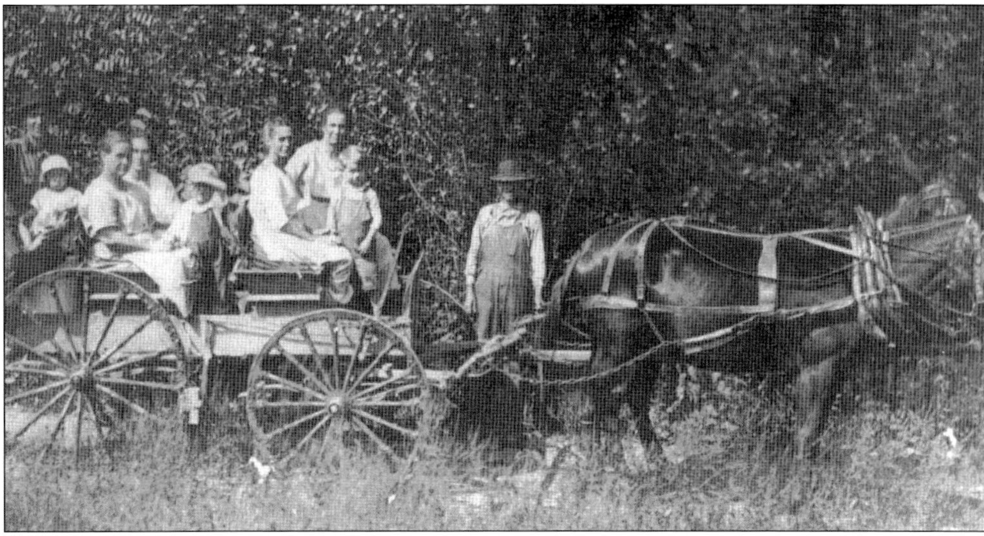

After the crops were laid-by (cultivated for the last time) in the midsummer months, it was time for berry picking, which was done mostly by women and children. Blackberries would be the first to ripen. After the blackberries were gone, it was time to climb the slopes for blueberries. Homemade berry baskets, made of strips of poplar wood, would be used to place the berries in and would fill up fast. Baskets were used to carry most anything, and each one had its special shape and use. Eggs, blackberries, laundry, and garden vegetables all went into baskets. This the Shields family, possibly on a berry-picking trip. (Courtesy of George Shields.)

By the 1930s, homes and land in Cades Cove were taken through eminent domain, causing families to have to pack up and find a new home. Most of these families moved to the other side of the mountain, where they could still see their beloved cove. Many would return periodically to their home place to enjoy the serenity of the area where they had lived. Some families went willingly, but some fought to the very end. All had many precious memories of Cades Cove. Polly Gregory Shields is cleaning up after a picnic at her former homesite. (Courtesy of George Shields.)

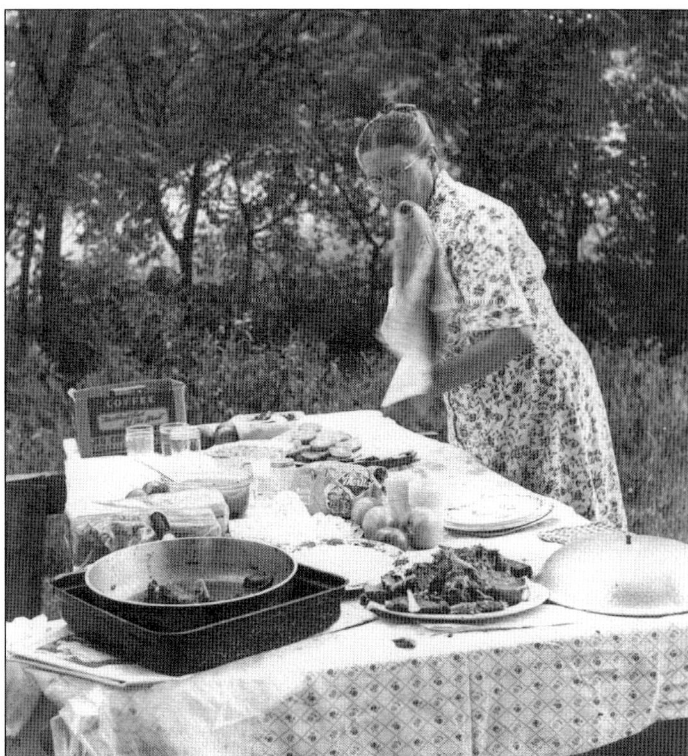

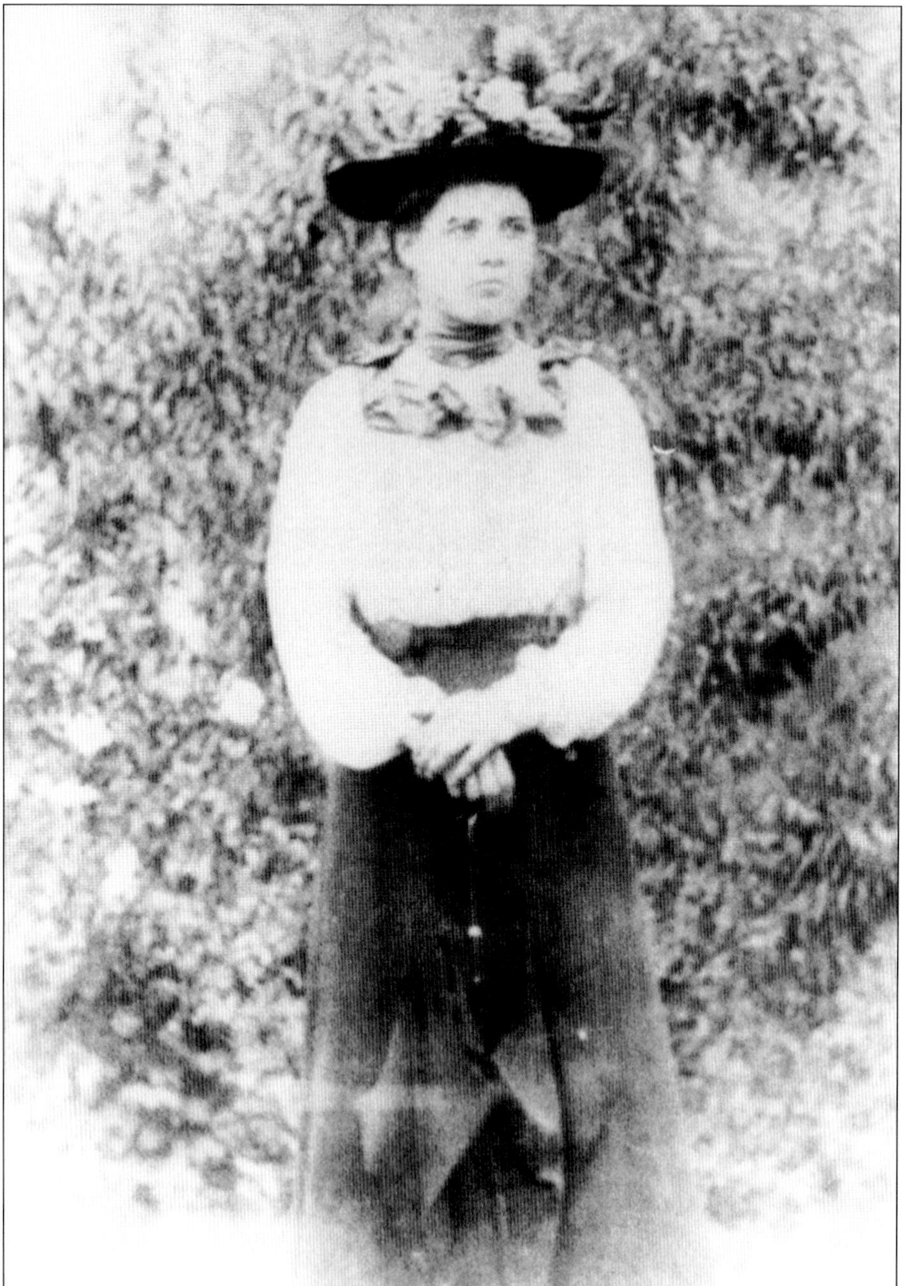

Cordelia "Delia" Myers was the daughter of Peter Adam "Pete" and Margaret "Maggie" Shields Myers. She married George Caughron and set up their household on land that she grew up on. George and Delia lived above a rich hollow adorned with dogwood and mountain magnolias. One of Delia's favorite things to do was work in her many gardens. She tended gardens all over the farm and grew many wonderful vegetables. Delia also had many chickens that would run loose in her yard, and she was concerned about hawks bothering them. Delia believed that putting horseshoes in the fireplace would keep the hawks away. This was just one of many beliefs that Delia and all the other cove residents had. (Courtesy of NPS.)

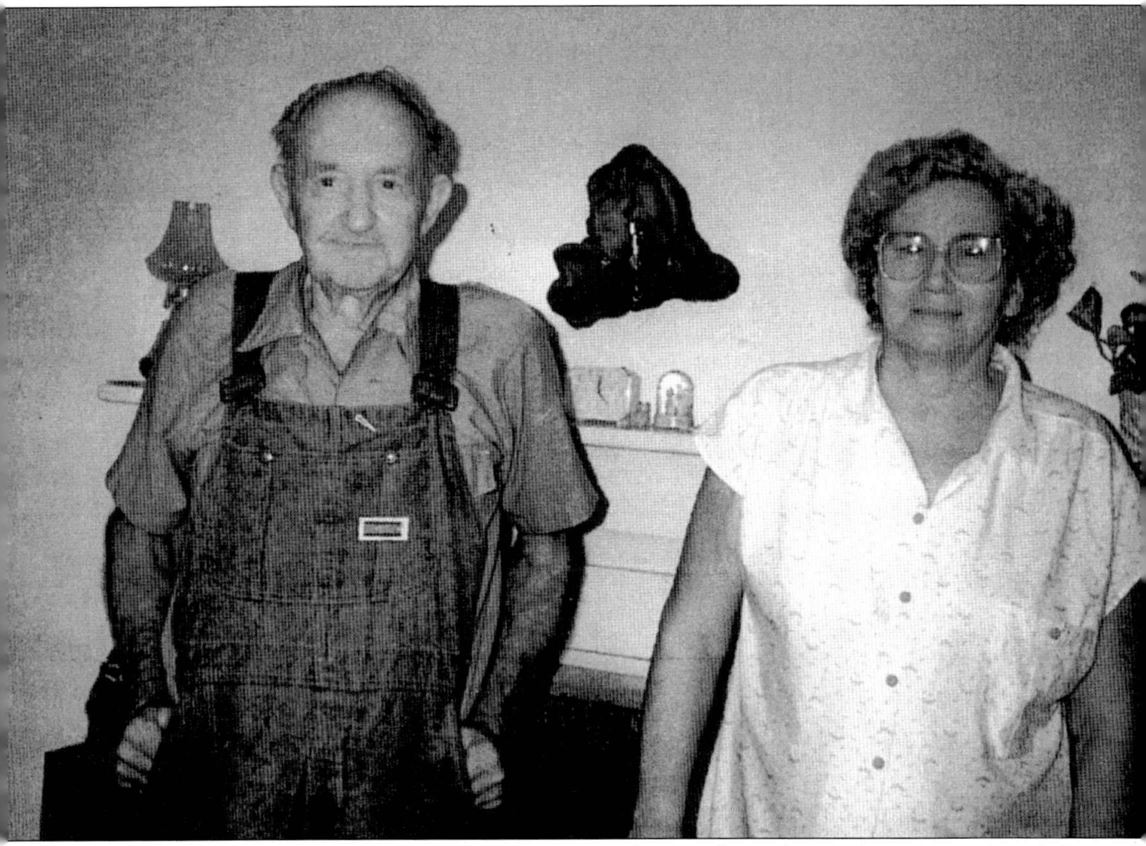

Kermit Caughron, often known as "the bee man," was born and raised in Cades Cove, and resided there until his death in 1999. Kermit and his wife, Lois, lived under the special-use permit in the Great Smoky Mountains National Park from 1942 until Kermit's death. Lois Shuler married Kermit Caughron when she was 17 years old in 1942. Their four children were born in the cove and enjoyed their years of growing up there. The Caughron family always had large gardens and fruit trees to provide them with plenty of food. Kermit had many beehives on his farm, getting his first two hives when he was 18 years old. Around 1955, running water came to the Caughron house by use of a waterwheel and water tank built by Kermit. Lois washed the family's clothes in an iron washtub with a washboard until about 1946, when she got her first gasoline-powered washing machine. When Lois moved out of Cades Cove in 1999, she was still cooking on her woodstove. Kermit often spoke of the Smoky Mountain wind that would come every fall; he said years ago they referred to that wind as the "chestnut knocker." (Courtesy of Ruth Caughron Davis.)

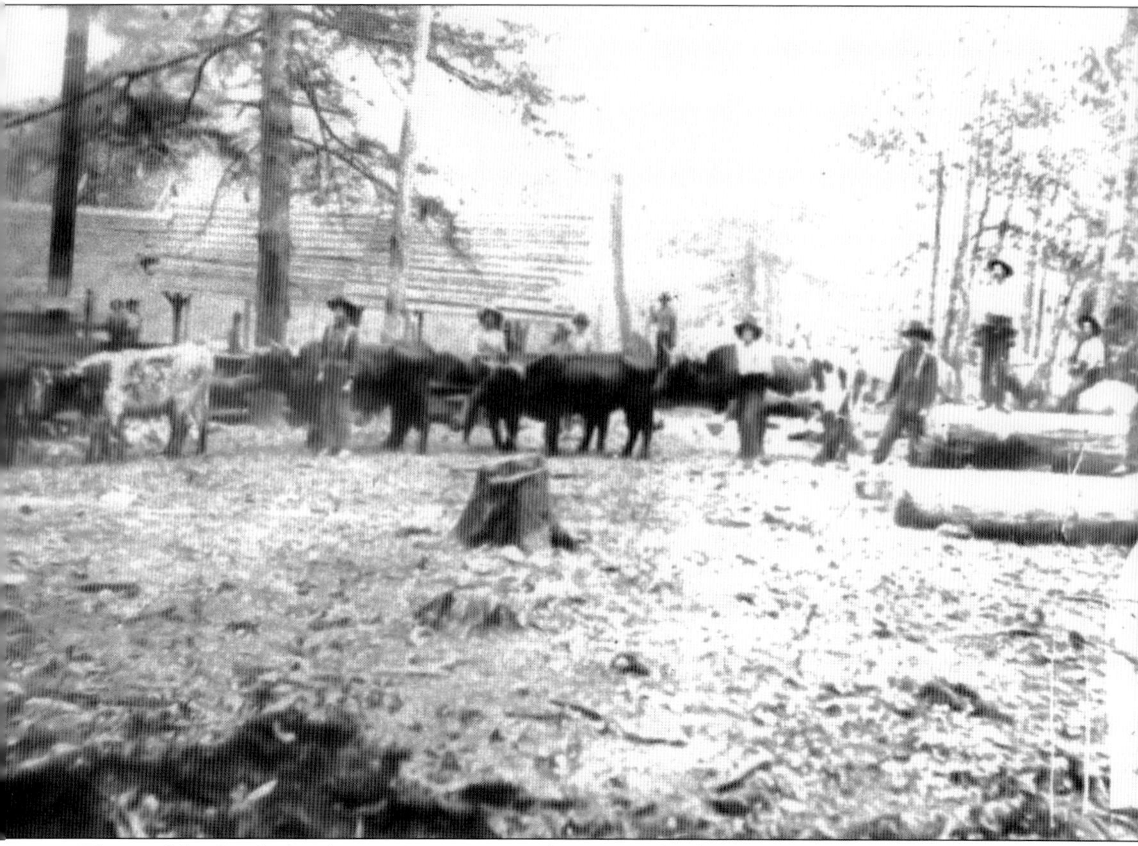

Three of the Sparks brothers—Sam, Tom, and George—had a logging camp known as Eldorado located between Rich Mountain and Cades Cove at the headwaters of Hesse Creek. The time was about 1905, when logging was a popular occupation. Oxen were used to skid the logs. A shelter was built over the circle saw and steam engine in order to keep the belts dry. If the belts got wet or damp, it would make it impossible to saw the wood. Oak, yellow poplar, and white and yellow pine were the best types of timber to cut. The Sparks sawmill was bigger than most portable sawmills of the time. The steam engine was mounted on skids, and when it was set up to saw, steam was piped from the boiler, which was on wheels. Different sizes of saws were used according to the diameter of the log to be cut. (Courtesy of Leon Sparks.)

The men and women of the cove were always wearing something to cover their heads. Women wore sunbonnets, while men wore hats. Carson Tipton (left) and Luke Lawson are wearing the wide, heavy-brimmed felt hats that most of the men in the cove had at the time. To them, it was considered a safety hat: offering protection from falling limbs, keeping them dry in the rain, and shielding their eyes from the hot sun. (Courtesy of NPS.)

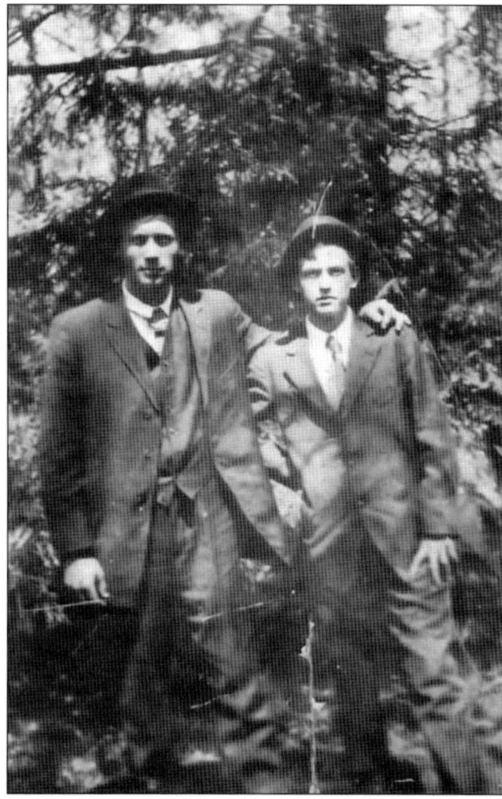

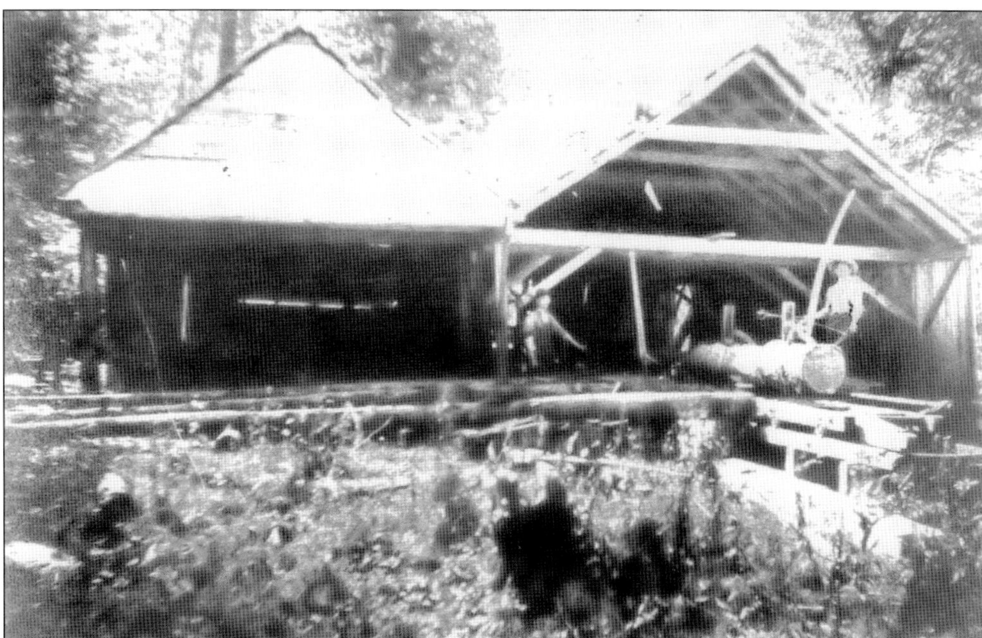

This steam-powered sawmill was in operation in 1908 and was located in the Lawson Sugar Cove, near Mill Creek. Local families logged most of the accessible hollows, and the lumber was used to build homes and barns. (Courtesy of NPS.)

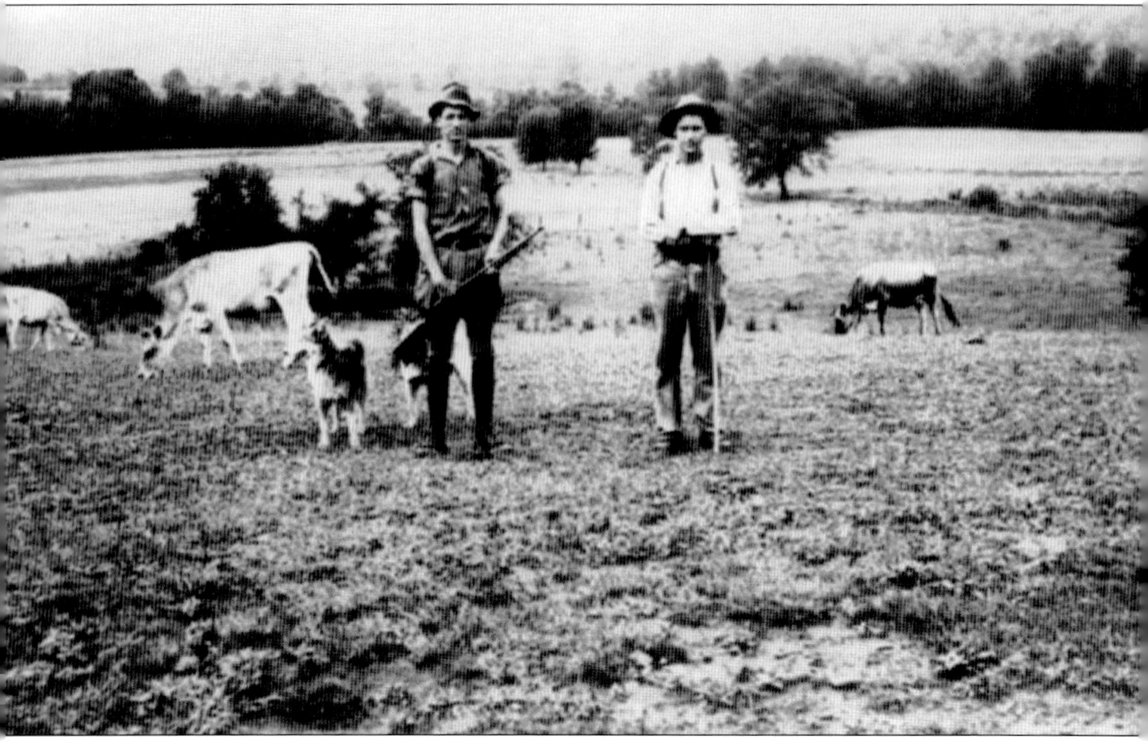

Clay Oliver (left) and his cousin Frank Oliver would go to the top of the mountain and work as herder boys in the summer months. John W. Oliver had built a one-room log cabin atop the mountain that the herders would live in. The cabin was located close to Gregory Bald. Cooking was done over a fire in iron kettles or in Dutch ovens. The owners of the cattle would place a bell on the lead individual; the herders became familiar with the tone of each owner's bell. Sheep, pigs, and horses were also taken atop the balds for the good grazing. Salt licks or salt blocks were put out by the herders for the livestock. If the owner brought his own salt, the herder would only charge $1 per head. If the herder had to provide the salt, the charge was $1.25 per head. (Courtesy of Margaret Oliver, John W. Oliver collection.)

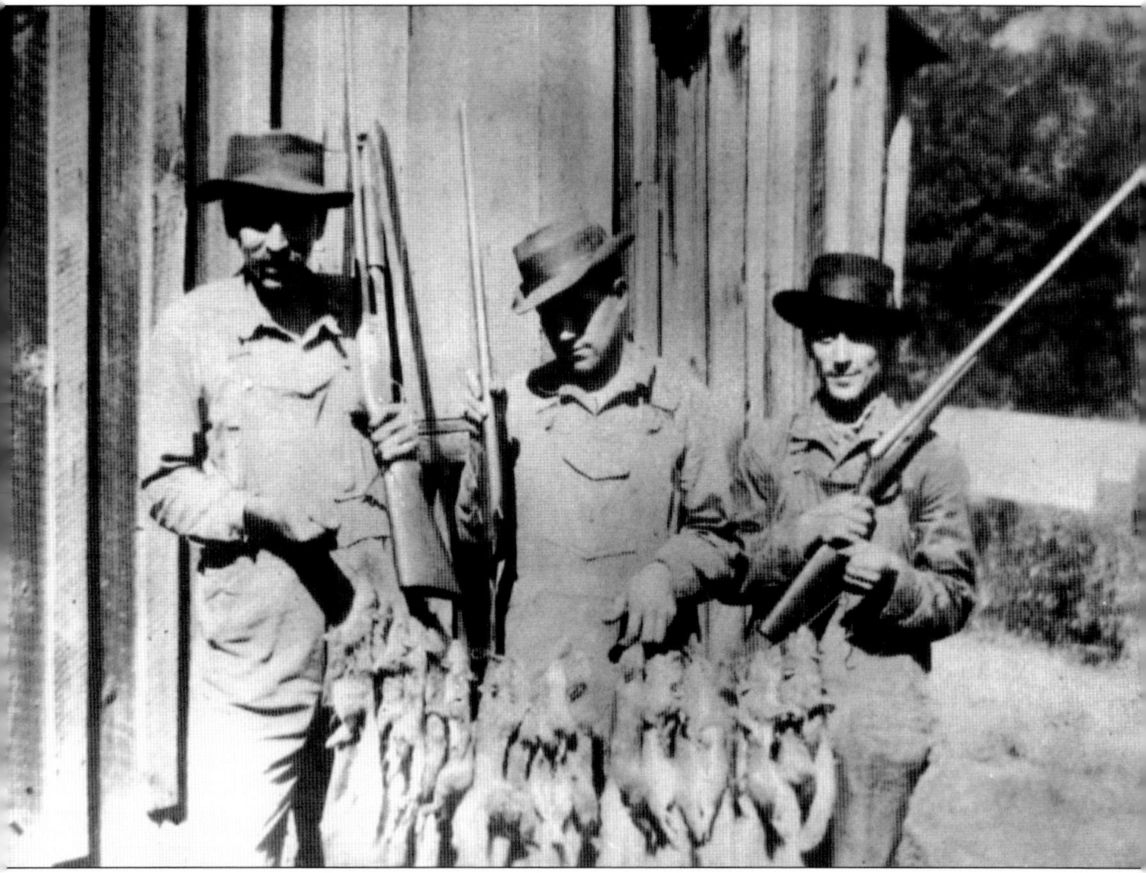

John McCaulley (left) was a well-known hunter of wild turkeys. He also loved to hunt raccoons, which was often the main course on the McCaulley supper table. John would cook the raccoon himself after it had been parboiled and seasoned. It was then put into the Dutch oven and placed over hot coals in the fireplace. The selling of raccoon pelts provided for the McCaulleys well. Chestnuts were also plentiful on the ridges of the Smoky Mountains. From the first of September through October, John McCaulley and his family would travel up to the ridges and gather the nuts that had fallen from the trees. Wagons full of chestnuts would be taken to Maryville or Knoxville to sell; the money would be used to buy winter clothes for the family. Pictured with John are Carl Brown (center) and Bun Whitehead. (Courtesy of NPS.)

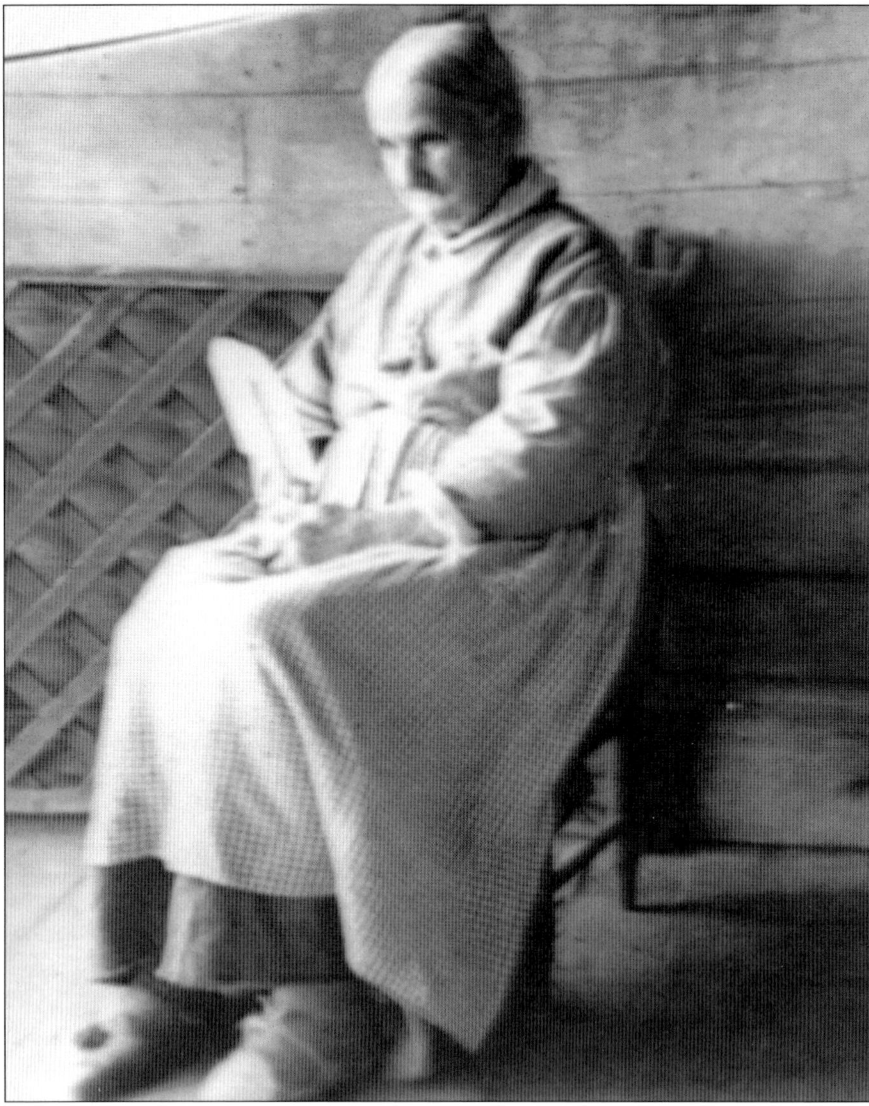

Rebecca Ann Cable, known by many as "Aunt Becky," did work that was usually reserved for men. She could be seen taking her cattle up to "Becky's Sugar Cove" or plowing the fields, not wearing any shoes at all. Aunt Becky could independently operate the Cable Mill. She was familiar with the use of flax and wool and would make essential clothing for her family. Cooking was something that she enjoyed, and she always put a big spread on the table. To control the flies, Becky had a fan at her table made from torn newspapers. She also offered the hungry a place to eat. Becky was a good friend of John McCaulley, who was an accomplished coffin-maker. When she became gravely ill, she asked John to make her a coffin. Payment was in the form of wool socks, which she had made. Becky recovered from the illness and lived many years after. Her conclusion was that "Jesus wasn't ready for me yet." (Courtesy of Roy Coada.)

The young people of the cove were involved in many social activities. One of the most popular would be the corn huskings and shellings. After the harvest, young people would gather for a husking. If a male found a red ear of corn while husking, he could kiss the lady of his choice. Pictured at right is Golman Myers as a young man. (Courtesy of NPS.)

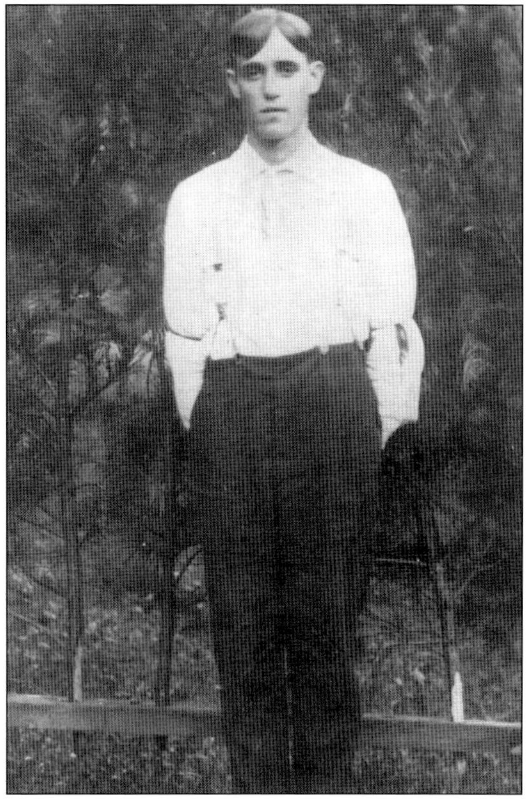

The family of Jesse Simeon Brown III and his wife, Rutha Myers Brown, is seen here. From left to right are (seated) Jesse and Rutha; (standing) Melvin, George, Mary, and Elizabeth. The Brown family was active in the Missionary Baptist Church. Jesse was the son of Richard Henderson and Sarah Elizabeth Headrick Brown. Rutha's parents were Dan Myers Jr. and Luranie Angeline Gregory. (Courtesy of NPS.)

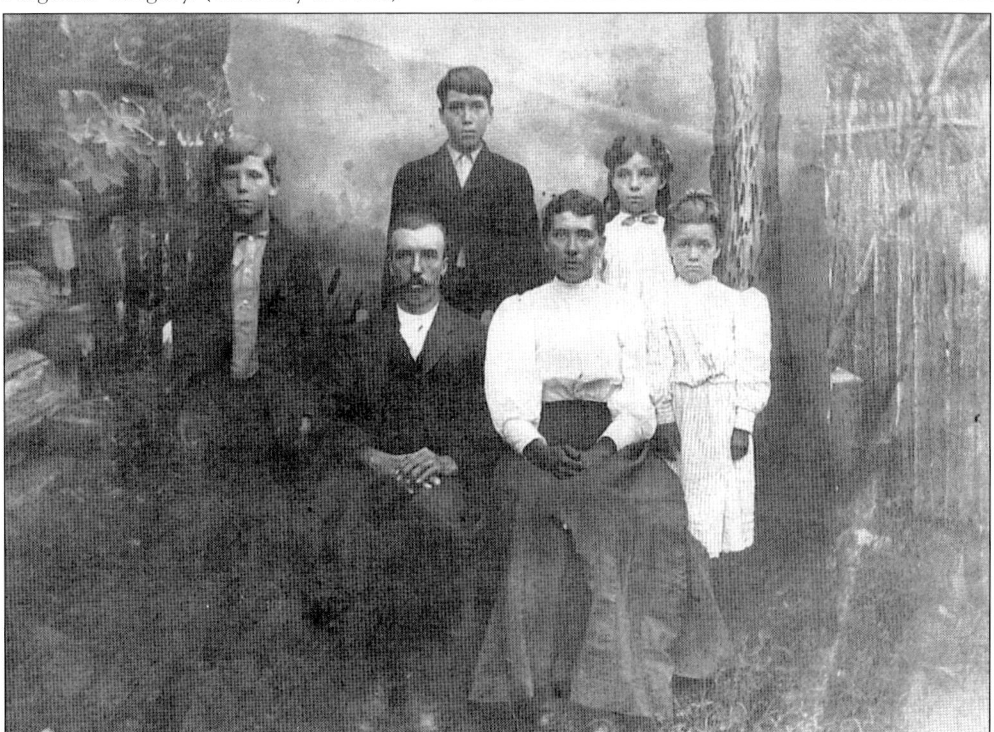

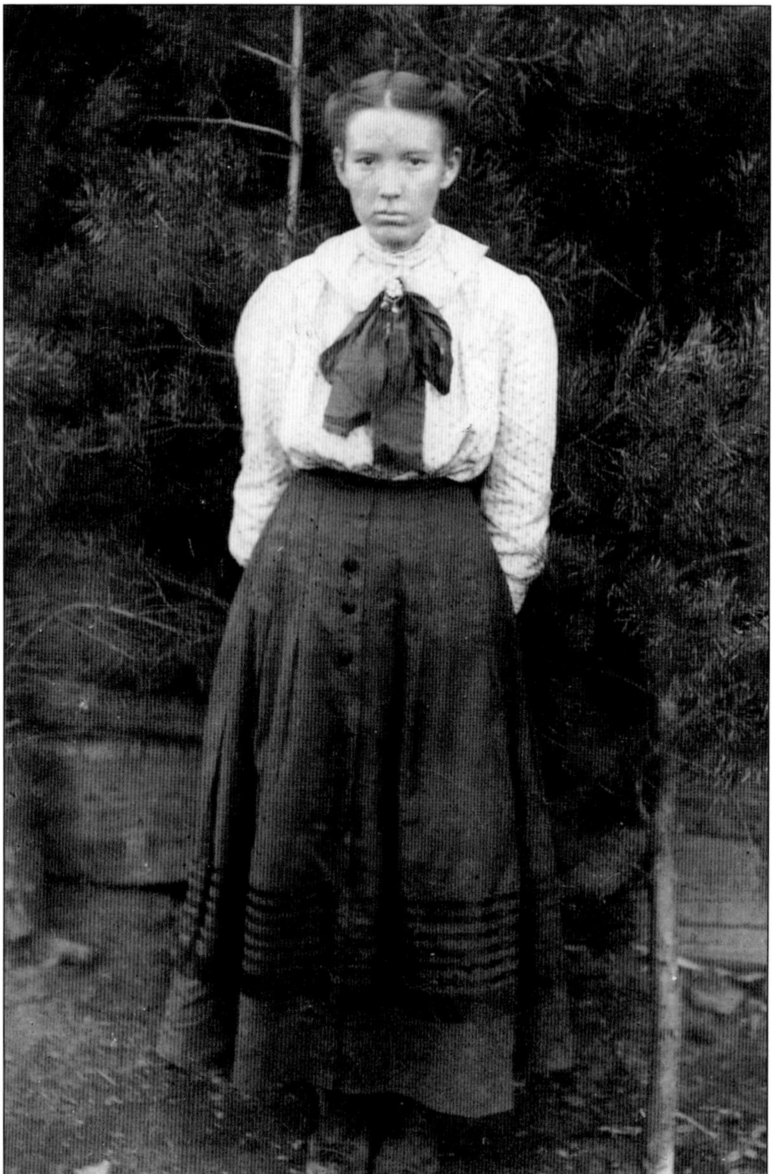

Sally Garland was born to William Charles "Charlie" and Myria Miller Garland. According to records, Sally died at a young age. Charlie was born in 1859 in Mitchell County, North Carolina, and around 1880, he married Myria and settled the family in the Beard Cane area near the headwaters of Hesse Creek, where most of their children were born. Charlie had many home places within the Smokies, and he included logging and farming among his vocations. He fathered 16 children and established himself as a legendary mountain man through his exploits. (Courtesy of Sylvia Garland Galde.)

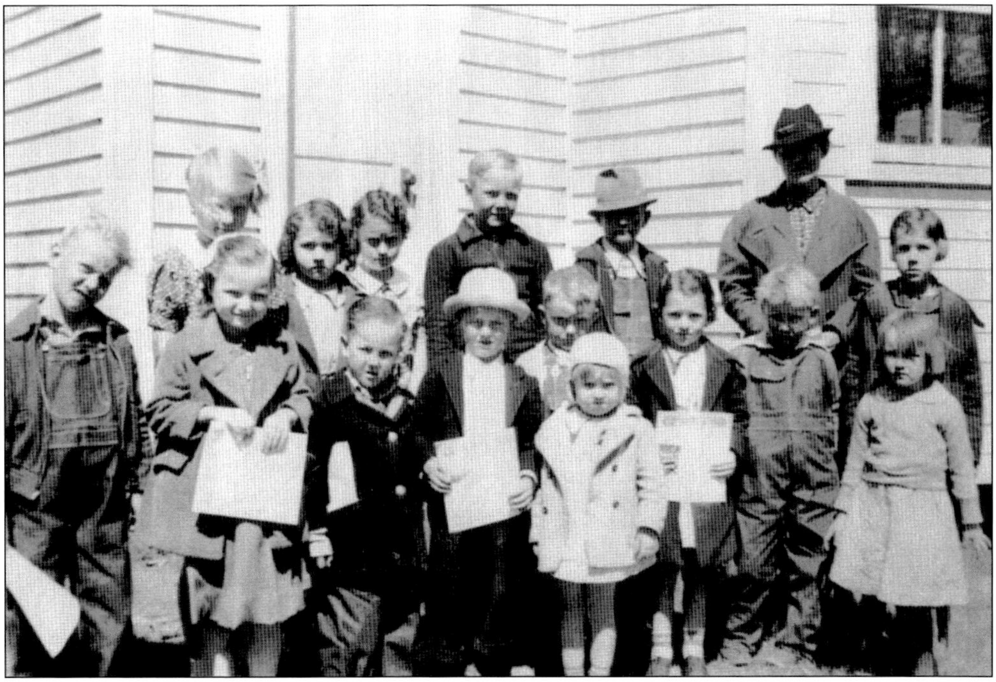

These children are in a Sunday school class at Cades Cove Missionary Baptist Church. There were no classrooms to meet in, so the classes each gathered in a different corner of the sanctuary. The people in the community of Cades Cove were very religious. The education the children received in church provided the religious foundations for their adult lives. (Courtesy of Margaret Oliver, John W. Oliver collection.)

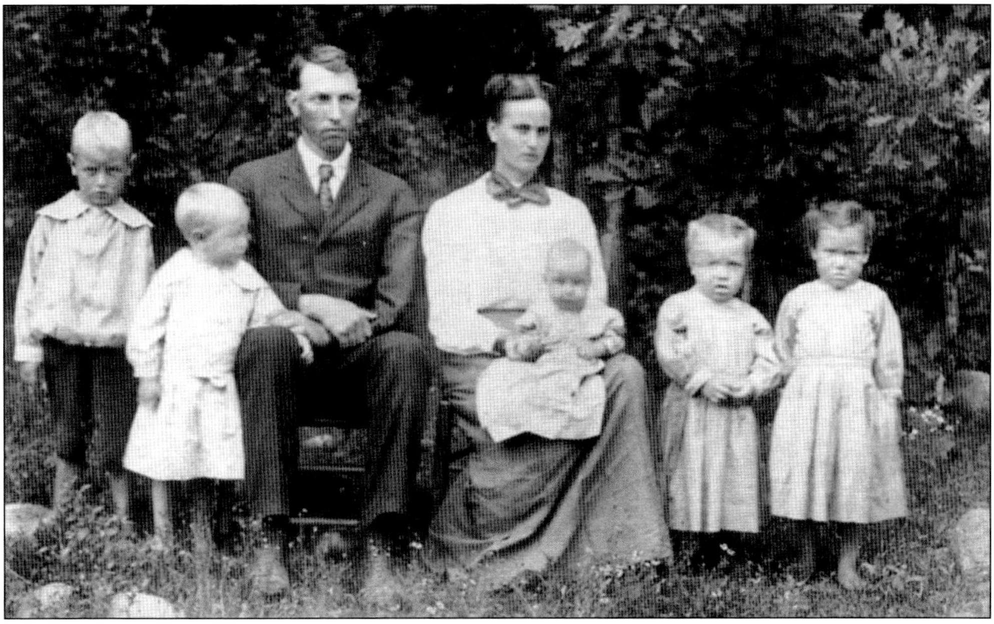

Pictured are Andrew Preston Roberts, son of Samuel J. and Martha Jane Shields Roberts, and Martha Angeline Roberts, daughter of William Howell and Elizabeth Jane Gregory Oliver, with their children. (Courtesy of Margaret Oliver, John W. Oliver collection.)

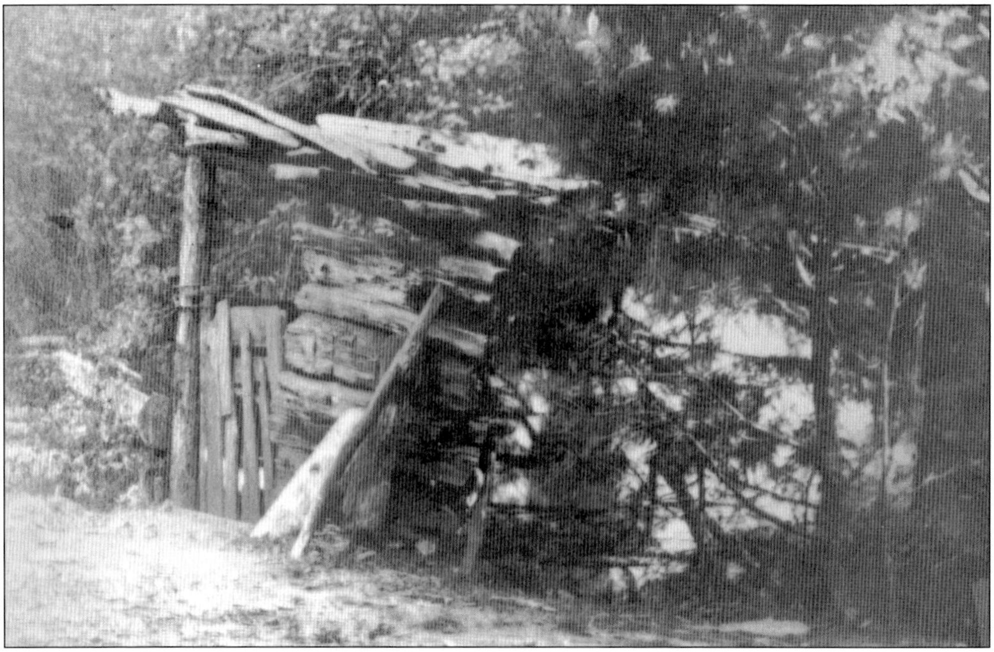

Samuel "Long Hair Sam" Burchfield ran a tub mill (pictured) in the Chestnut Flats area on Panther Creek. Burchfield was known as "Long Hair Sam" both because there was another Sam Burchfield in the cove and because of his long, flowing hair. He was the son of Wilson and Elizabeth Burchfield and married Evelyn Davis. (Courtesy of NPS.)

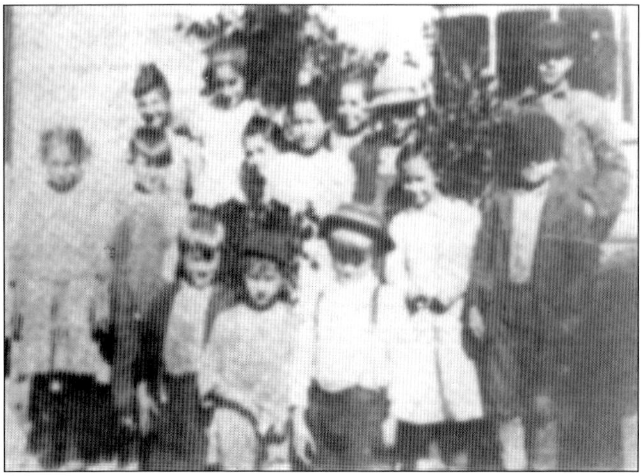

After the loss of the Flint Hill School in a fire, a frame school was built in 1911 for the Chestnut Flats area. The new school, Laurel Springs, was about half a mile closer to Forge Creek. The nearby Taylor Whitehead home served as a boardinghouse for several teachers here, among them Willie Sparks Burchfield in 1919, Elsie Yearout in 1920, Lester Shields in 1924–1925, and Stella McNeilly in 1926. Laurel Springs closed in 1927. (Courtesy of NPS.)

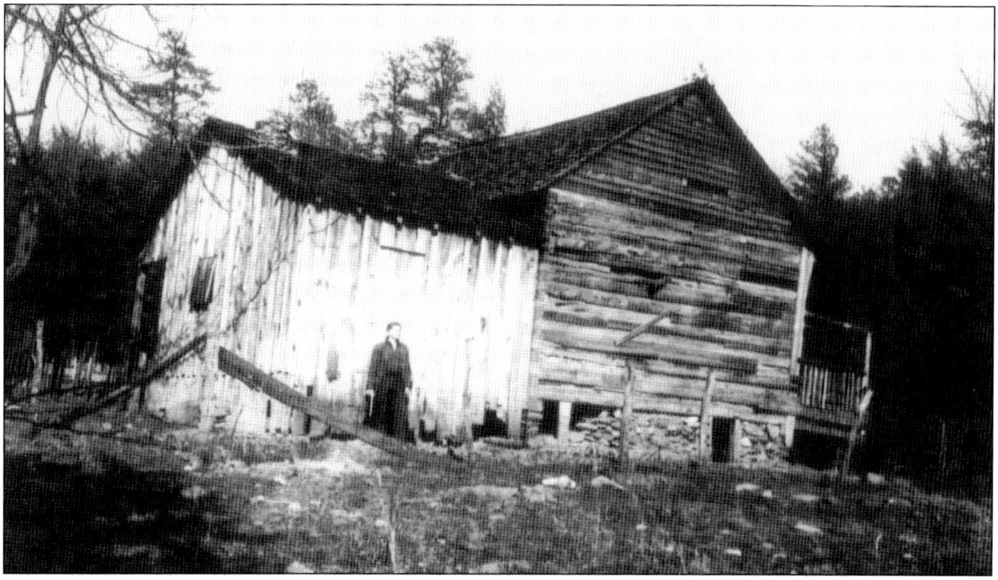

This is the George Tipton cabin, located on Chestnut Flats Road in Cades Cove, Tennessee. The National Park Service took this photograph in 1937. According to park records, Tipton was the last resident of the house. This is thought to have originally been the Jurd Wilcox home. Tipton was the son of George and Tuckaleechee "Tuck" Burchfield Tipton and was first married to Lula Burchfield. After her death, he married Katie Proctor. The person in the photograph is unidentified. (Courtesy of NPS.)

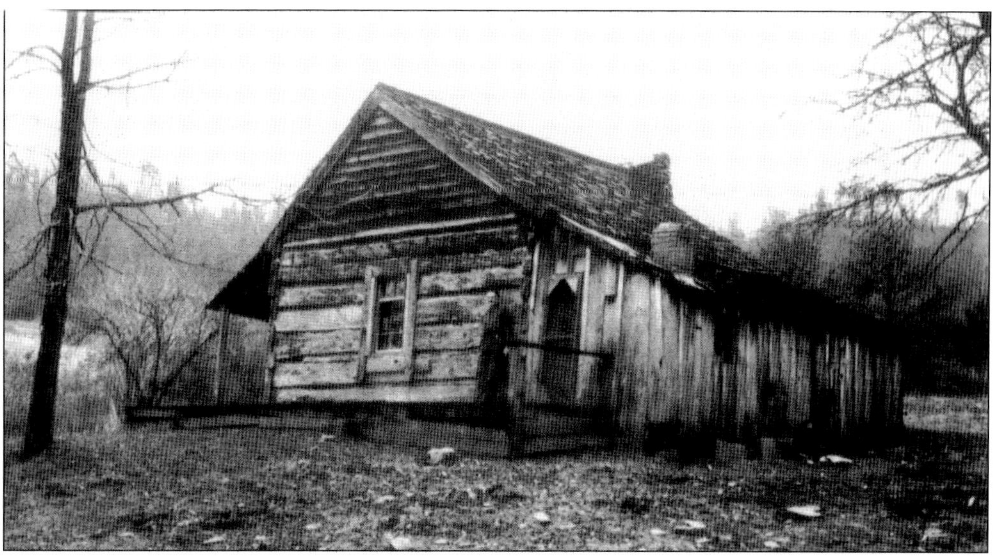

William Carson "Cars" Tipton, George Tipton's brother, also lived on Chestnut Flats Road. Their homes were not far from each other, and pictures of both Tipton homes were taken in 1937. Cars was always one to be acting a fool and always wore a black hat. He first married Irene Cable and later married Myrtle Hatcher. (Courtesy of NPS.)

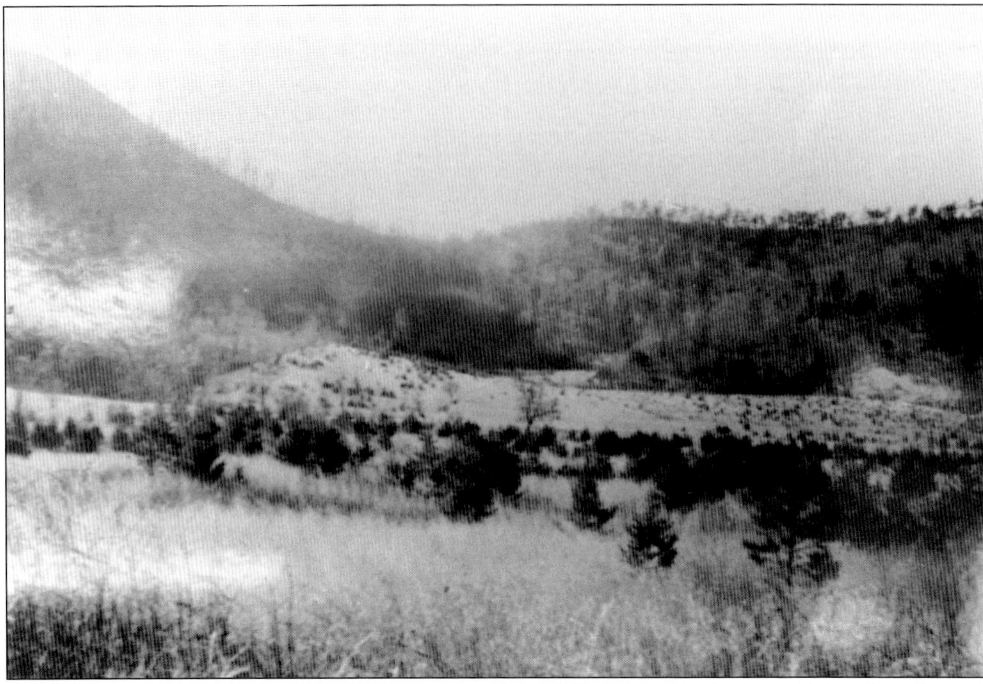

White Oak Sinks is a secluded area on the outskirts of Cades Cove. At least 10 families chose to settle here and raise their families. Many of the children that lived in the White Oak Sinks had to attend school at the Red Bank School in Dry Valley, Townsend, Tennessee. (Courtesy of NPS.)

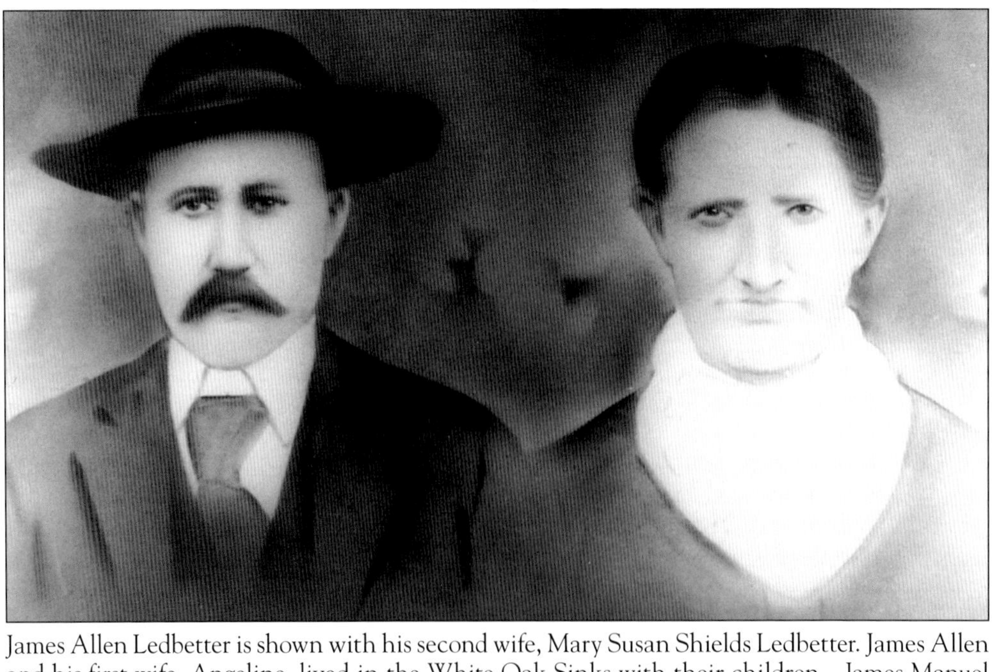

James Allen Ledbetter is shown with his second wife, Mary Susan Shields Ledbetter. James Allen and his first wife, Angeline, lived in the White Oak Sinks with their children—James Manuel "Mann," Mary, and Caroline. After Angeline's death in 1887, James Allen moved his family to Cades Cove to live in the Finley Cane area off Laurel Creek Road. (Courtesy of David and Paulette Ledbetter.)

James Manuel "Mann" Ledbetter married Betty Jane Anthony in 1899 and lived in the White Oak Sinks. Mann was the son of James Allen and Mary Susan Shields Ledbetter. Betty Jane Anthony was the daughter of John T. and Sarah LeQuire Anthony. After the death of Betty Jane, Mann married Anne Louraine "Lurena" Shields, daughter of Andrew Witt and Anna C. Walker Shields. (Courtesy of David and Paulette Ledbetter.)

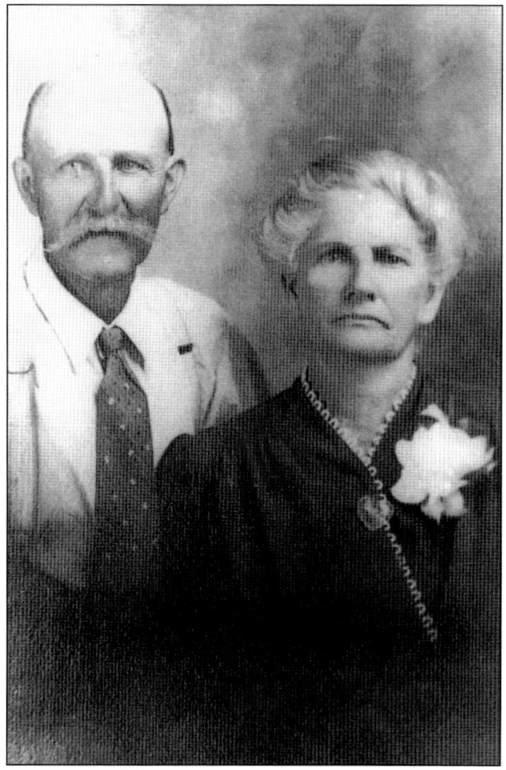

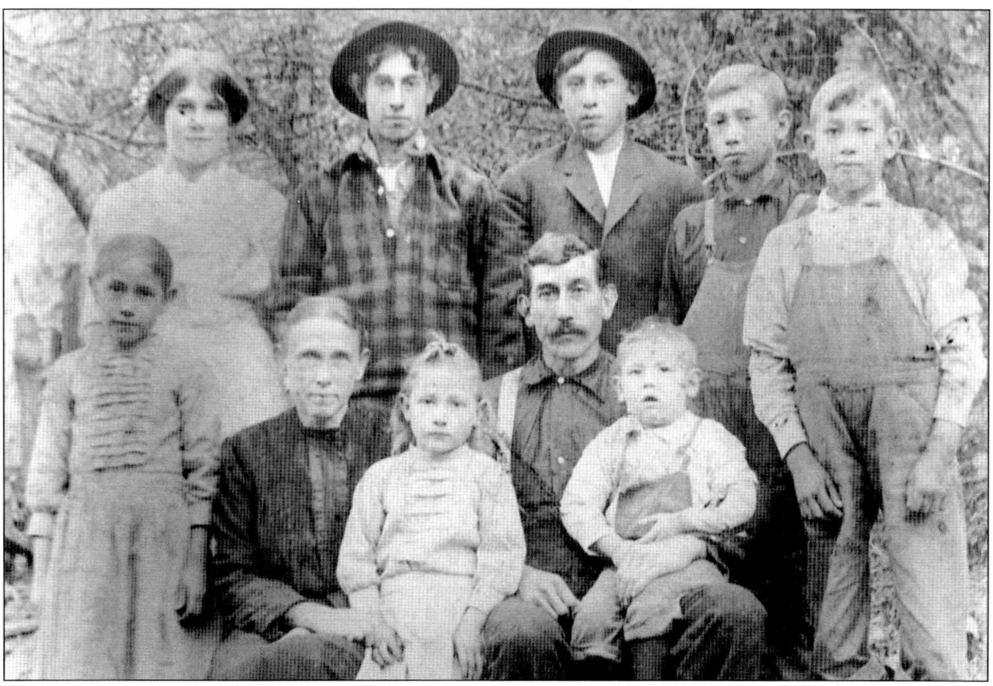

Jacob "Jake" and Roxana Burchfield Dorsey and their 10 children lived in the White Oak Sinks. Many families had children in a large age range. The older children would tend to the younger ones while their parents did the daily work. (Courtesy of NPS.)

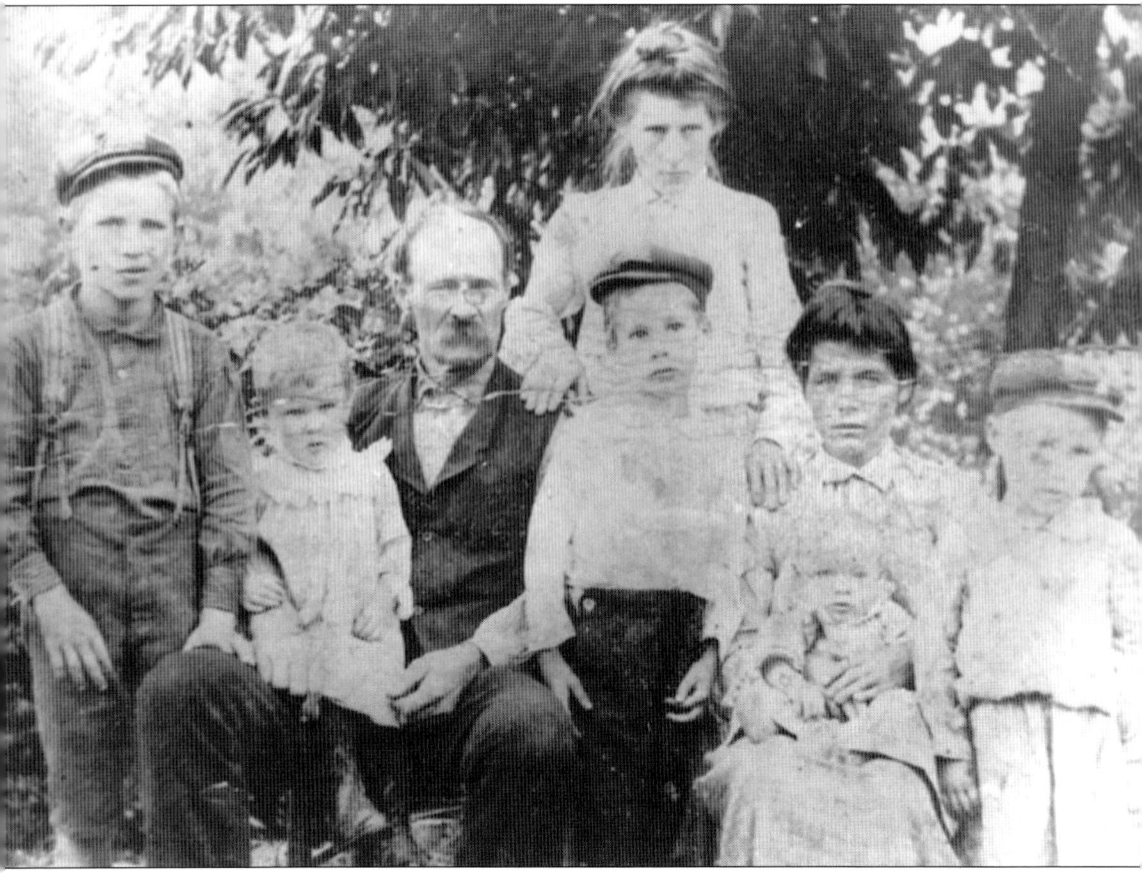

Matthew Manuel "Bud" Ledbetter was born in 1856 to Daniel and Elizabeth Forester Ledbetter. He married Mary Ann Sands, the daughter of Anderson and Mary Ann Sands, in 1878. Before their marriage, Bud had bought land in the White Oak Sinks. All of their children were born in the White Oak Sinks and learned at an early age what hard work was. Mary Ann Sands Ledbetter died in 1893, and Bud married to Drothea McClanahan, the daughter of Dave and Leah Burchfield McClanahan. All of the children that they had together were born and raised in the White Oak Sinks. The Bud Ledbetter family moved out of the White Oak Sinks in 1928. (Courtesy of David and Paulette Ledbetter.)

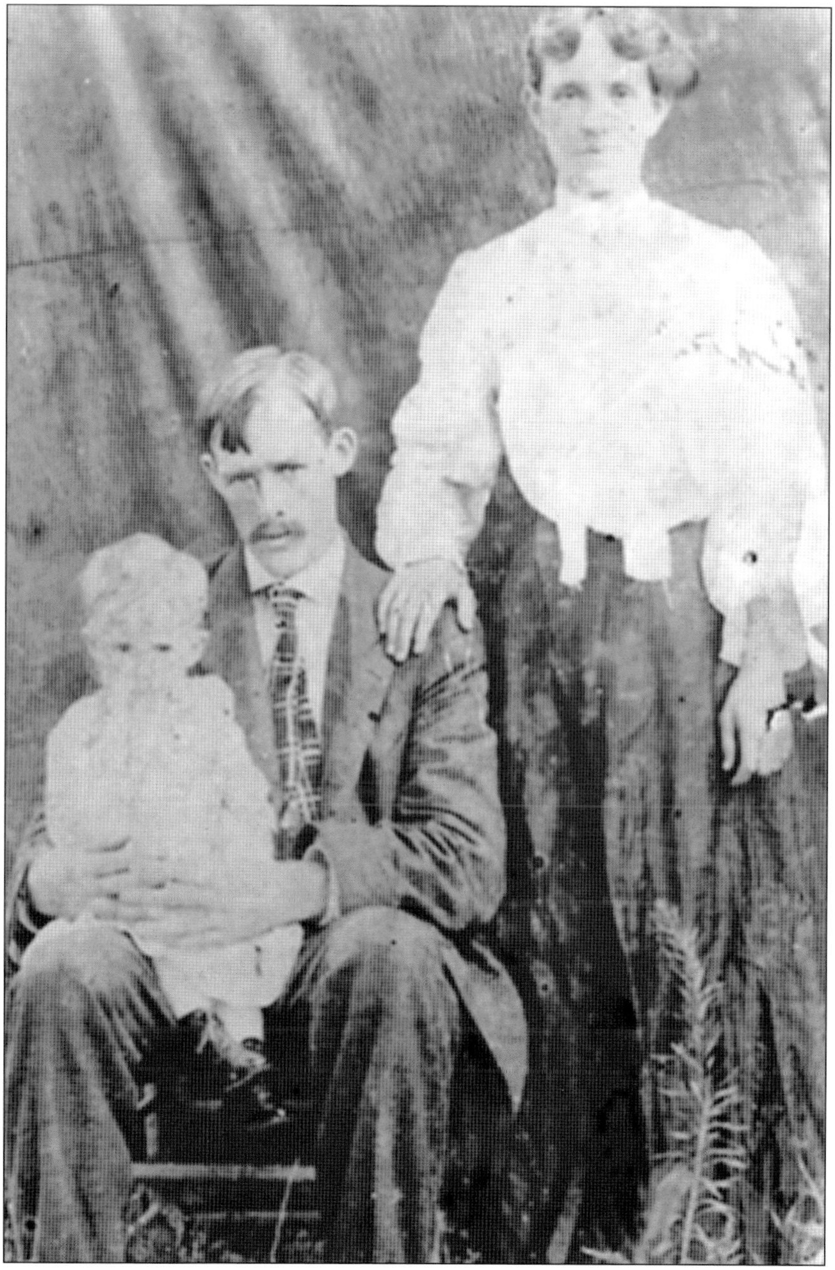

Daniel Calvin "Cal" Ledbetter was born in 1882 to Bud and Mary Ann Sands Ledbetter in the White Oak Sinks. He married Annie Rebecca Shields in 1905. She was the daughter of Dave and Phoebe Jane Walker Shields and was raised in Cades Cove. Cal and Annie eloped and were married on horseback on top of Rich Mountain. Annie was wearing all five of her dresses. As they were going down into the White Oak Sinks, her father came in search of them. He could not find them, so he shot down into the woods. He reportedly said, "I guess I killed 'em" and left; the shot hit no one. After he thought about this marriage for a week or so, he made his mind up to go and check on them and straighten things out. Pictured are Cal and Annie with their son Elvin. (Courtesy of David and Paulette Ledbetter.)

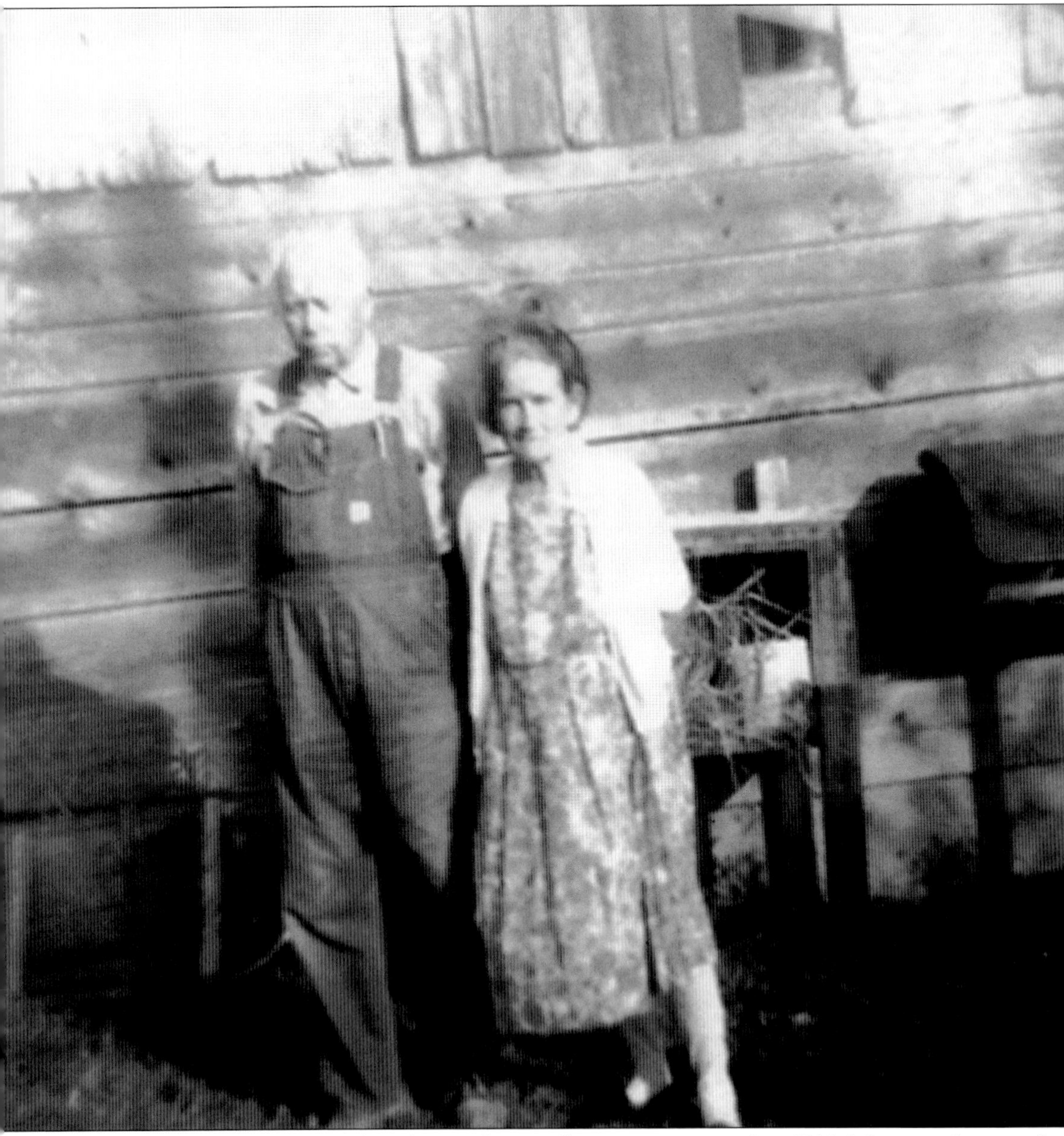

John Andrew Bryant and Ruth Angeline Ledbetter were married in 1912. John was the son of Fonzie and Annie Jane Headrick Bryant, and Ruth Angeline was the daughter of Allen and Mary Ledbetter. John and Ruth lived in the White Oak Sinks area for some time, then moved to the nearby Meadows. They had 10 children while living in these areas. (Courtesy of Johnnie Bryant Sparks.)

The children living in the White Oak Sinks had to travel over the mountain to the Dry Valley to attend Red Bank School, seen at right. Below is a picture of a school group. Many of the children are residents of the White Oak Sinks. (Courtesy of Sylvia Garland Galde.)

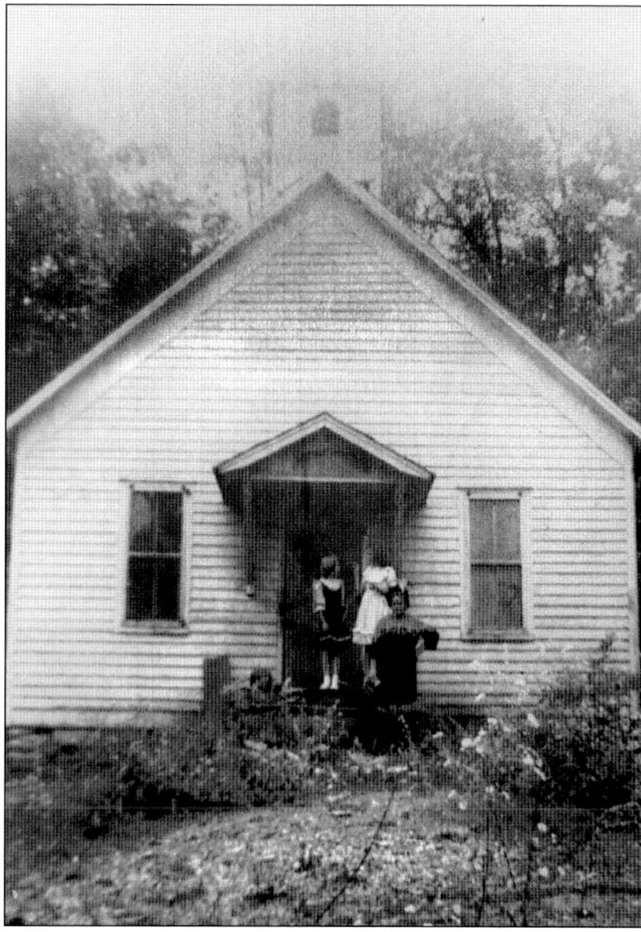

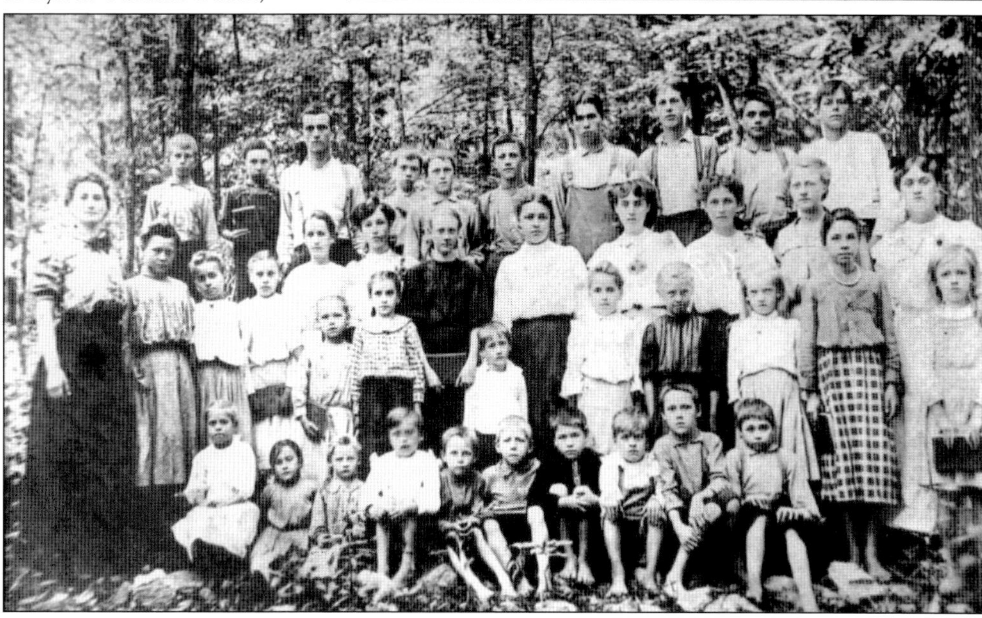